The World
of the
Blue-Collar Worker

The World
of the
Blue-Collar Worker

**Edited with an Introduction by
IRVING HOWE**

QUADRANGLE BOOKS
A New York Times Company

Library of Congress Catalog Card Number: 77–190132
International Standard Book Number: 0–8129–0251–3

Contents

Introduction
Irving Howe

This book has grown out of a special issue of *Dissent* magazine, published in Winter 1972, which was devoted to "The World of the Blue-Collar Worker." About two-thirds of that issue now appears here, containing material that seems likely to be of lasting interest. It is a book that speaks for itself, so I'll confine my few introductory remarks to some points about our intentions and results.

Our main interest in bringing together the reportage and analysis that follows was to discover some of the realities of American working-class life today. We wanted to discover those realities with a minimum of political or intellectual preconceptions. What, we asked ourselves, are the actual experiences, feelings, opinions, and problems of those millions of people who work in factories and shops? I mean the men and women who, as a rule, aren't as quick with a phrase as college students, the men and women who don't get interviewed on TV shows or written up in "sensational" articles, yet who clearly are of the greatest importance in our political and social life.

We started with at least one assumption—that the currently fashionable notions about blue-collar workers are probably mistaken. We doubt, for instance, that most American workers are deep-going racists, though it seems likely that, together with most other Americans, they have their share of prejudice. We doubt that American workers are potential revolutionists, though it again seems likely that, like many other Americans, they have serious complaints about the society they live in. And we were morally repelled, as must be anyone

3

of humane feeling and democratic persuasion, by the stereotype of the last decade which has it that workers are clods whose only interests are guzzling beer, staring at the boob tube, and whistling at girls. Not that we suppose them to be nature's noblemen—it's by no means clear that nature has any noblemen. But we do believe that there is an unusual amount of ignorance about American workers, as well as a considerable degree of contempt and ideological preconception floating through both intellectual and popular life.

An example comes to mind. A TV "special" was recently produced about the life of black people in Detroit. Many important elements of that life were shown, but nowhere was there a word that tens of thousands of black workers in Detroit belong to and some are active in the United Automobile Workers Union; or that a good many of them have begun to occupy posts of influence and power within UAW locals; or that one of them, Marcellius Ivory, has become the director of the UAW on the West Side of Detroit, thereby heading more than fifty thousand black and white unionists. By contrast, some "militant" demagogues, ranting violence but probably commanding no more than a handful of followers, were given much attention on this program.

Now, for our part, we think that a serious social analysis has to stress the growing numbers, strength, and influence of black workers in unions like the UAW, and that such trends, though not readily appealing to the people who make TV "specials," are far more important than the sensational ephemera of the moment.

So our first and deepest concern was simply to break past the barriers of ignorance, indifference, and contempt. The reportage in this book that is most valuable is that which gives one a feeling for the quality and flavor of working-class life: what it means to live in a town like Cicero, how a local in the auto or steel union functions day by day, what the experiences are of Jewish and black workers in the New York garment industry, and so forth.

Intellectually, we have tried in this book to break out of the fixed categories which the Left—and, of course, many contributors to this book are people of the Left, the democratic Left—has accumulated over the years. One paradox about the American working class that has always bedeviled left-wing and especially Marxist intellectuals is that American workers have frequently been tremendously militant, even violent, in their day-to-day struggles for better living conditions, yet have seldom accepted the programs and premises of socialism. In Europe, by contrast, the working classes of the more advanced countries, as well as some of the backward ones, inherited the tradition of socialism as their "natural" outlook, yet in their daily struggles they were seldom as combative as American workers. Whatever the explanations for this, and they are several, it had first to be accepted as a reality. But radical intellectuals in the United States, especially when burdened with an ill-absorbed or vulgar Marxism, found themselves driven to all sorts of intellectual dodges in order to avoid this reality.

Many of us who appear in this book believe that the workers form a crucial segment of American society; we believe that trade unions, whatever their limitations, are an indispensable and indeed central component of any political alignment for social and economic reform; and at least some of us believe that there are inherent tendencies within American society making for continued conflicts of interest between capital and labor. Yet all this has little, if anything, to do with romantic or authoritarian versions of Marxism that look forward to an apocalypse out of which the proletariat (or, more probably, a party apparatus acting in its name) will take power. We see little reason for anticipating such a development in the United States, and given the moral credentials of those who propose it, less reason to desire it.

One of the most unhappy consequences of the effort to impose traditional Marxist categories on American social life is that unrealizable expectations concerning the working class are aroused. Once these are inevitably frustrated, there follows a terrible souring, a "disillusionment" that soon ends in cynicism. Instead of regarding the workers as the human beings they are, with all the strengths and weaknesses, desires and disappointments of other human beings, the ex-Marxist has a way of turning upon them with the gall of disappointed love. He then declares them mere brainwashed clods, hopelessly "one-dimensional," mere creatures of the belly who are manipulated by the Establishment and the mass media. Such nasty elitist notions ran riot through the thought and writings of the New Left during its brief moment on the American scene — though, in that case, the condescension shown toward the workers was due not merely to the crabby elitism represented by Herbert Marcuse but also to the social fact that a good number of the student "revolutionists" came from affluent, and sometimes wealthy, families. Not having known in their own experience the pinch of need, they could afford to be contemptuous of unions which merely — merely, indeed! — improved the day-to-day living conditions of millions of people.

Now, in recent years one encountered a curious melding of snobbist feelings toward the workers, a melding from both Left and Right. You could hear young Buckleyites talk about workers and unions in accents not very different from those of young New Leftists. More important, you could hear young New Leftists talk about workers and unions in accents not very different from those of young Buckleyites. During the last years of the '60s, however, an apparent counter-trend set in. Articles about Joe Worker and the alleged backlash he threatened began to appear in the magazines. Insofar as these articles made clear that the affluence of the American worker was largely a myth, and indeed that he was having a devil of a time just paying his bills, such articles served a certain purpose. But too many of them were tainted by an unspoken condescension: "You had better pay attention to these guys, otherwise they might raise a lot of hell, and many might even go over to the racism and reaction of George Wallace." In short, what these articles often represented was not an intrinsic interest in or concern with the experience of American workers but a prudential admonition as to the consequences of neglecting them.

In this book, I think, the reader will find a different approach. Even those writers whose approach is analytical rather than reportorial speak with a sense of community and fraternity toward the men and women who work in factories and shops. They are writers who, as a rule, don't allow the statistic to blot out the man. They recognize, almost always, that their theories matter insofar as they help to illuminate the problems of human experience. And since each contributor speaks for himself, it is only natural that there should be disagreements among them.

Yet some dominant impressions can be summarized:

¶ While they share, of course, those experiences which are pervasive among all human beings in this country, blue-collar workers have problems, outlooks, and modes of behavior distinctly their own. The concept of social class, if applied with some flexibility and without ideological preconception, still seems a useful one for noticing and explaining differences in conduct and response between large groups of people. And blue-collar workers find themselves right now, despite notable improvements in conditions over the past few decades, in a very tight spot—squeezed economically, disturbed socially, uncertain politically.

¶ The trade unions remain a major factor in their lives, even if they attend meetings only occasionally and grumble about them frequently. Several of our writers report that when crucial issues arise, like forthcoming contracts and the election of officers, workers respond with sharpened interest. The relationship between them and their unions is very complex, not reducible to a formula that pleases ideologues of Left or Right. One major point of differentiation seems to be age. Younger workers, unburdened with memories of depression and sharing, to one or another extent, the free-spoken critical attitudes of their generation, are more likely than the older workers to criticize unions and their leaders.

¶ One of the major internal developments within the unions

during the next decade is likely to be the growing numbers and strength of the blacks. Hardly a report in this book fails to mention that groups of black workers are steadily increasing their political power within the locals, and then, more slowly, beyond them.

¶ There remain all sorts of problems concerning working-class and trade-union life which are touched upon or discussed in this book: Are workers more inclined to be "authoritarian" in their responses to civil liberties issues than other segments of the population? In what ways do ethnic loyalties criss-cross class involvement within unions and in working-class neighborhoods? Is there developing a "new working class," composed of relatively skilled technicians and professionals, which will significantly change our sense of both the social composition of the working class and the probable nature of the trade unions? What will be the role of labor in a "post-industrial society"? About these complex questions there is nothing for me to say here, since they are fully discussed in the essays that follow; but let me note the discussion by Herman Benson of the problem of democracy in the trade unions, which seems to me a splendid example of how it is possible to be simultaneously a loyal supporter of the principle of unionism and an active critic of its shortcomings.

There are, of course, omissions here of important topics concerning American workers and their institutions. An especially important one is their political role in the party system: How much influence do the unions exert in primaries, elections, and lawmaking, and how does this influence vary from area to area, moment to moment? Such a study was projected but didn't materialize. Still, there is more than enough here to warrant discussion, debate, disagreement.

I. Life, Work, Neighborhoods

No Pride in This Dust
Bennett Kremen

Young Workers in the Steel Mills

On a Greyhound speeding through a dark, icy night toward Chicago, I return to old memories of packing lunch bags and pulling on greasy overalls each morning before rushing desperately to beat the factory time clock — months and months of this drudgery my reward for temporarily dropping out of a Chicago high school during the mid-1950s. Now I head once more toward that muscular city on the lake, to struggle again with time clocks and lunch bags — this time driven not by necessity but curiosity.

Only seven others, mostly students picked up in a college town, share the heavy darkness inside the bus. And now, with recent memories of a tough month I've spent in Detroit futilely searching for work in the car plants, I can't help wondering about the boy nearby with the backpack, the long-haired one behind him, the shoeless girls in front of me. For though they're all dressed as insurgents in a rebellion against technology, they surely know little of the sooty bowels of industry, where millions their own age labor each day. Yet I quickly hear bitter voices behind me as we reach the flame-tinted skies over Gary:
"Wow — look at that mess!"
"Yeah, they're even burning up the clouds!"

BENNETT KREMEN is a free-lance writer whose work has appeared in the New York Times, *the* Village Voice, *and other publications. This article will be the first chapter of a book by Mr. Kremen to be published in 1973 and appears here with the kind permission of Dial Press.*

11

"Why don't they just turn it all into a frisbee field?"

Laughter travels through the bus, and a flurry of conversation continues all the way into Chicago's Loop. And though I've heard similar exchanges countless times, I can't help being impressed again by such intense expressions of "alienation from the tools of production" by these fortunate people, even if it's only fashionable prattle. For they're the ones benefiting the most from industry and grunting the least in its service. What about those who grunt the most?

The sun isn't up yet and the "Hawk," Chicago's cruel wind, lashes down on the thousands of workers huddling at bus stops. Even in my heavy laborer's clothes, this frigid journey to the Southworks is an agony. That mile-long mill owned by the United States Steel Corporation squats on the damp shore of Lake Michigan. The final bitter reward for playing the early bird is having to queue up now in the frost outside the gate, waiting for the seven o'clock shift to start.

"That's when they open the employment office, isn't it?"

"Uh-huh."

The fellow I'm talking to has a huge, blond mustache and is wearing an army jacket with Vietnam markings on it; he seems as disgusted as I am.

"Been looking long?" I ask.

"Three months. But I think they're hiring here."

"They are," I assure him. "Maybe we'll get lucky."

"Lucky . . . ?" He shrugs and looks up at the rows of smoke stacks and blast furnaces, ". . . if you want to call it that."

When the gate finally opens, he rushes into the employment office like the rest of us and quickly fills out cards passed out by a guard. This haste, however, is only a wasted effort. The hours trickle away in this increasingly crowded room without a word said to most of us. All we can do is wait and stare.

All around me are young people, many fresh out of high school and the Army—or off the streets of the South Side. Most seem remarkably free of that classical, humble, hungry look of the job hunter. Throughout the morning they stream in like locusts. This isn't only the ordinary consequence of unemployment: crowded into this room are men who were conceived during the baby boom in the 1940s and '50s, now hitting industry as once they did the country's school systems. And this pounding on the doors can only intensify as the average age of workers in mills and factories continues to tumble dramatically each year—as it has since 1968. By the end of the decade, 68 percent of the labor force will be below thirty-four, a sharp reversal of the age distributions during the '50s and early '60s. Already men in their twenties comprise a third of organized labor's entire membership.

As I look around, unpredictable things are confronting me. Where are the Polish kids who traditionally flock to this mill? For decades legend has always designated the Southworks, the huge mills next door in East Chicago, and the industrial wilds of Gary below it as a land flowing with *kolbassi* and boilermakers. Yet 70 percent of those here are black—yes, young, black, and beautiful. For they aren't wearing the overalls, that drab, humble uniform of the working stiff: their "vines," man, are their own—purple silk shirts with collars hanging halfway to their waists, fur coats, four-cornered velvet hats, and bright, multicolored shoes that mock this somber environment where roughly 9.5 percent of all U.S. Steel's raw tonnage is poured. Watching these men filing one by one into the interviewing section, their loose ghetto walk declaring the assertiveness of the mean streets of the city, makes me wonder if the steel industry has produced a *confidential* document similar to the gloomy one put out in Detroit in 1969 by Malcolm Denise, Ford Motor Company's top labor-relations man.

"More than 35 percent of [Ford's 1968 work force] . . . ," he confided at a company management conference "were non-white, compared to 15 percent in 1960." Then, after predicting unique labor troubles because of that anticipated flood of young workers into industry, he concluded with this warning: "Another feature of the landscape in which we will be operating [in the '70s] is our increasing dependence on blacks to get our work done. Whatever some may feel about the black issue in general, we are in fact dependent, and will continue to be, on black people to make this company go."

"Hey," I whisper to the fellow next to me with the big, blond mustache, "are there always so many spades looking for jobs around here?"

"Sure."

"What about in East Chicago?"

"Oh, those dudes are workin' all down the lake, even past Gary."

"What's happened to the Polish people who used to work these places?"

"They're still around—the older ones mostly. A lot of 'em moved away though and never want to come back around here anymore."

"Will working with all these black guys bother you?" I inquire suddenly. For a moment he eyes me warily before responding:

"Will it bother you, man?"

"No."

"Well, I don't give a damn either."

We keep on talking, trying to beat the boredom of this incessant waiting. He tells me that even the local union president at the Southworks is a black man. Since this local is a large one in one of the largest steel-producing regions in the country, that's probably quite important, I tell him. Well, not only Local 65 but the whole region, he figures, will probably be mostly black in ten years.

"Then for the first time, we'll see *black power* with real muscle behind it," I tell him. "And even if the blacks here don't really know it yet, that power probably already exists."

A sudden thoughtfulness — or is it distress — hovers in my young friend's eyes. And quickly I shift away from talk about race, even though he seems too indifferent to really care about it either way — and though that very indifference, if real, intrigues me. For such a sentiment would be a striking departure from the monolithic hatreds that flourished among the men I worked with in this city less than fifteen years ago. These questions must remain hanging, for I'm being called for an interview.

Early the next morning, I'm in a room again with about twenty others — most of them young, many of them black — listening to a black personnel man in expensive tweeds playing the lay-it-on-the-line role:

"What I'm telling you now is the same for blacks and whites — there ain't no difference, because at least five of you, that's 25 percent," he says, "won't even last out the six-week probationary period — blacks or whites. But jobs are tight, so more of you might stick it out this year than last. Listen, I ain't going to lie to you — some of those foremen are nothin' but bigots, and I know that. But you don't settle things by hittin' 'em up side the head. And listen," he says with sudden urgency, "you just gotta come in every day; you just **gotta** come in on time!" And though he speaks now about not keeping valuables in our lockers because dudes searching for marijuana or money will wrench them right open, he expresses far more concern in another plea for us "to get in here every day. If you can't make it, you gotta at least call in and let them know. Man, I don't know why guys don't even call in!"

Though this lecture is inappropriate for the beefy, red-headed fellow next to me droning on about fringe benefits and buying a house with a paneled basement, I'm sure that the man in front of us isn't simply wasting his breath on ominous predictions. And as we're being loaded now into a bus to be taken to our assigned locations, I'm almost convinced that what I'm about to experience may have little resemblance to my working days of—well—*long ago*.

Yet some things are ageless, like this ride through the teeming, fenced-in mill past flatcars loaded down with huge, glowing ingots of raw steel that cast their heat like giant radiators. We bump along past dozens of roads, ore docks, rail lines, and shops, some a block long and hissing and clanging with the sounds of hammers, alarm bells, and deadly molten metal that rears from the furnaces like harsh sunshine. Awe—and a touch of uneasiness—shows on the young faces of those sharing the bus with me, their feelings surely paralleling my own. For to the uninitiated, it seems impossible that all these steaming slag piles and ore boats, blast furnaces and cranes that travel on tracks far above us can be managed by 8,200 mere workers, though they labor around the clock in three swing shifts every day of the year.

"If they ain't got a lot of machines to do all this goddamn work," I announce in a fool-around tone, "we're all gonna have a sore back!"

"I'm hip—better they use a dynamo than Little Joe. They ain't got no spare parts for me, man!"

The laughter is heavy, though only the driver and a few new workers are left in the bus—Little Joe among them. And now, smack on the shore of the lake, where the wind hits like a razor, the driver calls out his last stop—our stop.

"This is #2 Electric Furnace—only a half-hour walking time to the gate."

He is smiling when he says it, but none of us stepping out into the damp cold shares his amusement.

"You gotta be jivin' man—you mean from now on we gotta hoof it!"

"That's it, Little Joe—coming in and going out."

A low, angry grumbling at the thought of this cold, payless walk each day fades only gradually as we follow the driver through this noisy, dirty building to the foreman's office. When we enter, the grumbling is over, but a sullen silence remains.

"OK—each of you have a number on the card they gave you. Memorize it, because that's what you're going to be called around here."

31-445 then, is who I am to the pair of foremen in blue hard hats who've just given each of us a bright yellow helmet worn by production workers on labor gangs. For $3.19 an hour then, with a bit extra for late shifts and weekends, we now conclude these sterile preliminaries and don our hard hats, joining tens of thousands of other young workers thus initiated into the lowest ranks of the steel industry.

"Some of you young guys take too many days off! I just don't stand for that shit, or for you comin' in late either!" The sudden tough talk comes from Stanley, the smaller of the two foremen whose unpronounceable Polish last name is tagged to his helmet. The taller one, Mr. Lis, continues now, but in a gentler voice:

"Yeah fellows—you won't get ahead you know, if you do this AWOL stuff. And we want you to get ahead. So you try to watch those absences, huh?"

Neither this easy sell nor the shock tactics seem to ruffle the skepticism of my fellow workers, for they must have sensed, as I did, that Lis and Stanley were only going through a feeble ritual that neither of them really believed would prove effective. Behind Stanley's bluster and Lis's "sincerity" was a note almost of deapair.

Had the foremen I'd once worked for displayed such helplessness, I would've been startled. But I'd already heard young workers in Detroit barrooms and bowling alleys groaning about having to face another day of tedium on the assembly line and boasting about how often they'd gone AWOL.

"Your generation hated that line too," a clever old workingman told me in a bar off Cadillac Square, "but you had a lot of guys proud to work for them big companies in those days. Remember that type? These kids have a different outlook on life. They've never been broke the way we were, and they've got a hell-of-a-lot more schoolin'. You want to know somethin'—*they don't even know how to take the crap we took!*"

Though he didn't speak of affluence and alienation, of levels of aspiration and the breakdown of traditional motivations, that old-timer summarized much of what I'd heard for almost a month from union officials, economists, and worried business executives all over Detroit: a mood of quiet despair descends in those executive offices when they lay out the statistics on their absenteeism problem and speculate on its long-range effects.

"From 1957 to '61," I was told at Ford, "we averaged 2.6 percent of our production workers off on a given day. Each year since then, the figure rose until it reached 5.8 percent in 1968. On Mondays and Fridays though, the figure often goes almost to 15 percent. And that really hurts inside those plants. Right now we're averaging 5.1 percent for the year."

"You mean you're still averaging that high even after three years of recession and inflation?"

"Yes."

"Then you're going to need chronic economic trouble to cut that figure—or a catastrophe."

"I guess so—but believe me, nobody's praying for it!"

At General Motors I was told by a major official that productivity and the quality of cars coming off the line are affected adversely by absenteeism—and that it enhances inflation. "This is a serious matter, and we certainly talked about it quite a bit with the union during the 1970 negotiations. These absences are occurring in every geographical area—and all races and types of people are involved." Though only 15 percent of the work force at GM generates most of the late arrivals and absences, he went on, most of these men are concentrated among the newer workers under thirty-five. "They often take one or even two days off every week." When I asked him what he thought the outcome will be if this continues, I was given a brief lecture on the fall of Rome. Although this sort of instant Latin scholarship usually makes me impatient, I was impressed by his calm pessimism; for it was dramatic as perhaps only an immensely powerful man's pessimism can be when an element of habitual control is suddenly defying his grasp.

"It happened in the schools; it's happening in the Army—," Louie Streho, an old salt running the Detroit branch of the seamen's union, told me. "Why the hell did they ever think it wouldn't happen in the factories!"

In the mill now, as I lean leisurely on one of the brooms Stanley has thrust upon us, I begin to wonder about all this unexpected time I seem to have just to muse about things like Louie's bit of wisdom. I soon find out, from a few old mill hands, that these brooms we're pushing around often just keep us busy until enough men are AWOL—and we're really needed.

Yanagan, Charlie Chan, Scatterbrain, his brother Nobrain, Measles, Big John—almost everyone in the mills gets a nickname, including me after the second week:

"Out late last night, huh?" I hear while half asleep in the labor shack, a tiny room where the men warm up in this freezing, open building.

"Yeah," I tell Stash, one of the few older Polish guys still coming in here since the young blacks arrived.

"Chasin' whores, huh Ben . . . that's it—*Ben Whore!*" Everybody laughs except those still asleep, but they don't remain that way long:

"Get up—it's Biz!"

Four of my young friends leap up from their daze and dart out onto the floor away from the crotchety foreman: Stash heads upstairs where the electric furnace is blazing—and the big pay's made.

I follow Yanagan, the burner, who lights up his torch and starts cutting up scrap, but only until Biz passes out of sight.

"Come on Ben Whore—let's get away from here!"

"Hey, that's some name Stash gave me."

"Yeah—he's all right."

"Why do most of those guys upstairs stay out of the labor shack, Yanni?"

"Why?—'cause they're jive-ass bigots!"

"Are the younger workers the same way?"

"Uh-uh—some of those white boys are all right—not all of 'em; but a lot are gettin' hip. We wrote a petition to get a new union man for this shop, and none of those lilly-asses upstairs would sign it, but those young dudes did."

"What about the union—you for it?"

"You gotta be—or this company'll fuck you up good! But none of us really gives a shit about the union, 'cause no kind of big shot is goin' to make it any different in here."

"How do you want it to be different, Yanni?"

"I don't know man—just different, *real* different."

Yanagan leads me through a dark corner of the shop now, his eyes cast cautiously at the overhead cranes scooping up scrap for the insatiable furnaces upstairs.

"Psssst!! Hey!"

Hissing at us from behind a half-filled gondola car is Tommy Thumbs, and huddled uncommonly close to him are Little Joe, two vets recently back from Vietnam, and the new Italian kid.

"It's a downer day, man—let's lift it up!" Tommy passes a joint to Yanagan who draws the smoke deep, then hands it to me. For a moment I hesitate till Little Joe pats me on the shoulder and says: "What you waiting for? When you're feeling bad, you take medicine, right? Well, this place makes you feel sick, and you got the medicine right in your hand!"

The smoke striking into my lungs sends my blood leaping. And soon the flying sparks, the hot steel, the raging, exploding furnaces above us seem like frivolities on a carnival night.

Not all the mills in the country are quite like this one, I'm told. But old hands insist they will be, as the older workers retire in the next five years.

"Maybe some big doses of economic trouble will shape these kids up," a tough-minded company man told me in Pittsburgh. "But that's liable to murder us too. And I'd hate to see too many of this

breed out on the streets without jobs. I just don't think it'd be healthy."
Others both in Pittsburgh and Detroit reminded me that plenty of the
younger workers—indeed many I've met—are diligently paying off
mortgages and working hard for a second car, "and when that other
type gets older and has a few kids, everything'll probably settle down."
Yet when I asked what would happen until then, I got only a shrug of
the shoulders. A few clever economists, however, point out that the
steel industry has invested more than $10 billion in capital expendi-
tures since 1965, but that the expected soaring increases in productivity associated with such a huge investment haven't materialized. The
"productivity puzzle" is what this unprecedented mystery, found not
only in the steel industry, is being called. And it's haunting the financial wizards of Wall Street and Washington. I recommend they spend
a few days in a labor shack getting it all straight.

"Tommy—you've been out for two days. Don't you miss
the bread?"

"I can get by. I'd rather have the time than the money."

"You know—if jobs stay tight, the company'll probably start
cracking down hard."

A sudden, angry silence falls, and all the men in the shack are
staring at me. But I keep on talking because after four weeks of digging choking lime from degasser pits, hooking scrap to cranes, and
sweeping miles of dust and grime into neat little piles the way they do,
I'm entitled to their trust. "What if they crack down, Yanni?"

"They don't own me, man! If I want a day off, I take a day off.
Nothin's gonna stop that!"

"What if they fire you?"

"Then let 'em fire me. I ain't seen 'em do it yet."

"Why not?"

" 'Cause the next guy who comes along is going to do the same
thing I am."

Everybody in the room is laughing—not at me or Yanagan but
at the company, that slightly ridiculous Goliath they so easily can
thumb their nose at. For just the other day when Biz, that old Yankee
workhorse, caught Charlie Chan sleeping in the locker room, he rolled
his cigar in his mouth and began barking:

"Get to work! You know you shouldn't be lying around in
here—go on now!"

"Fuck you Jack!" Charlie hissed up at him.

"Get your coat mister!"

"Shut up, or I'll shove that cigar right down your throat!"

"You get the hell home!"

Charlie is laughing now as he tells us how mellow it was hav-ing the rest of the day off even though he lost the pay, and how he came in ten minutes late the next morning and not a word was said.

"Don't you care at all about getting the work done, Charlie?"

"They don't care about me—whether I'm livin' or dying! Why should I give a shit about them!"

Not all these young men are so bitter, and some even work hard—when they show up. But neither whites, blacks, skilled workers, laborers, militants, nor conservatives—and there are conservatives—are thank-ful to the company for providing them with jobs.

"Oh—that's strictly Mickey Mouse," a young Polish mill-wright with hair flowing from under his hard hat said to me. "You find some guys upstairs talking that way—but not many my age. This com-pany is using me to make money: I use them the same way. And that's all. . . ."

Another skilled worker, this one with short hair, who averages at least $5 an hour and who moonlights as a cop in the suburbs where he lives, told me: "The job's not bad, but this company stinks. You don't get anything from them without a fight."

"What about the union?"

"You got to keep on their ass, too."

"Any niggers working in your unit?"

"A few."

"Don't they bother you?"

"No—why should they?"

"Plenty of the older guys can't stand them."

"Some of the younger guys can't stand them either—but I don't think we're so steamed up about them. I'll tell you something, a lot of those black guys won't take any crap from the company. I don't mind working with them at all."

A few weeks later Ed Hojinachi, the treasurer at Local 65 of the Steelworkers union, my local, told me that he first realized things were profoundly changing when Bob Hatch, a black man, was elected president of 65. I answered that I wasn't at all surprised this had hap-pened, "not after what I've been hearing in the mill. And you know, Ed, a lot of locals in the Auto Workers have been taken by blacks, too—with strong support from some young white workers."

"Well, it's about time. I guess they want a fighter these days—whoever he is."

"Yes, and maybe it's about time," I hear echoed from Ed Sadlowski, who nine years ago, in an era when local union power simply wasn't challenged, took the presidency of 65. He was only twenty-three then: today he's Bob Hatch's strongest supporter and, at thirty-two, has his eye on the leadership of the entire Chicago–Gary–Milwaukee–Joliet district—a crucial one in the 1.2 million-man United Steelworkers of America.

"Of course there are changes coming," he says as he tours me through the Bush, the neighborhood around the mill where the skies blaze every night and the barrooms are seldom empty. "In 1965—get this!—only a few hundred disciplines were issued to the guys in the Southworks. Guess how many the company gave out last year?" The number must have leaped, I was sure, but to hear just how much stuns me: ". . . that's right, 3,400 disciplines in 1970—for coming late, for not coming at all, for swearing, arguing, drinking. And the company guys are moaning. They'd love the union to play copper and get everyone in on time for 'em—sure!"

"What do you tell them?"

"No sir—that's not my job. 'Make life better in those mills!' That's what I tell them."

Eddie takes me for a shot and a beer to a bar with music from Durango or Huahuaca blaring from its juke box, an establishment run by a brother of his friend and colleague from Local 65, Johnny Chico; then through the black section of the Bush where exhausted frame houses hug the edge of the Southworks; and finally to Marti and Joe's at the mill gate where, this time, polkas from Cracow or Warsaw blast from the juke box.

Men fresh off the second shift with mill dust still in their throats eagerly belly up to the bar. Its blunt, plain mahogany and the heavy laughter of the men leaning against it would be home to John Garfield—except for the TV flashing images from outer space and the long-haired young worker next to us in the red-white-and-blue cleatless track shoes.

Soon Eddie begins talking to him and his drinking partner who works in the same shop. He asks why they don't come to union meetings, and they tell him that they're boring. He asks if they'd like to see things changing in the mill. They would. He asks if a lot of other young workers feel that way, too. Many do. Then what can be done to make those changes come about? Their answer is a feeble shrug.

"Listen," he says, "you got to give more if you want more. I don't mean just wanting cash—I mean a better life. The union has to give more too. Sure, bread and butter's important—but maybe we spend too much time just thinking about money. Those companies (if they know what's good for them) and the unions, too—everybody should be thinking, and soon, about giving people better lives."

Snow is blowing in through the open doors of the shop, and steam rising from a slag pile by the lake turns suddenly eerie as the late-shift moon breaks through the clouds. The month is coming to an end, and so are my last hours in the mill. Despite the ceaseless clanging of metal echoing through the shop, the early morning brings a rare calm.

"Say José — did they really used to fire you after only three disciplines?" I'm talking to an intense, talkative old laborer who'd been in the mill more than twenty-five years.

"Sure they did. Now some of these young kids got six, seven, even eight of 'em and they're still around."

"How does that make you older workers feel?"

"We laugh."

"No kidding!"

"Sure — 'cause those foremen used to be so tough. You'd stop shovelin' for a few minutes and they'd say, 'What's the matter, you tired?' Now they catch these kids sleepin' on a bench and they don't even say nothin'. We're laughin' all right."

"But aren't you mad at the kids, too?"

"Sometimes, especially when you gotta carry the load for 'em. But I'll tell you, they've made gentlemen out of a lot of those company guys — not the big shots, I mean the company guys right here in the plants."

"What's going to happen after you older fellows retire, and it's only younger workers in here?"

"I don't know — sometimes we wonder if there's gonna be a mill anymore. One thing's sure — it ain't gonna be the way it used to be!"

The sun is finally rising over the lake now, and tired men with dirt-streaked faces begin trudging into the locker room. After good-byes to José, I join the others at the huge wash basins and, imitating those around me, fiercely scrub the mill from my skin like a guilty man. How determined Yanagan, Tommy Thumbs, Charlie Chan, and even José are with that soap and water, for there's no pride in this dust, nor joy in the frigid walk along the lake to the gate where we hand in our cards to a guard and pass into the outside world.

"Hey," I say to Tommy Thumbs while we're standing in the street waiting for a bus, "should they turn this whole damn mill into a frisbee field?"

"Into what, man?"

"Forget it Tommy — it's just a stupid idea."

Young Women Who Work
An Interview with Myra Wolfgang

WEINMAN: Can you begin by telling us something about restaurant workers?

WOLFGANG: The restaurant industry provides low-paying service jobs. It is the one industry that gives married women an opportunity to work just from eleven in the morning to two in the afternoon. They send their children off to school and are back home when the kids return. Also, it's an industry that allows you to work days if your husband works nights, or vice versa, so that child-care responsibilities can be divided between parents.

Now, along come the unions with their preconceived ideas. We say join our unions and you'll have seniority which will give you the right to work eight hours a day, a full day! We don't even bother asking senior employees whether that's what they want. If we did, they'd probably tell us that they would prefer to work part-time, and let the new person be stuck for eight hours.

Also, we say, the senior employees will have a choice of vacations. That's commendable, I mean it's a vested interest that they

MYRA WOLFGANG is International vice-president of the Hotel, Motel, and Restaurant Employees' Union, as well as secretary-treasurer of its Local 705 in Detroit. She also heads the Coalition for Women's Advancement. This interview was held in Detroit in the spring of 1971 by Bernard Rosenberg and Saul Weinman.

have in the job. But the new employee says, "Oh, to hell with this, I don't want to work in a union house. I'll never have a chance to take a vacation with my kids. The employees with seniority are going to beat me out." I cite that as an example of how by not consulting with our people we lose touch with them.

Then, too, we have difficulty appealing to young people — and there're many in our industry — because of the position labor has taken on the war. It's fine for the head of the labor movement to say, "I support the military," and "We have to leave Southeast Asia with honor," when he is talking about somebody else's life and not his own. Young people feel that very much.

On top of that I think there are real injustices in the unions, through they're blown up out of proportion. For instance, you have the Nixon administration laying responsibility for unemployment among black building tradesmen on the alleged racism of the building trade unions. Now, when 22 percent of the members of your unions are unemployed, as is the case with the carpenters in the Detroit area, this isn't the best time to say to them, You should share with blacks. The blacks and whites who are building tradesmen would all be working if the Nixon administration met the needs of housing in this country. But it hasn't done that, and the result is that you have all of this propaganda about unions, although *some* of it is justified. Well, between the war position and the racism, there isn't too much to attract young people to the unions.

I'm particularly concerned about the young because, as you know, the restaurant industry is an entry occupation. It's usually the first job a youngster works at; he may be working to buy a car, if he's middle-class and his father says, "You want a car? Go out and work for it."

This kid is going to earn exactly enough for a down-payment on that car, the insurance, and gasoline money. He may even buy it in partnership with three other kids. Here they are, working in a restaurant and we come along and give them a big speech about job security. You know, they should join the union so they'll have security on the job. But they're thinking of just one thing — to make enough money to get the hell *out* of the job. We also tell them that if they stick around long enough, we have a very good health, welfare, and pension plan. Our pension plan is predicated on the idea that everyone in the union must be covered. If we start to make exceptions, then the plan is no longer actuarially sound, and we can't fulfill our commitment to our older people. But meanwhile, what do these young guys care about pensions?

So we are finding it difficult to give young people enough

reasons to join the union. I have come to the conclusion that those who do join want the union because they would like to have someone around who will call the boss an s.o.b. They are just dying to call him that but they don't dare because they want that extra money. So they look for a mouthpiece in the union. That is why my public posture has to be one of a general hell-raiser. I believe more people are going to the unions because they want someone like me to raise hell, generally, than are looking for pensions or seniority or vacations or other benefits.

WEINMAN: Does that have any strategic value? I mean raising hell?

WOLFGANG: Well, of course, it does. I assure you, I really am a very peaceful person. Why does that make you laugh?

ROSENBERG: Can you tell us about the racial composition of your local?

WOLFGANG: Our union, about four years ago, was reaching the point where the majority was black. This is now changing, and the majority is again becoming white. That is because of the general closing of businesses in the inner city. You have restaurants and bars closing daily in the inner city, and they are all going out to the suburbs.

ROSENBERG: That's nationwide.

WOLFGANG: It's nationwide, but I speak with direct knowledge of Detroit. What happens is the blacks simply do not follow their jobs out to the suburbs. Many of them are housekeeping employees. You have twelve Holiday Inns in the metropolitan Detroit area. The Holiday Inns here have more beds than the Statler and the Hilton combined. Now, the Holiday Inns are all out there at the edge of town, with the exception of one on Trumbull Avenue here. All of them are outside the inner city, and the black maids just haven't got the transportation to get out there. Besides, prices in the suburbs are geared to getting employees who live in the general area.

The housekeeping department at the downtown Sheraton Cadillac Hotel is, oh, I'd say 90 percent black, and I think that the reverse pattern holds in most of the motels in suburban areas. And that's true of the restaurants, too, except for gourmet houses. If you're talking about waiters, some blacks make enough money to own a car, so they can follow a job. No one else has made that kind of money; few can follow the job, and therefore the complexion of our union is changing.

I remember about fifteen years ago, there were five hundred organized restaurants and bars from Jefferson, where Detroit starts at the side of Canada, out to Eight Mile Road, which is the city line.

Right now, that's down to about, oh . . . fifty, and of the fifty, I'd say that half are manned by the owners. They may have a porter come in and clean up, or a waitress who works on Saturday night, usually a woman from the neighborhood. As far as the union is concerned, if we have a contract, we never can catch the girl because she's never there for thirty days. You know, under the Taft-Hartley Law we can't approach them until thirty days are up, and by that time they're gone.

This is no longer a small business. You take the Stouffer Restaurant Company. Before they merged with Litton Industries they were grossing $55 million a year, and even then it wasn't a small institution. Now they have merged with Litton. They grossed over $90 million last year, and they are going not only into the motel business, and very successfully, but also into frozen foods and in-plant feeding. Quite a merger.

ROSENBERG: Why does that disturb you?

WOLFGANG: Because they are not being organized.

ROSENBERG: Why not?

WOLFGANG: To explain that I have to be critical of the International Union, which is always bad politics.

However . . . I think it requires organizing on a national scale with national effort, not just by local unions as they are now structured. Historically, we have all of the gourmet houses organized along craft lines: chefs' and cooks' union, a bartenders' union, a dining-room employees' union. And we organized the white-collar people, too, into a separate union.

Now, even though structurally we are all in one council and make one set of demands on an employer, with one set of goals for negotiating purposes, still the local unions are separate, and that in itself produces the seeds of jurisdictional fights. The big thing in the restaurant industry right now is that it is becoming de-skilled. The person who cooks is also serving you. Go to any hamburger drive-in and you find that's the case. Not only are they cooking and serving you, but they are also taking your cash. So right there you have three unions, under our present structure.

In many of our cities, we have our dining-room employees in local unions based on sex, which I consider not only a bad approach but possibly illegal.

San Francisco may be better organized than any other city in our industry. Yet Union Street, which is covered with restaurants, has no union restaurants. This is a new phenomenon. It's not because they are franchised chain restaurants, but because—you should pardon the expression—these are "hippie tearooms." And that goes back to what I was saying before about young people being less interested in unions; they just look upon the job as a temporary thing and they aren't interested in unionizing it.

But we are not organizing the chains either, and they are the ones that are growing, and the mergers that are taking place are tremendous. Sheraton, for instance, is now owned by IT&T.

WEINMAN: I'm not clear on why it takes more to organize these.

WOLFGANG: Partly because of our approach. We've got craft unions, and you can't use a craft union approach in a restaurant when there are no longer any craft demarcations. That's one thing. The other is that one of the real strengths we had in organizing—at least I speak of Detroit and my own experience—has been the cooperation of the Teamsters, for instance.

Detroit is the only city where Stouffers is organized. The first strike we had at Stouffers, we of course had not only 100 percent support of employees working there, but when gradually some of them began seeping back in and the company considered bringing some staff people in from Cleveland, absolutely no deliveries were made. There was no milk, there were no vegetables, there was no bread, there were no lemons. Nothing went in there. That was the Teamsters helping.

Okay, the chain operations now, not only do they have their own deliveries, they have their own merchandise. Stouffers is not relying on anybody to make deliveries. They have their own frozen foods plant. So, what used to be our strength is no longer a weapon at all, and we have not as yet devised new methods.

We don't have to stop being a craft union, but we have to stop organizing along craft lines. Who works exclusively as a cook at a Big Boy Hamburger? Big Boy is about the ninth largest purveyor of food in this country, and that's starting with the United States Army as number one.

WEINMAN: Is the model that you are talking about present anywhere in the trade union movement?

WOLFGANG: I'd say that the closest anyone has ever come to that is Local 1199, the Hospital Union in New York. The first thing they realize is that they are going to organize the whole industry and they have got to expand and have one union, regardless of the geographical area. Here for instance in my local I am not permitted organization north of Fourteen Mile Road, and if some restaurant just happens to be right on the corner of Fourteen Mile Road, then, boy, we've got to go to the Supreme Court to find out who can organize it. Local 1199 has its base in New York but is organizing even in Charleston. And in organizing in Charleston they have become the symbol of a fighting union interested in the blacks.

ROSENBERG: What happens when suburbanization leads to increasing black unemployment?

WOLFGANG: More and more conflict.

WEINMAN: What do you do about that?

WOLFGANG: One thing we do, although not too successfully, is try to redevelop the inner city. That's why my local union, for instance, is very active in working with the city administration, and trying to promote a downtown sports stadium that would at least bring people back into the city. We are very interested in the theater, not only because of its cultural contribution, but I, for instance, am on the board of directors of the Detroit City Theater because I have a feeling that if you do get people out of the house, you know, and away from the boob tube, they are going to wind up either having something to eat or going to the theater and then to eat.

General community problems become our problems because we cannot be separated from them. I personally and as a unionist working with women have been very much involved in the whole question of equal rights for men and women. I am unequivocally for equality. But I just believe that the Equal Rights Amendment is the wrong instrument.

I am particularly concerned with the recklessness coming from liberal women who should be more responsible in their arguments for the Equal Rights Amendment. The classic one that they use all the time is, 78 percent of the doctors in the Soviet Union, but only 9 percent of the doctors in this country, are women. They go on to say that the reason for this difference is that women are so badly discriminated against in medical schools. And I am certainly not saying that discrimination against women hasn't existed with us. But I am saying that in the Soviet Union the reason why so many women were able to become doctors was that the government by legal decree established legislation which made it tenable for them to become doctors. The legislation was designed specifically for women, it gave them special benefits.

Consequently, when a woman is interning to become a doctor in Russia, the hospital is not permitted to let her work on Sundays, on holidays, or on any days her children are not in school. But this is a recognition of the role of the mother, and, incidentally, special protective legislation that would be outlawed with an Equal Rights Amendment.

ROSENBERG: Would the Equal Rights Amendment benefit some women?

WOLFGANG: Most of the women who are sponsoring it are business and professional women. Possibly it would help them, although in employment it only affects public employees. The Equal Rights Amendment does not control the private sector of society, where most of the discrimination takes place.

WEINMAN: Well, then, why would you fight it?

WOLFGANG: Because the Equal Rights Amendment, even though it wouldn't affect the private sector, would automatically repeal all legislation that applies to women only!

California has a minimum wage law of $1.65 an hour for women. I don't know what the reasoning was, but the California legislature didn't include men. Bear in mind, for instance, that women are farm workers, and are covered by the federal law, which is $1.30 an hour; but in California, because of a state minimum-wage law, they are paid $1.65 an hour. It's $1.30 versus $1.65. If the Equal Rights Amendment were passed, and with the turnover on your farms there, growers could cut the pay of women workers 35¢ an hour. And let me tell you something—that's quite a price for working women to pay in behalf of a mythical equality that professional women are supposed to attain through an Equal Rights Amendment.

WEINMAN: Are the majority of your members women?

WOLFGANG: Yes.

WEINMAN: What is the sex distribution?

WOLFGANG: The majority of bartenders would be males; also the top cooks usually are males. You know, it's a very strange thing, the question never dawned on me until this moment. . . . You take the Culinary Institute, the country's leading school for training chefs. I don't recall ever seeing a woman student there. And I am pretty sure it's because none applied. And our International contributed funds to the Culinary Institute. It was a fine institute on the Yale campus. They gave men a skill and a very great skill, one that is much needed in this country. But I never recall seeing a woman being trained there. Now, if you just will look at the school's statistics, it would appear that there's great discrimination. I think, frankly, that there is discrimination in many, many cases, and no doubt about it.

Still, you do have more women cooks coming up in the industry now. At Stouffers it's almost entirely women.

ROSENBERG: Let me know if I am wrong on this, but isn't it so that in early America there were only waiters and at some point women appeared as strikebreakers?

WOLFGANG: I think you've had that kind of history in all our industry. Originally the blacks in Detroit were used as strikebreakers. The black waiter was brought to this city through the Detroit Athletic Club because we had a strike there in 1921. That's how they broke the strike. It represented the first appearance of black waiters in Detroit. The second occurred during a strike we had at the Statler Hotel when, once again, they brought in black waiters. Unfortunately, that's the history of black breakthrough in this area.

I recall long before we had an FEPC in this state, many people thought that there was something "high-class" about a black waiter rather than a waitress working a banquet. We would be driven absolutely crazy on weekend orders, particularly for Bar Mitzvahs, when someone would ask us to please send waiters with white gloves. White gloves were a big deal. I sent out a letter about fifteen years ago to every caterer in the city pleading with them not to specify female, male, white, or black preference. "You will get the person who's first on our numbering system."

One of the elegant clubs here, the most expensive of upper-middle-class clubs, is the Franklin Hills Country Club, originally set up by Meyer Prentice, the only Jew in the General Motors hierarchy. Along came Mother's Day and Franklin Hills Country Club was determined to have waiters with white gloves. We had a contract that gave the employees seniority, and if they were not fired, for instance, in the 1968 season, then their seniority carried over to the 1969 season. In 1968 they had all women there, so I said, "You're crazy. You're going to have the women who worked there last year." They insisted on white gloves. I said, "Well then, okay, put white gloves on the women, but you're going to have women." We had a war of nerves. And do you know, they figured if they asked these women to wear white gloves, that the women would quit because it was so ridiculous. The new manager was from the Country Club of Detroit which is *the* place — you know, the Fords who only talk to the Sloanes who only talk to God. Well, Mr. DeHart, who had been manager at the Detroit Country Club, came over, and he wanted to bring the black waiters with him, and at Franklin Hills they were dying to have approval from those Country Club people. Finally I sat some of them down and said, "By the way, do you know where the white-gloves tradition comes from? It has absolutely nothing to do with cleanliness. It was simply that in the old days in the South, black skin was not palatable to the plantation owner while he was having his dinner, so he had his slaves cover their hands with white gloves." That produced a certain sense of shame, and it ended the business. No more white gloves.

ROSENBERG: You have a reputation for some flamboyance in this city, recently because of incidents at the Playboy Club.

WOLFGANG: *Playboy* magazine announced that their next club would be opened in Detroit. We knew that they were not paying bunnies any wages anywhere in the country. I was concerned about whether that was going to be their policy here, too.

WEINMAN: They got *no* wages?

WOLFGANG: I mean no wages, nothing.

ROSENBERG: All commission?

WOLFGANG: All tips. We finally negotiated for commission. Well, when they were getting ready to open here, they advertised for help. They got a location on West Grand Boulevard near Second. I simply had to find out what and whether they were going to pay anybody. It was our intention to put a picket line on the place, protesting their labor policy. My daughter was then seventeen years old, and I dressed her up in a very becoming black-and-white checked skirt with an orange velvet top. Her hair was flowing, she had a guitar under her arm, the whole bit.

      She went down and applied for a job. She was interviewed by Keith Hefner, that's Hugh Hefner's brother. And they had a very good interview, and he hired her, and after she was hired, she inquired, "By the way, what will I get paid?" Answer: "You'll make $250 a week." She said, "I didn't ask you what I would make. I asked you what I get paid."

      At last he admitted that they didn't pay anything. "Well, then how will I make $250 a week?" "On tips." "OK, that's what the customer will be giving me, but what will you be giving me?" So, he repeated himself, "You don't get paid." "What about the uniform?" "We furnish that." End of interview. And she was hired. I then knew for sure that they were not planning to pay any wages.

      So, we put a picket line out, a very dramatic one, to stress the evils of working for no wages, you know, Sodom and Gomorrah, hell on earth. It got very Biblical. The television cameras arrived and newscasters wondered how we knew Playboy wouldn't pay wages. They weren't even ready to open, I said, because the damn fools just hired my seventeen-year-old daughter. In those days our liquor-control law didn't permit anyone under the age of twenty-one to work in such an establishment, which is why I had made the point that she was seventeen. The result was that for years, whenever I told my daughter to stay in school (she is about to get a second M.A. degree and I've kept her in school now for seven years), her answer was, "But I could make $250 a week as a bunny. Why go to school?" It wasn't until I explained to her that it wouldn't be long-lasting that she decided to become a professional.

WEINMAN: Was this episode related to the strike in New York?

WOLFGANG: New York followed. There a very interesting thing happened, only they won their argument and we lost ours. Our national agreement with Playboy International requires that whenever we reach a 51 percent majority of the membership in a given area, the company agrees to become bound by the highest contract of that area. However, that's for cooks, bartenders, waiters, buffet workers; as far as bunnies are concerned, they are supposed to be covered by a national agreement presumably because of the interchange from one city to another. The theory is that you guys get tired of looking at the same face, if anyone bothers looking at a bunny's face — but anyhow, they keep sending them from city to city. So the agreement has the usual language according to which no one shall be fired for union activity, but it goes on, unfortunately, to state that the employer may discharge a bunny for "loss of the bunny image."

Now, in New York, the bunny who "lost her image" first, naturally, was the shop steward. Very quickly New York charged that she was discriminated against for union activities, and the contract there required arbitration. They refused to go into arbitration. The courts directed that they do so and this bunny was reinstated with full back pay, about $4,000.

Here in Detroit the same thing happened. It involved not only the shop steward but a member of the bargaining committee. Five cities elected two bunnies to sit on a national bargaining committee. And everyone thought this was going to be a ball, that they were going to have some real fun.

Our own international officers were startled at the approach of these girls. They understood unions. Most of them were married to union members. The two Detroit bunnies who sat on the national bargaining committee — one girl was married to a fellow who works at the General Motors Tech Center and is a member of the UAW, the other girl's husband was a member of the Musicians' Union.

Well, when they came back from the national bargaining, the member from the Detroit team, who was called Bunny Jo, within a month's time was fired for loss of the bunny image. Jo was anxious to test the agreement she had negotiated. One part of the agreement stipulated that the employer could not arbitrarily fire someone for loss of the bunny image, but the bunny could name a committee of three of her peers to adjudicate. Bunny Jo, naively and without telling the union, agrees to the appointment of a committee of three of her peers who immediately agree with the boss that Jo had lost her bunny image.

When I found out about that, I was just furious. I said, "Jo, you were a member of the bargaining committee, you were the shop steward there, did it ever dawn on you that the real reason you were fired was because of your activity in the union?"

She said, "Of course it dawned on me. I've kept tallies on how much money it has cost me to be steward, and all an employer has to do in our industry is give you a different station or different hours."

So we claimed that she was fired for union activity and asked the company to go into arbitration. They refused, claiming that she could not use two remedies of the contract, and that she had selected one of them, but still we went to court. The courts upheld Playboy International, but our International union has authorized that it be appealed to the higher courts, and we are going all the way with it.

In the meantime, we are also filing a case locally with our Civil Rights Commission, created by the Fair Employment Act we have here. It was recently amended to add age as an illegitimate basis for job discrimination. If we find that Bunny Jo is older than the other bunnies, we will contend that is why they say she has lost her bunny image. If somebody had told me thirty-five years ago that I would be worried about such a problem, I would have said he was absolutely crazy.

WEINMAN: There are also a lot of kids who work in department stores. Your situation sounds a lot like the Retail Clerks'.

WOLFGANG: That's right. They have exactly the same problem with the package girls and boys. You have the kids going to work for some immediate purpose, like accumulating enough money for college.

But about that, in our industry an interesting thing has happened. Chuck Muer, who has quite a few restaurants around the Detroit area, opened one in Ann Arbor called the Gandy Dancer. It's a charming restaurant. I was out there talking to some waitresses. The first three girls I talked to were college graduates—all three of them had their degrees in education, and all three couldn't get jobs as teachers.

I subsequently found out that every woman employee in the Gandy Dancer is a college graduate. All right. Now, I asked how long are you girls going to stay in this industry? One said, "I'll stay until I find a job teaching." But then she gave me a real broad smile and added, "but I am not going to look for a job teaching. I can't make the money as a teacher I can make here. I'm going to make it while I can and then off to Europe for two years."

ROSENBERG: It's like working to buy a car.

WOLFGANG: I admire that in the kids. They are living for now, as they really should do.

ROSENBERG: What effect does the present economic crisis have?

WOLFGANG: Very simply, we are the first to be hurt. Always the first to be hurt because you don't eat dinner out; you eat dinner at home. You invite six friends over instead of going to the movies. Incidentally, after World War II, when men came back and couldn't find the housing, they all bought small houses and built recreation rooms. That's part of how the suburbia bit got started—and on a Saturday night you invited five couples over, and you did whatever was at your particular level, played cards, had beer and potato chips, and that was it. For the next five Saturday nights, you were busy on return invitations. All of your social life began to center around the home. In the summer it was the outdoor barbecue, and in the winter it was the recreation room or beer bash. The result is that these people just don't go out and it affects our business immediately, which is why, as a local union, we are so very interested in theater or any social activity that will get people out of their home.

All that's left as a saving grace for New York restaurants is that tourists eat out, but we don't have tourism in this city.

We have one good month a year, which is January, when the Society of Automotive Engineers meets in Detroit.

We do have the summer clubs and the winter banquet circuit which is mostly fund-raising affairs and conventions. We depend an awful lot on conventions.

ROSENBERG: What about the war?

WOLFGANG: On the war issue, this local has taken a very clear position. We oppose it. Our International union has not taken a position; there's no doubt that if they did, it would be one supporting Meany.

ROSENBERG: Did you have any politics in the '30s?

WOLFGANG: Who didn't?

ROSENBERG: Were you a Socialist?

WOLFGANG: Yes, I still am theoretically. I never was a joiner! In other words, I didn't change, the world just changed around me. That was true for most of us who became leaders in the trade unions. We got our basic training in the working-class political movement.

Workers, Black and White, in Mississippi
Pat Watters

The big, middle-aged man, wearing his hard hat and heavy boots, breathes a long sigh as he pours himself a cup of coffee in the union hall (with such signs on the wall as "SST—Ours or Theirs?" showing the U.S. and British flags, and "Visit Your AFL–CIO Union Barber" and "Keep America Beautiful, Get a Haircut"). He has just come off the shift in the shipyard, and in some sense he is typical of the American labor force, just as in some way his union is typical of the American labor movement at the beginning of the 1970s. But in other, perhaps crucial ways, neither he nor his union is typical. Neither fulfills the expectations one might have of labor, of the working class—or for that matter, of the Mississippi white he is.

Raised on a farm and conditioned in the graces and disgraces of early twentieth-century white Southern ruralism, he has been buffeted during the past decade between the racist dogma of official Mississippi and the sane racial policies of his union. The majority of the members of the Mississippi AFL–CIO (perhaps 90 percent of all who are over forty) come from a similar background—though the conditioning of the black members has been different. All have come into the labor force less by choice than by the compulsions of cultural and economic change.

Race, politics, and economics—these, as across America, are

PAT WATTERS, Director of Information for the Southern Regional Council, is the author of The South and the Nation and Down to Now: Reflections on the Southern Civil Rights Movement.

the concerns of his union. But where he is puts these concerns in a tilted perspective. "It's hot today," he says, and he is expressing faith in the Southern belief that scalding coffee cools you off. Out in the shipyard in Pascagoula, Mississippi, where he has been working under a merciless sun in murky air, the temperature is upward of a hundred. "It's hot. Long about 2:30, I begun to see them little red monkeys in front of my eyes."

Where he is makes a difference—most of all as regards race. One does not come around asking glib questions in the latest catchwords. "What about all this talk about ethnics in the labor movement?" I asked Claude Ramsay, the rough-hewn president of the Mississippi AFL–CIO, himself one of those who came from a Mississippi farm into the labor force and movement (by way of a paper mill in Pascagoula). "Ethnics, hell. We ain't got nothing but black and white—and a few Indians and a couple of dozen Chinese families up and down the Delta." He recalled a recent talk he had given to a carpenters' union on strike in a small town. "I walked in there, and sure enough—the thing we are putting an end to—the whites were all sitting on one side at the meeting, and the blacks on the other. And who do you think had to stand up in the back? A bunch of Choctaw Indians."

Ramsay's leadership has centered on such matters as trying to end in Mississippi the South's old story of separation of black and white. To bring the two together on mutual economic interests has been from the beginning a fundamental goal for Southern labor, and Mississippi labor has been a leader in the South in seeking that goal. Ramsay's leadership has to be credited as the main reason, and another of those tilted perspectives becomes apparent about Mississippi and Southern labor in the fact that Ramsay is the only state president the Mississippi AFL–CIO has ever had. The State Council was not formed until 1959, with Ramsay working after-hours to get it organized. That he has been able to be re-elected during the twelve years of the Council's existence—sometimes with his racial policies challenged by opposing candidates—demonstrates that white Mississippi workers can resist the racist conditioning of their society. If nothing else, it shows that for many of them self-interest matters more than racism.

The best of this tilted racial perspective was expressed by another worker at Pascagoula, a younger man raised in northern Mississippi (where racism is stronger than down on the Gulf Coast):

White against black is just not as strong in the state as it used to be. Before, black and white couldn't get together. A nigger was a low-rated person. But I told my friend here [gesturing to a black officer in his local] I might not know what it is to be black. But I sure know how it is to be treated like a nigger by management. And blacks can see that whites are getting the same old shaft blacks get. We fought each other for a long time, with the company egging us on. But now we are — some of us — fighting together.

Some of the tilted economic and political perspectives were on display at the 1971 meeting of the Mississipi AFL–CIO Committee on Political Education (COPE) in Jackson. The 236 representatives were to make endorsements for the year's political contests in the state. The delegates sat at long tables in a narrow, badly ventilated room. Many of the white men had crew cuts, none long hair or a beard; none of the black men or women had an Afro. The seating was admirably intermingled. More impressive was that it remained so when the delegates went to lunch.

Part of their perspective is suggested by the list of questions each candidate had been asked by a COPE committee — whether public employees have a right to collective bargaining; whether workmen's compensation (among the least advantageous in the nation) should be increased; whether the state maximum weekly unemployment benefit might not be increased from $49; how taxes might be increased (the sales tax in this lowest per-capita-income state now stands at 5 percent); whether teacher salaries (among the lowest in the nation) should be increased; whether the state should enact, since it does not have it, a compulsory school attendance law; whether state employees should be put on civil service; whether absentee balloting should be available to all and not just to special groups such as servicemen; whether eighteen-year-olds should be allowed to vote — and whether, in the year 1971, Mississippi might not find it desirable to establish (not now having one) a state department of labor.

How limited the strength of the Mississippi AFL–CIO is in state politics was evident in the discussion of some candidates, which made it clear they did not consider a COPE endorsement entirely an asset. Though it has grown considerably in recent years, union membership remains around 85,000, by Ramsay's estimate, out of a total population of 2,216,912. Nor are all the locals affiliated with the State Council. Only North Carolina, with its union-busting textile plants, is a tougher state to organize.

One speaker at the 1970 convention said of political candidates seeking clandestine labor support: "They wanted our vote, but they didn't want to be seen with us. If they met with us, they wanted to make sure it was in a secluded area in the woods or in somebody's cow barn. So far as I am concerned, we have had it with that kind of candidate. Now, if my granddaddy was alive and a candidate, I would say the same thing about him."

At the COPE meeting, it was reported that one candidate for lieutenant governor, Cliff Finch, had said he would appreciate labor support but preferred not to have an open endorsement. This attitude went strongly against him in the screening committee and resulted in its approval of his opponent, William F. Winter (who later won in the November 1971 election). It was pointed out that Winter had taken the same stand when he ran unsuccessfully for governor four years earlier, but had since come to realize it was a bad mistake. Finch supporters got up in consternation to say that *they* had advised him it might be better not to have a public endorsement.

A prim and proper-speaking middle-aged white woman and an older black man were seated side-by-side at a table. She voted one way, he the other, and when he sat down, she said in the same bantering tone she would have used to a white man: "You just wait. I'll get even with you Monday." And he laughed and said, "I'd like to see you try."

The vote was, finally, to endorse none of the candidates for lieutenant governor. The same decision had been made, on recommendation of the screening committee, in regard to the governor's race. This suggested some of the deeper difficulties, still, of the union movement with Mississippi's racial struggles, and the personal dilemma faced by Ramsay. Ramsay's dilemma revolved around the black candidacy of Charles Evers for governor. Previously, Ramsay had been involved in the development of black political strength in the state—such affairs as the Freedom Democratic party, the Democratic Conference, a coalition of white and black regular Democrats, organizations of the state-wide Voter Registration and Education League, and the election of a black legislator, Robert Clark. But there had been bad blood between Ramsay and Evers for some time (though Ramsay claims an AFL–CIO voter registration drive had been essential to Evers's election as mayor of Fayette), and this came to the surface during the gubernatorial race.

In private, Ramsay accused Evers of being of the monied interests. "It took me some time," he said, "to realize that not all blacks are sympathetic with labor, with our economic interest." He was incensed, as were many Mississippi hard-core white liberals,

over Evers's urging black voters to support segregationist Jim Swan **in the** primaries on the dubious theory that he would be easier than **the** other white candidates to beat in a two-man general election race.

It is doubtful that Ramsay could have delivered the white labor vote for Evers even if he had wanted to. His disinclination to support Evers was one of several recent episodes that lost him prestige and support among black leaders. In the past, his rapport with such leaders and his influence on the increasingly strong black vote had been one of the assets (like the labor vote itself) on which the labor movement depended. In one way or another, this had hurt his image with the most powerful of the black organizations, the NAACP, the Freedom Democratic party, and the Delta Ministry.

In its internal liberal and black struggles Mississippi, more than any other Southern state, is a close community, in many ways like an extended small town. Personalities figure large and personal relationships are incredibly complicated. Aaron Henry, one of the most powerful black leaders, acknowledged some of Ramsay's difficulties, but said Ramsay still had considerable rapport with black leadership in such matters as voter registration. Many blacks, Henry said, feel that Ramsay wants to be the white voice for the black community — something not now, if it ever was, acceptable to blacks. But Henry himself didn't agree — and felt the thing about Ramsay that alienated some blacks was just his natural way, his loud and boisterous argumentative manner, for example, of the kind that often is second nature to a man who has fought his way up in labor. He might have added that in dealing with blacks just as he does with whites, Ramsay treats them with ultimate respect — as worthy adversaries.

Speaking of these difficulties, Ramsay expressed hope that a new black local leadership will emerge from such organizations as the Voters' League. In the national and even some of the Southern perspective, this might be described in scornful tones as pitting a set of Uncle Toms against a set of militants. But in the tilted perspective of Mississippi (and most of the South) this merely describes a reality, a natural sorting among blacks between those willing to try to wrest more reform (which has been considerable in the South) from the system, and those who despair of the system entirely. In Mississippi this could mean the difference between those blacks who view all the Mississippi AFL–CIO has done in the racial struggle as valuable, **and** those who see it as meaningless.

Since Ramsay became state president in 1959, he has been a spokesman for racial equality within the union movement and for racial and economic reform in Mississippi society. He likes to tell of dramatic moments of change within the unions, like the time after the murderous riot following the admission of James Meredith to the University of Mississippi, when a bunch of Pascagoula men organized what amounted to a Klan—burning crosses, shooting into the newspaper editor's home, and the like. Then Ramsay was still living in Pascagoula, and he went to the Metal Trades Council and warned that they were going to lose the shipyard if this kind of thing didn't stop—because of the yard's dependence on government contracts. "I knew some of our members were involved," he said. Ira B. Harkey, Jr., printed his speech as an editorial on the front page of the Pascagoula *Chronicle* and, sure enough, the trouble quieted down.

Because of that episode, and an early attempt by Ramsay (later successfully pursued by other groups) to force Federal Communications Commission action against Jackson TV station WLBT for racist practices, and because of the hysterical general violence of whites during the 1964 Freedom Summer when hundreds of civil rights volunteers worked in the state, Ramsay has been a frequent target of abuse. In those years he carried a shotgun in his car, warned threateners he would take some of them with him, and told local unions they had better decide whether they wanted to be represented by the Klan or the AFL–CIO. This was probably the strongest stand among Southern AFL–CIO state presidents, and certainly a performance superior to that of labor on the race issue nationally. "I decided at the outset," he said, "we were going to put the labor movement on the right side of crucial issues."

Ironically, the most dramatic and most publicized black-and-white organizational effort the South has yet seen, a "strike" of pulpwood cutters in Mississippi and Alabama this fall, was not an AFL–CIO undertaking. The strikers, independent contractors, are not technically considered hired labor. Ramsay's role in the strike was limited to advice-giving.

Ramsay's stand on race is an integral part of his goals for the labor movement in Mississippi. From the start, he has presented his analysis to the membership in plain, uncompromising language. He recites the dismal statistics of Mississippi's low social and economic standing (nearly always below the other Southern states, which means fiftieth in the nation) in per capita income, education, health care—all the indices. He tells how politicians, by making race the paramount issue, have failed to confront these crucial problems.

Ramsay relishes telling how agricultural interests in the state discouraged the rise of industry in 1910 with passage of a law forbidding any corporation to own more than $1 million in assets, and how, when Governor Hugh White in 1936 made the necessary turn to "Balance Agriculture with Industry" (the BAWI program), it was in terms of allowing government agencies to float bond issues to build plants for private industry. (The limitation on corporate holdings had been repealed in 1924.) Other BAWI inducements to industry have included tax exemption to plants for given numbers of years, a right-to-work amendment to the state constitution, and weak workmen's compensation laws. In 1960, the law on bonded indebtedness was amended to allow equipping as well as building plants. Industry so lured is almost always anti-union, often running away from a union shop in another state. Most are low-pay; clothing manufacture predominates. If such a plant is finally organized, owners simply pull out, as like as not to another town eager to float a bond issue to build a new plant. Ramsay inveighs against the whole system, urging the need for sophisticated unionization.

In all of this, he has stressed support of Negro rights on moral and constitutional grounds, but with appeals to the self-interest of whites as well. As early as 1966 he was saying in his speeches:

> Twenty-six counties in Mississippi have a Negro population majority. Many of labor's worst enemies in the Mississippi Legislature live in these counties. We have very few members residing in those counties; if these people are removed from office, it will have to be done with the Negro vote. To a large degree our legislative program is dependent upon our ability to form a political alliance with these people.

Violence done to organizers, a commonplace in the '50s and '60s — beatings, shootings, fire-bombings, police harassment, the whole arsenal used against civil rights workers — these have abated. Beat up and told to get out of town not too long ago, one organizer went to the county sheriff and was told laconically that he probably had better follow his assailants' advice. In 1967, the Laurel home of the Rev. Allen Johnson, a labor supporter and civil rights leader (now president of the Voters' League), was bombed. Since then he has had white support in developing a three-hundred-home cooperative housing project which bears his name and that of singer Leontyne Price.

But more sophisticated anti-union tactics continue, including efforts under the right-to-work law to discourage blacks from joining unions — a new version of the old divisive strategy. Against all this, Ramsay points to organization results — a doubling of union membership in the twelve years of the State Council. He is especially pleased that in the past five years much of the new organization has been in the northern part of the state — the seat of past resistance and repression. Union members tell gleefully of a town that resisted over many years but finally had its plants organized, and this year had Ramsay speaking to the Rotary Club.

There still is the grave lack of fuller industrialization in Mississippi. Average nonagricultural pay in the state is still a low $2.43 per hour, which includes an increase of 91¢ since 1960. Manufacturing still employs only 120,000 of the state's more than two million people. A mark of resistance to organization: according to the Bureau of Labor Statistics, 13.8 percent of nonagricultural employees in Mississippi belonged to unions in 1968. This compared with a national average of 24.8 percent. Only North Carolina (7.5 percent) and South Carolina (8.6 percent) were below Mississippi among the Southern states. Alabama, with aerospace and steel, had the highest percentage in the South, 20.1. In the face of such facts, Ramsay extols the state's real advantages for industry (natural and human resources) as boosterishly as any industrial council spokesman. The industries Ramsay deems desirable include paper mills, whose stench and wastes befoul much of the South's air and water. Like businessmen themselves, Southern labor leaders, by the nature of what they do, cannot face the question of whether industry is really a desirable goal. A worker whose farm home sits between two paper mills and catches the wind from one if not both may have his doubts. Why not land reform?

Attempting to win more friends in the legislature is only part of the union's political strategy. Another part is the effort to elect a House Speaker who is a friend of labor, because in many ways (partly because of the state's antiquated constitution) he has more power than the governor.

Its political strategy demonstrates the Mississippi union movement's potential. Other dimensions are suggested by the example of Pascagoula. There, in 1965, the state of Mississippi put $130 million worth of BAWI bonded indebtedness into expanding the shipyard Litton Industries had acquired from Ingalls, a local firm. The state also accommodated the plant with highway construction, and the federal government has done its part for Litton (despite some feeble liberal protest) with river dredging and more than $2 billion in defense contracts. The Pascagoula Metal Trades Council did its part, too—accepting a five-year contract in 1967 with top pay of $3.62 an hour (low even for shipbuilding) to "encourage" Litton. Litton did expand—building a highly automated assembly-line shipyard (called the "West Bank") on the Pascagoula River, across from the old yard. The separation of the two yards was used by the company as an excuse for trying to avoid seniority obligations under the contract and, more important to the unions, to try to blur jurisdictional distinctions—a complicated wrangle that wound up before the National Labor Relations Board. (The old-line union members in Pascagoula have come to despise Litton with more than ordinary anti-management spleen. Ramsay cites Litton as the example par excellence of the evils of absentee, "conglomerate" ownership, and of subsidy of private industry. If one-ninetieth of what workers at the plant casually accuse management of in wasteful, ignorant, corrupt practices should prove true, Litton would be a national scandal to make Lockheed look respectable.) The large number of new workers who did not join the union presented another serious threat to the Metal Trades Council. (The work force is being expanded from five thousand to twenty thousand.) Not a few of the nonorganized were black workers who were told the company's own race-relations committee could represent their interests better than local unions with a racist background. The Metal Trades Council had been one of those to withdraw eleven of its unions (all but the office workers) from the State Council in criticism of Ramsay's racial policies—some time after it had taken his advice about the Klan. But in 1970 it called on him in this new difficulty, and the locals are beginning to drift back into the Council. An organizing camapign built union membership up to 70 percent, and the contract was reopened for ongoing negotiations on the wage scales. Ramsay drew on resources of the International unions to develop a model program for the plant. Litton, at an unusual White House conference held in January 1971 (in part because of liberal congressional criticism of the Litton situation), was ready to accept Ramsay's program because its own employment program was encountering a dismayingly high turnover.

Ramsay's program included:

A nondiscrimination clause putting the plant in compliance with federal contract regulations. This required that 45 percent of all future employees be black, and it required advancement of 340 blacks then in dead-end jobs.

Establishment of a human relations committee in the Metal Trades Council (the first in Mississippi) to handle racial problems. Similarly, the union has established a relationship with a local Black Coalition and other civil rights organizations.

Setting up a recruiting and training office with U.S. Department of Labor manpower grants, with cooperation of the AFL–CIO Human Resources Development Institute and the Joint Apprenticeship Program of the Workers Defense League—A. Philip Randolph Educational Fund. This office works with new employees, in cooperation with Litton and the Mississippi Employment Service. But its most significant program is the recruiting and coaching of apprentices. Under the 45 percent black hiring policy, the program offers to thousands of blacks in the area opportunity superior to any previously available, and probably unsurpassed in the South.

Plans for a union housing project, which would, in effect, be a new town within Pascagoula to take care of the drastic housing shortage caused by the shipyard expansion. A nonprofit corporation took out an option on one thousand acres of land and sought federal funding to build houses, which the union would erect as part of a training program for the building trades. (Ramsay pointed out that when discussion of the project first got started, he casually told the Pascagoula union people that he assumed they realized such a building program and such housing would have to be integrated. No one demurred.)

The general program now is in effect. Bob Thomas, a black veteran of the Mississippi labor and civil rights movements, is in charge of the Joint Apprenticeship Program office. He has a black secretary and two white field workers, and a black expert in recruiting and tutoring who is on loan from the Harlem Joint Apprenticeship office to help get things organized.

Recruitment for apprentices began in March 1971. One of the white recruiters is B. M. (Shorty) Carnell, a union man since 1944 and a machinist in the shipyard since 1958. He gives to the job the same intensity and activity he gave, earlier, to an assortment of other union offices. He knows and loves shipbuilding, knows all the union and management ropes, and has an inexhaustible fount of contacts. He is an ardent union man; it can be expected that most of his recruits will be so, too, before he is done with them. "The young people want to talk about what the union can do for them; I ask them what they can do for the union. It has to be more than paying dues."

The initial response to the apprenticeship program has not been as strong among black and white young people as might be expected. But Shorty is confident that careful screening is necessary and diligent seeking (in the swimming holes, beer joints, churches, wherever young people go) will pay off. Currently the program is confined to the Pascagoula area. If the housing program goes through, recruitment can become statewide — including the Delta of Mississippi, which exports to Northern and Southern cities virtually all of its black and much of the white youth. Bob Sutton, the man on loan from the Harlem office, said the only difference he could see between such work in the

Northern ghetto and among the black youth of Mississippi is the necessity to indoctrinate the latter more in the meaning of unions. Young Mississippians, black and white, he said, tend to go after the quick money of unskilled jobs and to shy away from schools. "It helps when they understand this program will help them all the way through."

In Mississippi the appearance of things is often deceptive. Sutton dresses and speaks as though he might always have dwelt in Harlem. It turns out he grew up in nearby Gulfport. Shorty, who speaks and looks like a Mississippian, grew up in Cincinnati. The two don't quite agree about race relations in Mississippi. Shorty thinks all the trouble is over. Sutton sees change since he left for New York, but won't concede the millennium. Shorty tells about the black man who got trapped by machinery in a shipyard accident and a white man who gave him mouth-to-mouth resuscitation until he could be freed, saving his life. Sutton tells of the time when he was a boy and he and his father came upon an automobile wreck, and his father, a big man, literally muscled the car door open and reached his hand in to rescue the driver. The driver, a white man, stretched out his hand, then saw that it was a black hand extended to help him, and refused. Of such talk, point and counterpoint, is being built the real racial understanding of the future—in Mississippi and all over the South—outside the "liberal" and *de rigueur* radical bastions, among the people of both races who have suffered most from racism.

One of the young white apprentice-candidates I met, a native Mississippian, no longer is under the sway of the upbringing he got in the old racist pattern. He got to know a lot of "spades" when he was a racing-car driver and during his time in a Mississippi small-city "head-scene." He has nothing against "spades," he says, as long as they respect his right to be an individual, too.

A man in his fifties who works in a unionized paper plant tells how the thing worked out there. The personnel manager got the order to hire blacks and was afraid to. He told the older man he was going to put the order on the bulletin board and asked him to organize a protest over it. "Not on your life," the man replied. "You just hire those blacks and let them get out with those peckerwoods in the plant, and it won't be a week before they're matching for nickels and wrestling around with each other"—and sure enough, he said, that's the way it was. Perhaps that's the way the man wants to believe it turned out to be. Mississippi's racial antagonisms are so deeprooted and the weight of the past so much against blacks that it is no more reasonable to expect the millennium there than in the rest of the South—or the rest of America. But the difference in Mississippi, more than in the rest of the South and the rest of the American labor movement, lies in the groundwork Claude Ramsay has laid during the formative years of the Mississippi AFL–CIO. What he has done and does now transcends race. He wasn't talking, as so many liberals and labor people, about black people per se when he insisted on adherence to the Constitution as the guiding principle. He was talking about the rights of individuals — all people. And he knew that this principle was more important than immediate practical gain for the union.

Describing how conservative most of white Mississippi still is, a young International union representative said, "Why, they think Ramsay is a wild-eyed radical. In an industrialized Northern state, he would be considered conservative." But if a man like Ramsay is judged conservative in the standard national perspective, something is wrong with that perspective. In the same way, Ramsay's difficulties with elements of black leadership have left him open to attack as being old-fashioned. But all that Ramsay has done, whether correct or not in specific situations, has been to stay consistent with his primary values — constitutional rights in regard to race relations, which to him means integration and the rights of labor in economic and political matters (which in a few instances has pitted him against some blacks who would be willing to sacrifice organized labor's economic advantages to prevent it from being an influence on masses of black workers). Ramsay is no more likely to capitulate to them on the basis of color than he was to whites. And if, in a national or in some ways Southern perspective, this makes him old-fashioned and conservative, then the perspective needs to be examined. For Ramsay and many of his counterparts in the Southern labor movement have, indeed, been real radicals within a truly conservative society.

Perhaps soon, in some superficial aspects, the skews in the Mississippi perspective will disappear. But if Ramsay's value system continues to prevail in the Mississippi labor movement (and the same might be said for most of the rest of Southern labor), it will be more capable of coping than most of American labor with the kind of complicated problems that will come with success and largeness and power.

Bob Thomas, the black man in charge of the Pascagoula Human Resources Development Institute, has his own perspective. Blacks and whites, both, have been "re-educated" by recent union and civil rights history in Mississippi, he says. They have both learned they can't move by themselves. Anybody, black or white, who thinks otherwise is either mistaken or out to exploit people. He started in the union movement in Memphis "when the CIO was born, when they

opened up the unions for black people and said, 'Come all ye . . . .' "
He knew what it was to be "run out and shot at" during the civil
rights movement. When he talks about his work in Pascagoula, it
is not in terms of black and white, but the total community. "I've
never seen anything like it. It's the greatest challenge I've ever had.
And it's the greatest opportunity that community has ever had. . . ."

The Case of the ILGWU
Dorothy Rabinowitz

In the summer of 1900 the newly formed International Ladies' Garment Workers' Union could call its own a treasury of $30 and a few desks in the office of the Cloakmakers' Union. This modest enterprise was called into being at the behest of the New York Cloakmakers, who were spurred by necessity to appeal for a union of all crafts; the garment industry had become, by 1900, one of the largest in the country. As unions went, it was a time of great need and little choice. The old Knights of Labor were dead and took with them, it seemed, the problem of dual unionism. By 1900 the garment industry had absorbed great numbers of women and girls – a population in which organized labor had hitherto shown slight interest – all of whom, clearly, needed to be organized.

The collapse of the Knights and the commitment of workers to the AFL signaled the end of the quixotic dream of a union of a single, undifferentiated army of labor which would array against its adversaries a legion of all crafts and all degrees of skill. The "everybody in" school of unionism yielded, finally, to a *realpolitik* whose intelligence and shrewdness is incontestable three-quarters of a century later. Samuel Gompers and the AFL understood, as the Knights never

DOROTHY RABINOWITZ is co-author, with Yedida Nielsen, of Home Life, *a story of old age, and author of* The Other Jews: Portraits in Poverty. *Her literary and political essays have appeared in* Commentary *and other journals.*

49

did, the power of the craft union. They understood that the real power
of a strike lay in withholding skills. The period in which the ILGWU
began was also the time in which the withholding-skill theory became
entrenched. Workers who sought to join most unions generally encountered elaborate conditions of entry; the idea of preserving a
limited labor force had taken hold with a vengeance.

Precisely in this period of exclusivity, the ILGWU could
say that it was the open-door union. This was undoubtedly as much
the result of the peculiar nature of the work — and of the workers — as
of any ideological commitment on the part of the new union. No doubt
it was some of both. From the beginning, the work of the industry
revolved about the home. The skills, most of them, were easy to learn,
and immigrants who learned them could do so without leaving the
ghetto. Awful as it was, the ghetto was decidedly less threatening to
the immigrant job-seeker than the uptown of tall buildings: for the new
arrival who was sparsely, if at all, acquainted with English, it took
guts to leave home. The ILGWU was located in the heart of the ghetto
and thus, from the beginning, a unique sense of protection, of intimacy
and mutual ownership, characterized the relations of the garment
workers and their union.

While the industry kept the work force in the ghetto, it was
largely by way of the industry that many of them got out of the ghetto.
To make the leap from worker to boss, all an industrious man had to
do was earn enough money to rent four sewing machines. Contracting,
which would be one of the great evils of the industry (and remains
so today), had its origins precisely in the ease with which the system
permitted every man to become a boss, of a kind. In the worst days of
the sweatshop, a jobber might farm out work to several contractors,
all of whom had a steady supply of workers — women, children, new
immigrants, *landsmen* — to do the work. There were all sorts of advantages in the contracting system. One contractor might produce
well on one kind of material, another on just a certain aspect of the
garment, and thus the choice among contractors yielded the jobber
some advantages of specialization. But the greatest advantage, undoubtedly, was that contracting enabled the jobber to avoid responsibility in the matter of pay or working conditions.

The contractor was only somewhat better off than his workers,
and when he was unable to pay them, as was sometimes the case, they
could not look for redress from the jobber. So far as he was concerned, only the contractor worked for him. The very history of the
sweatshop was grounded in the contracting system, as indeed were
the major union battles. Workers might labor from sun-up to ten at
night for $10 or $8 a week, at work for which there was no stand-

ardization either of price or wage. Competition was so fierce among the contractors that the manufacturer could easily name his own price. And then the contractor would pass his price cuts down to his workers.

To civilize the relationship between the jobber, contractor, and worker was the central aim of the early ILGWU. Its two historic strikes—the revolt of the Shirtwaistmakers in 1909 and the Cloakmakers' general strike of 1910—were a direct attack on the system of subcontracting. The Shirtwaistmakers began, and the Cloakmakers concluded, a strike against this system which resulted in one of the great labor victories of modern times. The Cloakmakers got a standard rate of pay and fixed responsibility for that pay. The Protocol of Peace that emerged from the strike settlement provided for conciliation and arbitration. It established a preferential union shop. It set a maximum of two and a half hours overtime. Home work was abolished. It ordered a six-day week of fifty-four hours, with piece rates to be established by a committee of union and employers. A Joint Board of Sanitary Control would oversee working conditions. To be sure, the Protocol did not last. But its spirit did, beyond the wildest expectations of those who fought for it.

Those who organized and endured the two great strikes were characteristic of the high heroic tradition, the fiery moral stature with which the ILGWU was informed at its inception. Indeed, the self-image of the union today is comprehensible only by the illuminating light of that past: little Clara Lemlich of the Shirtwaistmakers, standing up against the pontifications of the union leaders at the Cooper Union hall to call for the strike; Rose Schneiderman, who led the first Triangle strike, and then, as Leon Stein describes in his excellent book on the Triangle fire, led the funeral procession for the fire victims, leaning hatless and coatless into the rain, informing everyone around her with her rage in the largest procession of working people the city had ever seen. There were the men of the Cloakmakers' Joint Board who prepared feverishly for their long siege; who published their English, Italian, and Yiddish *New Post* to rally workers for the strike which brought sixty thousand Cloakmakers off the job on a single afternoon and kept them off for weeks.

The Shirtwaistmakers themselves were women, many of them Russian Jewish emigrés who had tasted the wine of revolutionism. They had read Ibsen and Whitman. They came to the shops with stars in their eyes; they were literate, they had perspective, they could organize. Indeed, their bravura was of a kind the grimmer men of the Cloakmakers could ill afford, much less feel. (The men were in this work to stay: the women might marry.) The Shirtwaistmakers wore their best clothes on the picket line, and when molested by the whores and pimps employed by management, they defended themselves with hatpins. They found a great ally in the rich women who took up their cause. Members of the Women's Trade Union League befriended them. These were also the days when Judge Olmstead could sentence a picket, shouting, "You are on strike against God!"; days when Mrs. O. H. P. Belmont, society leader, would flounce into the same courtroom in her enormous hat and produce bail for the girls arrested that day.

Later there were different heroes, other struggles — perhaps none more decisive than the war for control of the ILGWU that raged between the Communists and the Socialists in the 1920s. The outcome of that war irrevocably formed the union as it is today. It was a battle that hardened the strong and routed the weak; its calamities defined and isolated those necessities of leadership to which the union would cleave for good. By 1921, the Comintern had launched its campaign to seize the trade unions, and thereon began the battle for control between Socialists and Communists which almost wrecked the ILGWU. (Among the latter was Charles "Sasha" Zimmerman, now a typical member of the reconstructed old guard that forms the top ILGWU leadership.)

It was an era of disastrous, party-directed strikes. It was the period in which Legs Diamond and Little Augie sent their mobsters out to do battle on opposing sides of the strike, with both under the control of that genial tactician, Arnold Rothstein. Out of the ruins of the 1926 Cloakmakers' Strike, which collapsed under the weight of the fanaticism with which the party leadership blocked every attempt at settlement, the ILGWU emerged poorer but tougher. The Socialists were in control, and some of the left-wing functionaries who had once supported the CP began to comprehend the Communist design on trade unionism. To be sure, there were bitter encounters yet to come as the party set up its various dual unions. But by the early 1930s, the ILGWU leadership had acquired that loathing for the totalitarian which marks men who have done business at close range with party-directed functionaries. They knew the party ideologue and the zealot, and the henchman always close by in the back pocket, and they knew them in the way given only to those who have tried to meet them in the spirit of openhandedness. By the end of the wars, the leadership had attained to that scarred sense of reality which persists to this day in its weary distrust of ideology, that abstract virtue behind which the totalitarian impulse so often cruises.

The present-day leadership of the International is marked by a reverence for reality and a loathing for abstract virtue which are more than an inheritance of ideological wars: they also provide the fuel with which critics have fired their attacks. It is a predominantly Jewish leadership, of which the bulk are in the tradition of the Social Democrats. There is a smattering, too, of ex-Bundists and ex-Communists. Perhaps the closest thing to an ideologue among them is the kind of union intellectual — there are several — who looks upon unionism as the last humanistic enterprise left to men. By and large, though, the legatees of the Socialist-union tradition are today confirmed pragmatists in the matter of human necessities. Health care, a living wage, and education strike them as values considerably more respectable than any of what they suspect to be liberal abstractions. Counted among those abstractions is the idea of proportional union representation on racial and ethnic lines, and the notion that there lies slumbering in every man a capacity for leadership that only needs rousing. (But of that, more later.)

That there exists in America a large body of people in whose lives economic necessity is no longer the determining factor is of little direct interest to a union whose rank and file will never see a day without economic necessity. Garment work has always been low-paying and, for the most part, it still is. Whenever the union has managed to raise the wage level, the manufacturer has sought escape by moving to depressed areas. The industry has moved to the farm belt, to Los Angeles, to Pennsylvania, anywhere it can escape organization and labor is cheap. In Mexico, labor now costs 16 cents an hour. If an employer moves there, he becomes a "multinational corporation" — with a showroom on Seventh Avenue.

The flight from organized territory has made an exceedingly mobile industry out of an always fiercely competitive one, and, from the logic of survival, it has always been a labor-squeezing industry. In New York, which is still the heart of the business, the average earnings for the least skilled workers are sometimes barely above the minimum wage. Between 1965 and 1970, employment dropped off almost in direct proportion to the overall wage increase in that period. Increased trucking costs and higher rents are also said to have contributed to the exodus from New York. Perhaps most important is the fact that the union is hard put to keep wages up in an erratic industry whose survival depends from season to season on such unpredictable factors as weather and women. The production of the wrong dress lengths can kill a manufacturer in a season. To save themselves from dying at the hands of caprice, the manufacturers got together on skirt lengths during a recent season and came to the union for help in selling that length. The union leaders did not think they should offer such help; though they could not have been very surprised that the manufacturers should come to them on such a matter.

The union's concern with "mere" wages and benefits, in the face of those rumblings of a higher nature which afflict the rest of American society, is the locus of no small blame from ILGWU critics. They are not as many as they are loud; and their charges of racism and corruption are particularly galling to the heirs and veterans of a tradition in which heroic battles were fought in the name of fraternity and a hint of corruption was enough to consign a union leader to oblivion forever.

There are the ironies: some of the items offered in proof of corruption, of dictatorial rule and racial discrimination are themselves emblems of the union's historical fight to stay free and clean. One of the more vocal critics of the ILGWU is Herbert Hill, National Labor Director of the NAACP, who has charged that the union ban on caucuses (except for a three-month period before conventions) is an instrument of racial discrimination. He has charged that the custom of keeping undated resignations for dismissing officers of the union is also an instrument of racial discrimination, whereby one-man control is assured and "Negroes and Puerto Ricans are . . . relegated to second-class membership." The undated resignations actually issued from the early years of David Dubinsky's leadership. Determined that no breath of scandal should disrupt the International, in what was already an age of union corruption, Dubinsky used the resignations to get rid of business agents whose conduct was irregular. The ban on caucuses dates from the 1920s, when the Communist dual union faction was at the height of its effort to divide and conquer the International.

Then, there are the charges which have their roots in a fine muddle of crossed traditions. To the complaint that there were no blacks or Puerto Ricans in Local 89, the ILGWU could answer that there were no Irish, Chinese, or Jews, either; that Local 89 was exclusively an Italian-language local and had been so since the era of mass immigration, when the Italians were organized. To this reply, union critics of Hill's persuasion countercharged that, in any event, such a local is against state law.

The weariness with which ILGWU leaders view such a charge, the ingenuousness that characterizes both sides, is symptomatic of a duel between antagonists who tarry over nonsense, lest they be brought too soon to that abyss where conflict must rage without hope of resolution because it has no aim but the expression of mutual enmity. Indeed, there is the sense that most of the charges brought against the ILGWU have to do with matters larger and more irreconcilable than those which are described: matters which are, in fact, not questions of union policy but trends of history.

The largest part of the new ILGWU constituency has no connection with the tradition of the Shirtwaistmakers or the Cloakmakers' General Strike. They have no family memory of sweatshops or union triumphs. They are aware of that which touches their present: that a good many of them are poorly skilled and low-paid and that, often, they do not understand the language of the men who represent them. In New York City the black and Puerto Rican membership is said now to be something more than half. There are also a sizable number of Chinese workers. Nationally, however, the union is still primarily white.

By the middle '30s Jews had already begun to leave the industry in great numbers, and by the end of World War II the Jewish and Italian membership, so long the bulk of the rank and file, dwindled to insignificance. What remained was the solidly Jewish (and some Italian) leadership, the reason for the most bitter criticism now directed at the union. It is charged that the top-heavy leadership has nothing in common with the black and Puerto Rican members in New York City and elsewhere (80 percent of whom are women); that, from the obvious paucity of their numbers in key union roles, there is a deliberate attempt to discourage them from reaching leadership. The ILGWU maintains, in turn, that part of the answer is that many blacks and Puerto Ricans are not union-conscious and feel that they have little in common, so far, with union interests. The fact that so many are women makes them even less likely to provide a large pool of leadership material: women want to go home and take care of their families, not to sit around for union meetings. Those that do, say the union leaders, lack no opportunity for leadership training. One ILGWU manager asserts that these will make up the significant numbers of black and Puerto Rican union leaders who will appear on the scene in a few years. But first they must be trained.

Critics charge that there is not a single black on the General Executive Board of the ILGWU. The General Executive Board is a twenty-three-member group that sets operational policy. (There is one Puerto Rican on the GEB.) In answer to this charge, one top ILGWU leader said with some irony that General Motors could afford tokenism: the International could not, and would not insult blacks by putting into positions of leadership men who would be plain figureheads by virtue of their inexperience. The General Executive Board, he pointed out, is composed of men of long experience, each one of whom is responsible for a large sector of union management. To such a working body, he added, the union is not about to add a figurehead in order to keep the peace.

One hears in this answer the special kind of reality of the trade unionist; that stubbornness which is an allegiance to his own history. The trade unionist is the forger of a slowly growing, infinitely patient success. He has won much: much that once appeared to be impossible has come round to fulfillment by the route of patience, experience, plain work. He knows that by now, he is accused of understanding the problems of management too well: yet he cannot understand how he should not know what he does know. It is a sense of reality which has grown increasingly alienated from the mainstream of received social opinion in America. And this opinion has it that much which appears to be impossible for any sector of our life is so because of the general impossibility of the American condition and the innate malfunction of the system. Thus is it possible to sigh over—and occasionally to dismiss—the achievements of organized labor as part of the malfunctioning system and, with it, all the outdated tools by which the labor union has known its progress: patience, experience, and work. (Only the trade unionist knows that the progress which came *after* the revolutionary ardor of the old days was no less progress for coming after.)

To the critics of the ILGWU, those tools appear as weapons of racial oppression, and the comparative optimism of the trade unionist seems a cruel disregard of the harsh realities of life *now* for minority workers. It is by now a commonplace of that opinion to describe the ILGWU as an oligarchy, a dictatorship, and even as an enemy of the working class. James Graham, activist and co-counsel during the 1968 New York Teachers' Strike on behalf of parents of Ocean Hill, cites the ILGWU in his book *The Enemies of the Poor* (Random House).

The manner in which the charges are made and the manner in which they are refuted are not insignificant. Many of the charges are ludicrous, as, indeed, are some of the answers the union makes, and that ludicrous aspect is part and parcel of the wild, mutual incomprehension which characterizes both sides. When, in 1961, Herbert Hill had Ernest Holmes, a black cutter, file a complaint against Local 10 (the Cutters' Local) with the New York State Commission Against Discrimination, saying that the local had refused to permit him entry, the union representatives of the local at first refused to make their records available. (The cutters are the most skilled and highest paid men in the industry.) In a fit of intransigence and anger, no doubt deeply felt, that a union with its long tradition of egalitarianism could be called to make such an account, the local refused to cooperate,

and thereby gave the Commission reason enough to issue a finding of "probable cause."

Thereafter, the union reversed itself and made the records available. A number of black cutters appeared on behalf of the union, in proof that the International did not discriminate. Herbert Hill claims that one day at the hearings, two black men followed him into the Men's Room to confess that they were testifying at the hearings because they were told to; that they then laughed and said their membership in the union was a great joke, and that their union books had just been issued them. For some time thereafter, Hill recited the details of this alleged bathroom encounter in a number of public forums. A subsequent check of the union books, however, indicated that the black cutters had indeed been members of the local for many months prior to the investigation.

Since 1961, the critics of the ILGWU have grown more militant, and not all of them are professional crusaders. One black former union chairlady, Florence Rice, recalls that in the fifties she was making very good money herself. When, as she said, she came to the realization that blacks and Puerto Ricans were systematically discriminated against in terms of work opportunity, she decided to testify at a hearing chaired by Adam Clayton Powell. She testified that discrimination was rampant in the union; that Cubans, Haitians, and Puerto Ricans were played off against blacks and each other, to threaten everyone and to keep wages down, and that when employers did this, the union looked the other way. Mrs. Rice says that, immediately after her testimony, "they started giving me bad work." Her salary, she says, dropped to $60, she was labeled a Communist, and she could get no job where she was not feared as a troublemaker. Mrs. Rice, now a private consultant on consumer matters, says that the union is now just what it always was: "that same old oligarchy at the top." She is also convinced that Adam Clayton Powell's downfall commenced the first day he held those hearings: when he incurred the enmity of David Dubinsky.

Mrs. Rice is not the first to believe that if David Dubinsky had cause to turn his wrathful attention on a man, he could destroy him. Indeed, the now retired Dubinsky once answered in response to a query about how he stayed young, "I do two things. I take care of myself and I take care of my enemies." The end of Dubinsky's leadership brought no surcease from complaints that the union was a dictatorship. The man was the personification of the ILGWU, and what might be said of him might be — and certainly is — said of the union. Paul Jacobs, a journalist of New Left cast, wrote in *Harper's:*

> The tragedy of the ILGWU is that its leaders do not understand
> the membership. . . . A far deeper cultural empathy and common
> tradition exist today between the Jewish ILGWU leaders and the
> Jewish employers. . . .

Dubinsky's Yiddish accent, Jacobs observed, was a factor in the
empathy between the Jewish union leader and the Jewish employers.
He stated further that the union's financial report "reflects the tight
hold of the past"; that Jewish and Italian organizations received far
more in ILGWU support than black, Puerto Rican, or Mexican groups.
One donation was for a Luigi Antonini Stadium in Haifa. (Antonini
is an old-time leader and now vice-president of the ILGWU.) Gus
Tyler, education director of the ILGWU, responded that the union
believed that $130,000 is not too large a contribution over three years
to help the children of the six million Jews exterminated by Hitler."
Noting that he was aware when he wrote it of the article's emphasis on
Dubinsky's Yiddishness and of his emphasis on the Jewish aspect of
the union, Jacobs reports, nonetheless, that he was shocked to receive
approving mail from anti-Semites, "horrible mail, congratulating me
on having exposed the role of Jews in running unions and even in-
viting me to speak at meetings of one anti-Semitic group in South
Carolina." Jacobs asserted that he did not intend to stop writing about
Jews—"one must write his perceptions of the truth" or not be a writer.
There is no evidence that the shock he received when anti-Semites
congratulated him has muted his sense of mission.

  That article was written in 1962. Now Louis Stulberg is president of the International and there is but one ILGWU local which
has a serious insurgent faction. As for the surprising lack of any more
insurgency, or any more vocal expression from black or Puerto Rican
workers, given all the charges, ILGWU critics explain that the
workers are afraid of retaliation. There is, then, only Local 155, about
75 percent black and Puerto Rican, in which an insurgent group puts
out a mimeographed newspaper with the headline "The Rank and File
Organizes." The paper is a series of allegations: that the manager,
Louis Nelson, is a czar, and that around him are his cronies who came
to the leadership when the union was built in the 1930s; that they do
not reflect the racial and ethnic composition of the union; that "most
of the 'girls' in the local—and all women are called 'girl' no matter
what their age—work as floor girls, operators, button hole markers,
etc."; that the union gets away with its low wages because of its ability
to divide workers "along racial, ethnic, craft and shop lines"; that in
most shops Spanish is more often spoken than English, and that it is
time the union made it a second language; that the ILGWU gave

$25,000 to Albert Shanker and the UFT during the New York City Teachers' strike.

In addition to the caucus in Local 155, an organization called "Fight Back" directs its attentions to labor discrimination such as that alleged of the ILGWU. Its spokesman, Jim Horton, repeats the charges made by Hill, by Mrs. Rice, and by the group in Local 155. He adds that he is neither a Communist nor an anti-Semite for asserting that the ILGWU is dictatorial and, in practice, racist. The largest part of Horton's scorn is directed at black defenders of the ILGWU whom he describes as "shameless stooges."

The union categorically denies these charges, as it has for as long as they have been made. It points to the extraordinary sums spent on its Training Institute to develop new leadership. It has run qualification courses for union officers, for example, in which any member could enroll before running for election. Ninety percent of the applicants to the Training Institute, the union reports, were black and Puerto Rican, of whom one-third graduated. These, presumably, will make up the ranks of top black and Puerto Rican leadership, after the necessary period of field experience.

As to discrimination in wages, the union responds that the worker is paid by the standard piece rate, which sets the rate upon the work and not upon the worker. Indeed, the union looks to the achievement, long ago, of the standard piece rate as the strongest instrument of the workers' civil rights. To the charge of work discrimination, the union asserts that to be a cutter, a man must first learn how — to which minority spokesmen might retort that it is easier for some to learn than others, when the spoils of nepotism rule; that the Italians in Local 89 can bring their cousins in to learn, while blacks and Puerto Ricans have no such entrenched relations. The union in turn can point to a very substantial number of black and Puerto Rican cutters, even as there are a good number of blacks and Puerto Ricans among the 58,000 retirees from the union.

Answer for answer, whether in the matter of discrimination in wages, nepotism, or lack of black or Puerto Rican leadership opportunity, the ILGWU can explain and explain. But it will not matter, for it is engaged, finally, in the conflict with the times that all unions face. Among those who make opinion, it is a time of fearful mistrust of unions generally. And it is no small sign of these times that Charlton Heston, of the Screen Actors' Guild, retiring after several years of the presidency, had to defend that union against certain charges of the independent slate (led by Western star Bert Freed). Heston's union, like the ILGWU, is charged with having more in common with the industry than with the actors; with having no proper representation of ethnic minorities. Heston characterized these charges as "racist slander." He is, Heston notes, particularly bitter inasmuch as his union pioneered in taking in Indians, blacks, Chinese, and Mexicans.

The sadness of the ILGWU battles, charges, and counter-charges is no doubt greater than that of the Screen Actors' Guild. Given its long history, such spectacles are no doubt more painful for the ILGWU than for any other union in the labor movement. Still, it is just that: it is a union among other unions in a sad time for old values and for old trade unionists. One of these, a former Bundist, reflects the enormities the times have visited upon him and men like him. He was one of a remnant that escaped death at the hands of the Nazis. Now, as in the early days in Poland, he can look back upon a life con-secrated to a faith: that unionism is a humanistic endeavor. His grave eyes reflect the wonder — yet by now it is no surprise — that he is to be counted among the "racists" and the "reactionaries" of the world. It is not true, of course. But there is no bitterness in him as he assesses the charge: only a slight, disputatious glint at the fate that could cast him and his tradition in the role of oppressor, in any man's eyes. It is not in his book of rules to dismiss these things; still less is despair in the rules. There are resources to bank on: for him, there is still the absolute commitment to the practical, to patience, and to hard work. And there is the ILGWU itself, and the pride of accomplishment that is its psychic trade mark, as clear a symbol in its way as the union label on the garment.

Silent in the Supermarket
Leonard Kriegel

One talks to these retired garment workers, these small, stooped men and women, and finds they have aged as they have been used. Time is supposed to weather, not crumble. Things are not supposed to take the place of people. But I walk into the neighborhood supermarket and I note how the new neon-lit organic food section is crowded with the very same people who hum with the rhetoric of fashionable radicalism, while those whom our government describes as "senior citizens living on a fixed income" walk carefully down the aisles, pause as if the decisions were momentous, shrug their shoulders, and pull out the cheapest package of tasteless, preservative-puffed bread. It is simply a question of snatching at reality in bits and pieces. Try standing in such a supermarket while the historical vision of the longed-for millennium flashes across the mind. "We are at the gates of heaven!" cried Liebknecht. The supermarket insists on different prerogatives. A pound of its own preservative-puffed bread is now 29¢. So much for the gates of heaven.

The ILGWU Cooperative Houses is a Title One middle-income housing development situated in the heart of the Chelsea neighborhood on Manhattan's West Side. Its ten standardized high-rise

LEONARD KRIEGEL, Associate Professor of English at the City College of New York, is currently a Guggenheim Fellow and is at work on a narrative of the lives of Jewish, Italian, and Irish working-class people in the Bronx. His most recent book is Edmund Wilson.

apartment buildings and grass lawns are bounded on the east by
Eighth Avenue, on the west by Ninth Avenue, on the south by 23rd
Street, and on the north by 29th Street. Remnants of old Chelsea are
scattered throughout its grounds. The Cornish Arms Hotel stands
on 23rd Street; a Roman Catholic church and school, once largely
Irish but now predominantly Puerto Rican, occupy the center of 25th
Street; a run-down Protestant church with a neon cross is on 26th
Street; a small Episcopalian church with an exquisite nineteenth-
century interior that speaks of better days stands on the corner of
28th and Ninth. But these vestiges of Chelsea's past do little to lend
Penn South, as the development is known, architectural individuality.
In fact, Penn South can serve as a prototype for the kind of development architecture that has so infuriated such critics as Jane Jacobs and
Ada Louise Huxtable. For better or worse, Penn South has changed
the neighborhood. Where most of Manhattan continues to deteriorate,
Chelsea seems to be on the way up. And whatever reservations one
may have about its architectural blandness, the cooperative has
succeeded in providing moderately priced and comfortable apartment
housing for more than 2,800 families.

Even its architecture speaks of its being a "union co-op." The
ILGWU sponsored and financed it, and ILGWU members were
given first opportunity to purchase apartments. But Penn South was
not designed exclusively for union members, and its population embodies many of the contradictions and trials that can be found in New
York. By and large, the older people who live here look upon the co-op
with a certain pride; most are union members for whom labor consciousness has provided the most profound sense of group identification they have ever known. On the other hand, the parents in their
thirties and forties who live here are usually not union members.
They are usually college-educated professionals who have chosen to
bring their families up in New York City and who recognize that Penn
South is as good a housing buy as one can find in Manhattan. A good
many of them look upon the trade union movement in much the same
manner as their Park Avenue and Great Neck peers. One might speak
of them as spiritual refugees, drawn to the very heart of that for which
they feel a certain contempt. They distrust unions and scorn those
whom they label "hard hats." And while they enjoy both the moderate
rentals and the air-conditioning, they begrudge the cooperative its
lack of style. If they are not what Tom Wolfe had in mind when he
coined the phrase "radical chic," it is not for lack of sympathy. Earning between $15,000 and $25,000 per year, they simply do not possess
sufficient status to penetrate the world of radical fashionability.

The stores and businesses that rent space in Penn South are

probably similar to those one finds in any private development in New York. On the corner of Eighth and 23rd, there is a branch of the Carver Savings Bank, still one of the few black-owned banks in the city. There is another bank on Ninth Avenue and 25th Street. On the whole, however, there are only two tenants that are slightly out of the ordinary. In the basement of the co-op supermarket stands a theater devoted to revivals of the classics. Occupying the top floor and roof of that same supermarket is the Mid-Town Tennis Club, where for $680 per year two people can play thirty-one hours of tennis. The theater attracts a number of young people to performances of Shaw and Shakespeare; the tennis club, a number of chauffeur-driven limousines to a neighborhood not yet affluent enough to witness with equanimity the arrival of a Rolls Royce Silver Cloud. Occasionally, one can see one of the young prostitutes who operate around Madison Square Garden come down here to try her luck with a tennis player. The retired garment workers and furriers stand by and watch silently, their mouths drawn; the young mothers walk along quickly, their heads reaching into New York's ripening air, their children marching to a quicker pace.

Let me call him Jacob. A good enough Jewish name. Jacob is close to seventy. But he is still angry. He has been angry ever since he can remember, although he had always assumed that the anger would dissipate as he grew older. But it hasn't. He is angry at those whom he calls "liberals," a word he does not so much say as spit. He is also angry at college students, black militants, the American Civil Liberties Union, Mayor Lindsay, the leadership of the unions, even at the Socialist party of the United States of which he remains a dues-paying member.

     A former organizer for the Fur Workers, he has been retired for more than two years. We are sitting on a bench in one of Penn South's two playgrounds watching children. I am watching my youngest son, who is four, and Jacob is watching his four-year-old granddaughter, who is the playmate of my son, as well as his two-year-old grandson. He speaks without looking at me, his eyes on his grandson who is jumping happily up and down in the sandbox.

> Why I distrust liberals? That's what you want to know? Because they never learn. The more they live, the less they know. They just jump from one place to another, from position to position. Always they look to blame somebody. Yesterday, they discovered that there was racism in the country. Until yesterday, they didn't know about it. Until Martin Luther King told them, they didn't know. Their eyes they didn't believe. **They needed Martin Luther King to tell them.**

His grandson falls and hits his head against an empty watering can in the sandbox and begins to cry. Jacob runs over to him and picks him up. He rocks the boy back and forth, then swings him in the air until the boy laughs. When he returns to the bench, Jacob's face, which is usually stern and distant, relaxes. He smiles. This is the way it is supposed to be, even in the bad books one has read. The grandfather comforting the grandson. Even among retired organizers, the image of the *shtetl* grandfather remains.

When he returns to the bench, I try to get him to talk some more about his politics. But he wants to speak of other things now. He tells me of what it was like working for the Fur Workers as an organizer. Toward the end there had been little left to organize. The fur market was dying. To hell with it. He is angry with his union, with all unions. But he doesn't want me to misunderstand. He had come to this country a militant trade unionist at the age of fourteen, and he would die a militant trade unionist. He had been born a Socialist, he would die a Socialist. But he wanted nothing of the American Left now. Politically, he trusted nobody, not even people on the Left.

> I came to this country in 1917, during the war. I went back to Russia in 1925. I wanted to see the Revolution for myself. I was tired of listening to all the old Jews on Eastern Parkway, the Socialists on one side, the Communists on the other. I wanted to see for myself what it was like. They were asking for skilled workers to return to the Soviet Union to help build socialism. So I went back. And you know what I learned?

He does not wait for a reply.

> I learned that the Socialists on Eastern Parkway didn't know what they were talking about, and the Communists on Eastern Parkway didn't know what they were talking about. It wasn't their blood that was being called for. I spent two years there. I worked in a steel mill, and by the second year they asked me to stay and help run it. But I came back. I was tired of the lies. I was tired of watching workers get kicked around in their own state. Maybe it was necessary. Maybe there was no other choice, like they said. But I couldn't stay.
>
> I came back here and began to work as an organizer. Here it was different. The problems were immediate. They had to be solved without theory. To get the best bargain for the workers. To organize working people. How do you make the only thing a workingman has, his ability to work, how do you make that into a weapon? It's a big problem. But it's not like what I was doing in Russia. Not like changing a society. A man can work better with problems when he can see

an end. You see, the job of a union is to make life easier for its members. The job of a revolutionary is to make a revolution. In Russia I was a revolutionary. We thought we were building a new society. But all the time I had to remind myself that I was working for the future. It was going to be different. And then, one day, I just couldn't work any more for the future. So I came back. A few years later and Trotsky is kicked out. Another ten years and Bukharin is dead. What a world!

He sits back against the bench and lights the pipe he has been holding in his hand. He clears his throat, shakes his head, as if he were forcing himself back to the present. These are an old man's memories. When he speaks again, it is about what is happening in New York. The longing is gone from his voice, the anger is back. He begins to talk about black militants. He does not hate Negroes. How could a Socialist hate any group of people? He does not even hate the Poles or the Germans. But the bitterness is deep and random, arrows hurled against the encroaching times. Always the need for victims. From the Left, too. And from him. He is angry at the Panthers, who are rabid anti-Semites; he is angry at William Kunstler, who is a corporation lawyer; he is angry at civil libertarians, who do not understand that if a man cannot walk the streets in safety then he has nothing of value.

By them, everything is police brutality. In that building on Ninth Avenue, where that woman was killed in the hallway, I hear they have a defense fund. Because the person who knifed her was Puerto Rican or black. I don't remember which. I met a woman whom I knew from the union. "Jacob," she says, "do you want to join us? Do you want to identify with the oppressed?" I should join her. Goddamn fools!

He shakes his head. I want to talk with him some more. I try to ask him how he passes his days now that he is retired, so as to get him away from politics. But he puffs on his pipe furiously, occasionally muttering at the overcast sky. He has damned a world that offers him no place. The simple times died in the twenties, even before they could be born. All the while he eyes his grandson, who is happily building a pile of sand in the otherwise deserted sandbox. Jacob stops talking to me. He turns away. He is finished.

I know his wife, Sophie. It is easier to talk with her. She is five years younger than Jacob, and she still works in the needle trades as an operator. As a child she emigrated with her family from Russia to Canada, then came to New York as a young woman. "You know, I didn't know Yiddish very well when I first arrived here. At home we spoke Russian. When I arrived here, before I married Jacob, I first learned Yiddish well. I did some acting. And I began to sing."

But she had earned her living as a garment worker from the beginning. "When I first came to America, I worked for Hattie Carnegie. It took two weeks then to make a suit. Today, you make a suit like that; even suits for the rich." She snaps her fingers at the ceiling. "It makes it even more necessary to have the union, and it destroys trade unionism at the same time." Like her husband, she believes that unions have grown old, have lost their idealism. But this does not really upset her. She simply considers it inevitable. She admires a few of the younger labor leaders, especially Victor Gotbaum. I am sitting with her drinking coffee in her kitchen on a morning in early June, a day after Gotbaum's union has virtually closed down New York. Across the hall, a neighbor's radio is blaring forth the news of the day. Everyone, it seems, is angry at Victor Gotbaum, except Sophie who chortles with delight as she listens to the comments. "That one I like. He knows his workers. He listens." She nods and smiles knowingly. "It's a different time. In the trade union movement, the leaders are following the workers now. Before, it was the workers who followed. There was greater trust."

I ask her how she and Jacob live.

I'm not retired yet. Jacob is. It's difficult for him. There's not enough to do. So he's angry. And I'm not sure he knows why. He spends a great deal of time reading. A lot of newspapers. All the retired people in this co-op read newspapers and magazines. A great deal. By me, it's a disease. I don't agree with Jacob all the time, but I understand how he feels. In a way, all the older people here feel like he does. It's too difficult to understand the world now. There are no sides that we can take. Except on something like Vietnam.

She sips her coffee and shakes her head.

Jacob and I don't have the problems that some of our friends have. Inflation hasn't done to us yet what it has done to them. I'm still working. That's what makes the difference. But I know men who live with their wives on their social security pensions and maybe $50 a month in union retirement benefits. So what is that? I tell myself it's a lot better than it used to be for old people. At least, you have a little bit of dignity, a little independence. You're not a horse, to fall down and die in the shop. What we want is what our friends want. Not to be dependent on our children. I'd rather die than that I should have to be dependent.

I ask her about how her friends live, what they do.

It's not what they do. It's that they don't do anything. It's hard to grow old; especially today, in this country. You don't belong to anything. With us, thank God, there is my daughter and her husband and the grandchildren. A friend of mine also has grandchildren. He visits them once a year in California. For two weeks. For him, for too many of my friends, there is little besides each other. A memory here, an old acquaintance there. The biggest problem is when you wonder if it was worth it. All those years of working, of organizing. It's not like when you build something like a business. That's yours. It's in the family. But unions you build for others. And you don't want your children to do what you've had to do. They grow up and they don't know too much about what the labor movement was. They become teachers, doctors, accountants. Would you want your children to work in the garment industry?

She pauses, stares at the ceiling. She is thinking, remembering, and I feel out of place. I cannot enter her world after all.

Why are the problems today between minorities? More and more, between minorities. Is it America that makes it this way? Listen, I owe this country a lot. But I worry. I look at what it does to the blacks and I tell myself that they're right, they should be militant. Like labor. Always the people who rob you want to judge you, too. And then I look at those Jews who are so frightened, the ones in that Jewish Defense League, and I tell myself that they, too, are confused and frustrated. So this is what we've come to. After all these years, this adventurism, this stupidity. But I can understand. A trade unionist has to understand. They're workers, too. Or else small shopkeepers. And the Italians, them too. And they all resent what is happening to them. They're confused. So they line up, one against the other. When I was working on the bench, it was side-by-side with Italians and Negroes. Conditions were lousy for all of us. And now, one group against the other. Am I an exploiter? Am I living here off the fat of the land?

She waves her hand at the ceiling.

Years after the battles have been fought and the politics defined, their social relationships are still shaped by the politics of the past. Sophie tells me of receiving a telephone call from a friend who had remained a Communist sympathizer long after Jacob and she had recognized that salvation would not come through the Soviet Union. He asks her to come over. She is surprised, she has not heard from him for twenty years. But she goes. They talk and drink coffee and laugh about the past, and then he brings out a tape recorder. "Would you mind," he asks, "if I ask you to sing? I want to record some of the old Yiddish worker songs. For my daughter. She has begun singing." At first Sophie is annoyed, then touched. There is a bond between them, a past. For the moment, the old wars shrivel. The Left is united, somewhere back *there,* in her own vivid blending of memory and fantasy.

The neighbor has turned her radio off. The silence seems threatening until Sophie speaks again. She tells me how she has always dreamed of seeing Switzerland, ever since she had read *The Magic Mountain.* When she retires, maybe even before, she and Jacob will take a trip to Switzerland. To see the mountains. I am suddenly thrust back into my own childhood, and I hear working people listing names like Tolstoy and talking about something they called "culture" which they did not "understand" but strangely revered. Trade unionism and socialism—somehow they would bring "culture" to working people. How ironic that the novelist of the German bourgeoisie should have found an impassioned reader in Sophie. To go to Switzerland to see the mountains.

Sarah has been retired for some ten years now. She lives in Penn South and just manages to get by on her social security and her small union retirement pension. In the past an ardent radical, she remains contemptuous of the ILGWU leadership. They have knuckled under to the bosses, she tells me. A sweet, frail old lady in her late seventies, she has walked with a cane ever since, some five years past, she was mugged and punched to the ground. Her hip was broken. She does not really blame the muggers. Rather, she blames "the system," and the mugging and Vietnam have become one in her mind. In her insistence on the totality of "the system," she reminds me of my students.

Sarah had lived in her own apartment, but after her hip was broken she moved in with her sister who has an apartment in the same building. When I meet her in the street, she is still a remarkably cheerful, even vibrant, individual for someone so frail and old. Like most of the former trade unionists who live in Penn South, she remains very much interested in politics. She identifies herself politically. She is a "progressive," a kind of password that she does not realize is out of fashion. But she has never been particularly analytical when speaking of the boundaries of her political world. In this she remains in the tradition of the Jewish Left, which has, perhaps surprisingly, never really been able to analyze itself in this country.

> I like your young people [she says to me]. The only thing that hurts me is what some of them say about Israel. The Holocaust, that is

part of all of us. We lived through it. There are no alternatives to
Israel. But everything else, what they are doing about Vietnam, about
the injustice to black people, in this I am with them 100 percent.
These students you teach, they are the hope of this country.

She likes my children and has always been alert to changes in
their appearance. She has no children of her own; she never married.
She continues to amaze me. She lives on next to nothing. She seems
to feed on air, so frail is she. I have never known her to travel. But
there remains in her a quality that I have found in so many of these old
Jewish radicals and trade unionists, a determination to see life through,
to welcome change and, above all, "progress," and yet cling to the
values of nineteenth-century egalitarianism. A strange mixture of
sentiment and toughness, a willingness to stick life out. That much,
at least, they carried out of the past.

The view from the supermarket remains the same. Day after day, it
does not change. It is a peculiar thing—shopping in a supermarket
demands a kind of aggressiveness that one would automatically assume
comes naturally to union people. It is really very much like a picket
line. But it bullies them. The co-op supermarket is supposed to be
their supermarket, just as Penn South is supposed to be theirs. No
one really knows why. But it is an idea given reality by the fact that
once a year, the prices, which are no better than the prices of other
supermarkets in the neighborhood, succumb to the men and women
who bring their year's supply of sales slips into the market so that they
can receive a rebate. "It's better than nothing, isn't it?" says a retired
garment worker. I nod. He shrugs. Still, it is better than nothing. His
2 percent rebate comes to $15.17.

Like Penn South itself, the supermarket embodies a certain
sense of disillusionment that many of these older Jewish workers feel.
One does not resort to such stock terms as "alienated" to describe
their condition. It is not from society that they feel estranged, it is
from their own pasts. And these men and women are not so much confused as disappointed. For this is it. This is all there is. In certain
respects, Penn South, with all of its limitations, is as close as they
have come to the commonwealth of their dreams. And it was their
dreams that distinguished them from other ethnic working-class
groups in this America, just as it was their dreams that separated them
from their children and grandchildren. For they reached beyond the
traditional American concern with the self, to project a collective
salvation. And collective salvation, like any other kind of salvation,
turns out to be drab. They still walk cautiously through *their* super-

market, which may be better than nothing but which shrinks their vision to such minutiae as the weekly shopping price list that is slipped under each door on Tuesday. They are still afraid on the streets of *their* co-op, and they are aware that one cannot walk with dignity when one has to walk with safety in mind.

The past haunts them. After the union meetings and the picketing and the folk songs and the politics, after the causes and petitions and speeches have blurred into one another, they are left with little more than a sense of having been shortchanged. And this is true of all of them, regardless of their past politics. It is as true of the fiercely pro-establishment ILGWU organizer whom I meet in the mornings with his *New York Times* under his arm, his strong, stocky frame belying his seventy-five years, as it is of the old woman in the laundry room who furtively glances at her copy of the Communist *World,* her face frowning and defensive.

Their relationship to America is a mixed success and failure. The success of the labor movement afforded some of them their greatest sense of personal achievement. When one speaks to them of strikes or union activities in the past, there is recognition, a participation that creates a selfhood at the very moment that the memory is sentimentalized. But all of this lies in the past. The Jewish workers in the garment industry are being replaced by blacks and Puerto Ricans, and the fur industry is dying—a victim of changes in fashion and the kind of sentimental ecology that has seized thousands of Americans, who believe, apparently, that the numerous plagues upon the land can be cured by insuring the preservation of the wild mink.

And so I watch them shop in their supermarket. I could speak of them as victims of their own success, but that would be a hollow mockery. Waiting for the end in America leaves one little but memories. Success should be more tangible, thicker. Anyway, it is one thing to storm the gates of heaven, and quite another to participate in the construction of a union. The first fulfills the messianic urge, the second simply slaps a patch on the mundane world in which one lives. The Penn South Housing cooperative is theirs, and the co-op supermarket is theirs—and, God knows, these are not the gates of heaven.

Yet they retain their belief in organization, in limited goals. Penn South is still a better place to live than where they had lived in the past. If the small pension from the union—some of them receive a mere $40 per month—combined with the social security check—some of them never made enough money to approach the maximum—dwindles each month in the face of a raging inflation, they have not been reduced to penury. Scarcity was theirs by inheritance, as was caution; they never really expected that to change. And this housing development, *their* housing development, has become for many of them a source of pride. The lawns are carefully tended, and vivid flower beds break the monotony, however slightly, of the standardized buildings. It is air-conditioned. Inside the cooperative, humorously, perhaps even pompously, the old wars continue to rage. In this way, too, the reality of the present is shut out. One seventy-year-old retired garment worker turns his face away from another seventy-year-old retired garment worker in the elevator. In memory's narrow eye, trade unionist and radical, Social Democrat and Communist, damn each other to similar perditions.

I place them against their cooperative and I ask myself what has been left to them. Few of them, I sense, hold a country of the mind in which a workingman occupies a place of his own. The nation has passed them by, and our new radicalism is more than willing to leave them to their fate. Their time has passed. Fashion now is the rage, and the truth of the matter is that they are not found interesting enough. Theirs are not the kind of lives out of which one creates drama. Radicalism must now set forth on new goals, and retired Jewish fur workers and garment workers are an old and rather boring story.

I fantasize about them. I tell myself it would be different if only one of these old men could adopt a posture, could conceive of himself as once again being *in* history. If only one of them could stand in the playground where the mothers watch their young children and do something out of the ordinary, sing "Solidarity Forever" or scream to the smog-ridden New York heavens that the rights of labor are the rights of man. Not that it would do anything to alter his fate. Most of the mothers who sit in the playground have gone to college, and they would undoubtedly sing along with him.

One frames them, finally, against their isolation. Perhaps it is enough to offer them a single moment of recognition. I think of a man walking cautiously down the supermarket aisles. A man who carries a scar on the bridge of his nose from the fur strike of 1926. Organize the unorganized, build a union; better still, be part of a union. There is not much there to stir the imagination. Still, there was a time in this country when such a fate seemed rich enough. It finds its echo now in the voice that expands with pride when it recites the remembered names of shops organized, meetings attended, speakers listened to. And in *their* housing cooperative, in *their* supermarket, with money, admittedly much too little, from *their* union pension and *their* social security, they walk down these well-lit aisles to buy the air-filled preservative bread. Of such bargains is the future made. With such strides does labor march.

Organizing Neighborhoods: Gary and Newark
Richard J. Krickus

Except in the labor movement, working Americans have rarely participated in mass-action organizations. Sociologists have found that the college-educated American is more likely to participate in voluntary interest groups than the American who didn't finish high school, drives a truck, and lives in a working-class neighborhood. The political science literature indicates a correlation between education, income, social status—and participation in political activities.

Let us consider, against this legacy of low blue-collar participation in community affairs, CCC—the Calumet Community Congress of Lake County, Indiana—and the North Ward Democratic party of Newark, New Jersey. Both communities are predominantly working-class, and blue-collar workers have played a prominent role in both the Lake County "Congress" and the reform of Newark's North Ward Democratic party.

Lake County, Indiana

Lake County's population clusters around the grimy industrial cities that were built along the shore of Lake Michigan early in this century. Gary, the largest, was founded in 1905, when the U.S. Steel Corporation purchased a massive tract of land for development. In the next

RICHARD J. KRICKUS is writing a book, with Vic Fingerhut, on the prospects of the Democratic party in the 1970s. He is an associate of the National Center for Urban Ethnic Affairs in Washington, D.C., and teaches political science at Mary Washington College in Virginia.

few years, swamps were drained and dunes leveled, a railroad to Chicago was constructed and a port dug. Soon coke ovens and blast furnaces mushroomed, forming a large industrial complex. Other industries followed the example of U.S. Steel, and other, smaller industrial cities — such as Hammond, Whiting, and East Chicago, Indiana — sprang up along a twenty-six-mile stretch of Lake Michigan.

Immigrants from eastern and southern Europe migrated to this corner of northern Indiana to work in the factories and mills and on the railroads. When World War I cut off this labor pool, blacks, Southern whites, and Spanish Americans followed in the footsteps of the Serbs, Croats, Lithuanians, Greeks, and Italians who had come before them.

Today Gary is a predominantly black town and has elected its first black mayor, Richard Hatcher. Mayor Hatcher's color is not the only novelty of his administration, for he is both honest and dedicated to the welfare of the city's residents — indeed a novelty in Gary and Lake County, where corruption has persisted for more than half a century. This old fact of life has resulted in a cynical view of politics. Lake County residents have suffered additional exploitation through the "legal" activities of corporations, which have deprived them of clean air, pure water, and — as Nader's Raiders now are attempting to demonstrate — from unfair personal-property and real-estate tax arrangements. Within the memory of most voters, their elected officials always have loyally responded to the tug of the corporations. Politically savvy residents charge that the destiny of Lake County, Indiana, is decided in Pittsburgh and Wilmington, not in Gary, Hammond, or Whiting.

While the worker may win significant victories at the plant through his union, the coalition of interests controlling the laws in his community is generally immune to his demands. Workers charge that the union leaders wield power in an autocratic fashion, that they concentrate their efforts on mill issues but ignore the problems that plague the rank and file in their neighborhoods, and some will tell you that the "big boys in the union are in too tight with the County Democratic machine."

In the 1968 Indiana primary, Robert Kennedy swept the black districts of Gary and the white ethnic areas of the county. In November, however, many of the whites who had supported Kennedy in the primary voted for Wallace.* This prompted pundits to conclude that Lake County's working-class whites were moving toward the Right.

---

* Wallace captured 16.4 percent of the votes cast in Lake County in the 1968 presidential race.

Jim Wright, who was a staff member of the Lake County Inner-City Task Force, a coalition of churches working with Gary's blacks, rejected this analysis. Wright, a six-foot-three, 205-pound former steelworker, was convinced that Wallace's appeal to his old workmates was a result of being disenfranchised from decisions that profoundly affect their lives. Wright saw that it was time to enlist them in bringing about long overdue progressive changes.

After much hustling, he wrangled support from the area's clergy for tuition to attend Saul Alinsky's Industrial Areas Foundation in nearby Chicago. In February 1970 he returned with Mike Barnes, a one-time Catholic seminarian, who had been active in community organization on the West Coast, then in Cicero and in a Mexican American neighborhood in Chicago. Barnes and Wright canvassed Lake County's bars, churches, streetcorners, mills, union halls, and shopping centers.

Most people they spoke to were still in the grip of rugged individualism: "I'll take care of my own problems." Collective action — it sounded un-American. Yet people grumbled about pollution and high taxes, and they knew the county's public and private institutions did not pay proper attention to them. But they had lived under these conditions for so long they thought it futile to resist.

Yet some people, made of sterner stuff, prepared to fight back through neighborhood improvement associations. There was Joe Sedlak, a Cedar Lake Catholic priest, who was active in a host of community activities ranging from educational reform to pollution abatement. And there was Carl Kafentaris, a draftsman and part-time VFW bartender, who for years had pestered his neighbors to get together and force the contractors who had built their homes to fix the faulty sewer system. Wright was certain that the organizational experience blue-collar workers had acquired in their unions would prove an asset in a fight to form a mass-based citizens' organization. Although the national media might call the workers of Lake County "conservative," Wright was confident that when provided with alternatives, they would move in a progressive direction. They needed experience in organizing their communities and in developing tactics that could produce results. And they could use the boost of a political victory.

Wright jumped at the opportunity to work with a small independent labor local, some three hundred strong, in its strike against Dupont Chemical in the Lake County town of East Chicago.* The

* The Chemical Workers' Union has been unable to gain a foothold in the Dupont dynasty. The workers in the Dupont plants belong to independent locals.

union wanted to write into its contract a pollution clause, to curtail the fumes the workers suffered in the plant and the filth that was fouling the air, water, and land where they lived. Herbicide wastes, hydrochloric acid, and sulphur dioxide were being dumped into shallow holes, excreted into the Calumet River, or pumped into the air. Management had told the workers that their pollution abatement demands were non-negotiable.

Wright asked Joe Sedlak to help him enlist members of the Izaak Walton League, the Indiana Save the Dunes Council, and other public-spirited citizens into a single organization that could provide the strikers with community support. Sedlak knew nothing about pollution, and he lived in Cedar Lake, some thirty miles from the East Chicago plant—why pick him? Wright said he selected Joe because he was a Slovak, of the same background as many of the workers. He was geographically distant from the Dupont workers, but psychologically sensitive to their problems for he "had been there himself." Under Sedlak's leadership forty different groups, amounting to more than three hundred people, formed the Citizens' League to Upgrade the Environment—CLUE. In conjunction with the strikers, CLUE conducted neighborhood demonstrations, circulated literature on the magnitude of pollution emanating from the Dupont plant, and badgered company executives.

When CLUE was formed, the strike was in its fifth week. Several days later it ended. Within a couple of months Dupont agreed to a nine-point pollution abatement program. This first victory was proof that the people might take on the corporations and win.

Now other problems seemed open to citizens' action. From February through June 1970, Wright and Barnes, helped by volunteer organizers, conferred with approximately three hundred people. By now, skeptics who had avoided them inquired how they could become involved. Conservationists who had never dared to take on the corporations were impressed. Wright says, "They saw us as the guys who could deliver" and help them with problems of "wildlife, clean air and water, and recreation."

The Dupont fight also gave the organizers the opportunity to watch people in action, and the men and women who had demonstrated leadership gained legitimacy in the estimate of other organizations and spokesmen. A number of young working-class college students, "day students" living at home, joined in during the Dupont fight. The coalition of the groups mobilized against Dupont now began to organize a network throughout Lake County. During the strike, Mike Barnes and Carl Kafentaris worked with homeowners from seventeen suburban developments in Ross Township. For years every spring they had put up with the flooding of their homes, when a nearby river overflowed its banks and inundated the storm sewers that backed up into their basements.

Barnes organized the homeowners, and under steady pressure the developers were forced to deal with the problem. The solution was simple enough — and inexpensive. Sewer covers were cemented over and a faulty storm sewer system was repaired. The contractors had ignored the people because they had anticipated that the working-class homeowners would remain passive. They did, for seven years.

In the wake of the union victory at Dupont, Joe Sedlak returned to Cedar Lake to find a school crisis in Hanover Township. Some forty teachers had been fired, ostensibly because they were incompetent but in fact because of their union organizing. For the first time in his memory Sedlak observed genuine community interest in the Township's schools, and he decided the time was ripe to organize a citizens' action group to deal with education. Sedlak organized the Citizens for Quality Education. His immediate aim was to provide community support for the striking teachers; his long-term objective was to turn the residents' attention toward an issue they had long neglected. "Until we started to support the teachers," says Sedlak, "the average citizen of Cedar Lake did not know we had access to files of that [board of education] office by law."

The organizers of this expanding network were largely community activists and blue-collar workers who at the outset had scoffed at the need for research. Pollution, health, schools — whatever the issue — they soon found it was necessary to gather facts. And they discovered, in turn, that by gaining a clearer understanding of a problem, the necessary tactical action would present itself. Faced with facts, dates, and samples, many government officials and corporation executives demonstrated their ignorance. As the people observed these confrontations, they recognized that so-called experts often were uninformed, lied to cover up, and, thus exposed, were vulnerable to citizen action.

By late summer, grass-roots people, volunteers, and groups that had participated in past actions were ready to form an organization of citizen-action groups. They decided to call their regional organization CCC — the Calumet Community Congress. (This area, consisting of northeastern Indiana and parts of adjacent Illinois, is known as the Calumet region.)

A regional multi-issue organization had distinct advantages. A mass-action organization, spreading over Lake County and including parts of adjacent Illinois, would permit CCC to exert power over the entire region.* Unlike single-issue organizations, which often dissolve upon achieving their goal, a multi-issue organization maintains the interest of its members because, on this larger scale, fresh battles are always at hand. The CCC organizers observed that whatever the specific orientation of the members, their solidarity grew as they fought together.

As CCC won a series of victories, the fledgling organization began to gain notoriety throughout Lake County. After each successful battle new groups joined in. Soon the kooks on the Right and the old pols in the county Democratic machine took notice. The John Birch Society and the KKK, both of which had sizable support in the suburban and rural areas of the county, charged that the CCC was a Communist front and had national, subversive objectives. Organizers were threatened, leaders intimidated, and outsiders friendly to CCC were followed by seedy-looking heavies.

The County Democratic boss, John Krupa, said that CCC was "masterminded by the forces of godless, atheistic communism." Krupa formed a counterorganization, called it Americans United, and attempted to pick off supporters of the Congress through a red-baiting blitz. Several churches and clergymen withdrew their support, and some community groups dropped out. But, by and large, the growing number of people who had become involved in CCC stood firm.†

Perhaps the single most important supporter of the Congress at this juncture was the Catholic bishop of the Gary diocese, Andrew Grutka, who had been a steelworker in his youth. Bishop Grutka was publicly denounced by boss Krupa for endorsing the Congress. Behind closed doors corporation executives did their best to persuade him to withdraw his support from CCC—to no avail. Many skittish community people stood firm because the Bishop stuck to CCC. While his moral support was vital, his financial help was even more crucial: in the fall of 1970 the Catholic Church was the primary source of CCC funding. Bishop Grutka survived the charge that he was a soldier of "godless communism," and the party machine's failure to destroy CCC

---

* Since then CCC has been decentralized. Area chapters have been set up throughout the Calumet region.
† During this red-baiting campaign, Steelworkers in CCC reported that some union officials began to "bad mouth" CCC. Since then it has been alleged that the union has been pressing Steelworkers to withdraw from CCC. There are three schools of thought which purportedly account for the union's displeasure with the Congress. The first is that the union is playing ball with the steel companies because it fears that the do-gooders in CCC may in one way or another interfere with production and thus jeopardize jobs. Second, many union officials are a visible part of the County Democratic machine. Finally, the union leadership is fearful that, should the rank and file band together in an effective organization outside the mills, these same people may one day represent a threat to the present union leadership.

suggested to the people of the county that perhaps boss Krupa and "his boys" were not as powerful as most of them had believed.

On the frigid Saturday evening of December 5, 1970, at George Rodgers Clark High School in Hammond, the Calumet Community Congress was officially founded. One thousand delegates, representing 143 organizations, attended. A cross section of Lake County's population—workers, professionals, small businessmen, students and housewives, Republicans and Democrats, and even a few Socialists—cheered the guest speaker, Nader Raider John Esposito, when he indicted U.S. Steel for its failure to pay a fair share of taxes and for its refusal to take proper precautions against the pollution that poisoned the air and water in the communities surrounding its mills. Under the chairmanship of George Patterson, a retired Steelworkers' organizer and survivor of the 1936 Memorial Day Massacre at Republic Steel, the delegates elected officers and adopted a program. It was aimed at combating pollution, political corruption, and inequities in state and local tax laws. Thirty-year-old Ken Tucker, one of the union representatives who solicited Jim Wright's help for the Dupont strikers, was elected president. Other elected officials were union officers, welfare workers, housewives, working students, clergymen, a cook, a roofer, a municipal employee, and a steelworker. Black and Spanish American delegates were a visible part of the founding Congress.

J. David Carr, general superintendent of Gary Steel Works, U.S. Steel, responded to Esposito's charges by denying that the company had created any special health hazard and said that it was carrying its proper tax load. Then setting his sights on CCC he said: "It is incongruous that a coalition of religious, educational, labor, and ecological organizations would embrace outsiders to promote a unity of purpose locally . . . when such a move might well only lead to divisiveness and polarization which in the end could only harm the potential for progress in the community." Parroting the charges circulated by Birchers and the KKK, he claimed certain individuals and groups in the CCC had a history "dedicated to destroying the American way of life."

Three days after the founding Congress, an emergency senate was held. The agenda was to provide support for a coke-oven ordinance scheduled to be voted upon by the Gary City Council the following week. Through a previous variance, the coke ovens had been exempted from an air pollution ordinance. U.S. Steel had convinced the City Council that there was no known method of controlling coke-oven pollution. The Calumet region was the only area in the United

States with a major coke-oven problem not controlled by law. According to Gary's Air Pollution Department, U.S. Steel's coke ovens produced 59,400 tons of air pollution annually. The U.S. Department of Health, Education and Welfare reports that, at levels of 100 micrograms per cubic meter, persons over fifty are subject to increased death rates and young children are likely to experience an increased rate of respiratory disease. In Gary, air particulate counts average over 130 micrograms per cubic meter annually and at times exceed 400 micrograms per cubic meter. The rate of lung disease is four times as high as the average across the United States. Because Gary did not have a coke-oven ordinance, the city stood to lose several hundred thousand dollars in federal "pollution funds."

When U.S. Steel saw that its old dodge for excluding coke ovens from the pollution ordinance had lost credibility, it went on the "economic offensive." Company representatives publicly speculated that, if the variance were repealed, U.S. Steel might be forced to close down the offending mills. In the past such utterances would have been seconded by Gary's mayor. But Richard Hatcher responded: "We are shocked by the thinly veiled blackmail threats that the corporation might have to close down the mills if it is compelled to clean up its mess."

Just prior to the council session held to consider the ordinance, CCC learned that three councilmen planned to vote for U.S. Steel, two for the ordinance, and four were undecided. Right up to the final day, community groups led by CCC lobbied for the ordinance through neighborhood meetings, phone calls, and letters. In the City Council chambers the councilmen faced a packed crowd and voted 9 to 0 to repeal the variance. U.S. Steel was stunned by this reversal and reputedly dispatched three PR men from Pittsburgh to Gary to investigate what was going on.

The repeal of the coke-oven variance, less than two weeks after CCC was founded, had an intoxicating effect on its members. Brimful with confidence, CCC, throughout 1971, slashed away at the corporate Leviathans of Lake County. It won a partial victory over the Northwest Indiana Public Service Company which, according to CCC, had bilked customers out of their deposits, arbitrarily calculated rates, and cavalierly shut off gas and electricity. Inland, Republic, and U.S. Steel all have been cited for their failure to pay their equitable shares of real-estate and personal-property taxes.*

---

* CCC has charged that Inland Steel's Indiana Harbor Works in East Chicago had been dramatically underassessed. According to CCC's evaluation of public records (i.e., taxable real estate and business property) and the company's own estimates, Inland should have been assessed $20 million more than it was in 1971.

CCC officials assert that the steel companies have employed numerous dodges to escape an accurate assessment of their taxable property. It has been a practice of U.S. Steel to calculate its own taxes, and for years the collectors have accepted the company's figures. The company had refused to take out building permits or to specify what specific installations it had built; consequently the city could not accurately assess the company. CCC is working on this score with the Washington-based Lawyers' Committee for Civil Rights Under Law, which is building a case for the city against the steel companies.

CCC has demonstrated that through collective action working people can force government and industry to act in the public interest and not merely serve the rich and powerful. Perhaps the most important point CCC has made in Lake County is that decisions affecting the common welfare had been made by corporate executives who had not been held accountable for these actions—and that, instead, the people must be given sanctions enabling them to check on "antisocial decisions" made by private interests.

Some of CCC's early, most avid opponents have been won over and have joined. Even in Lowell Township, a focal point of the KKK and Birchers, residents asked CCC to help them get repeal on a decision to rezone their area for a massive trailer camp—and under CCC pressure, county officials, who had refused to budge, were forced to comply with the residents' wishes.

CCC now offers the people of the Calumet region the option to participate in a progressive movement for change led by men and women from their own communities through a democratic organization. There are numerous working-class communities in the United States where it would be feasible to build similar organizations for people power.

Newark's North Ward

In the early 1950s, Newark's large Irish and Jewish population began to flee the city for the suburbs. Today the single largest white enclave in Newark, a city where 61 percent of the population is black, is the North Ward. The North Ward's population is 100,000—consisting of 70,000 whites of whom 90 percent are Italian American; 20,000 blacks; and 10,000 Puerto Ricans. When the Italian immigrants settled in the United States, they, like other ethnic groups, sought shelter among their own. The Italians brought with them an extended family system and a keen distrust of outsiders which was exacerbated by nativistic discrimination. These strong family ties and primary group relationships have fostered among their children and grandchildren an unrivaled attachment to their original neighborhoods. And so many Italian Americans still reside in the nation's "Little Italys," despite rising urban blight.

Were the Italian Americans of the North Ward to leave the city, the consequences would be grim. For Newark is already revenue-starved, and North Ward residents pay a disproportionate share of the city's property tax, which is one of the highest in the country.

The Italian Americans who have chosen to remain in Newark share with their nonwhite neighbors the grave urban problems — crime in the streets, declining services, and troubled schools — and they compete with them for jobs, living space, and services. This competition has fostered fear and suspicion in both communities. Out of the ashes of the 1967 riot, two militant spokesmen emerged for their respective communities. Imamu Baraka (LeRoi Jones), the black nationalist poet, reputedly spoke for a dominant segment of the black community, while Tony Imperiale worked the white side of the street.

Tony Imperiale, state assemblyman elected in November 1971 on an Independent ticket, is a karate teacher, one-time city councilman and candidate for mayor, and the leader of the North Ward Citizens' Committee, a paramilitary organization that first attracted attention during the riot. Imperiale received national-media exposure after the riot. Brandishing a law-and-order platform, he subsequently won a City Council seat, a post he later gave up to run for mayor. He lost out in the primary, and Ken Gibson beat the incumbent Hugh Addonizio, who had been indicted for corruption. Italian Americans control the City Council today, but the demise of the Addonizio machine and the election of a black mayor produced a leadership vacuum in the North Ward and widespread concern among its residents about their future. Imperiale, a five-foot six, 230-pound hulk of a man, has tried to fill that void. Beginning in the mid-1960s, he won widespread support among the community's whites for his security activities (his men patrolled the neighborhood nightly) and his ambulance service. There are few streets in Newark the residents boldly traverse after dark, and "protection" from any quarter is welcomed. In a city where one often waits precious hours for desperately needed medical attention, the ambulance service — though only a part-time operation — is an attractive organizational ploy. Yet, though Imperiale remains an important symbol of security for many residents, another leader with a different kind of political organization has also emerged in the North Ward: Steve Adubato.

Adubato, the grandson of an Italian immigrant, was born in the old First Ward, North Newark's original Italian enclave. He has been a school teacher for fifteen years, and has the reputation of an odd-ball "nigger lover" for his outspoken support of the civil rights movement. Six years ago he decided to become involved in politics. Determined yet unsure of his prospects, he plunged into the rough-house politics of the North Ward's Democratic party. At that time one congressman, four county freeholders, three state senators, the sheriff, the county clerk, four of nine city councilmen, and two state assemblymen resided in the North Ward. There was competition for political offices and intraparty dispute, and candidates were wedded to a politics of patronage and paternalism. Politics was a business.

Adubato was fully aware of the odds against him when he set his sights on the office of Democratic district leader. He won his first election, and this victory allowed him to peer into the inner councils of Newark's Democratic party machine. As he looked behind the veneer of respectability that masked the city government, he was appalled. Intelligent, idealistic, but tough-minded, Adubato accepted the stark truth that patronage and self-aggrandizement motivated many politicians. And surely he was aware that politics provided a source of socio-economic mobility for white ethnic Americans of an immigrant and working-class background. But he was deeply disturbed to see the old pols ignore the needs of the people when it was within their power to alleviate community problems—they were too busy peddling favors and stuffing their pockets. Adubato astounded them when he suggested that the party become more responsive to community problems. He was threatened with bodily harm, verbally abused, and publicly ridiculed when he questioned the budget of his party's chairman.

Adubato, a man who is short, with broad shoulders and a rough-hewn face, has a tough mind and will that thrive on conflict. After successfully resisting the machine's effort to scare him off, he decided to take the offensive and run for chairman of the North Ward Democratic party. The chairman, who is elected by the ward's ninety-eight district leaders, has the potential of considerable power in city and county politics. Adubato hoped the office would provide him with a platform and leverage to develop a new style of politics in the Italian American community.

The old pols scoffed at his candidacy. The machine had firm control of the chairmanship. Few people voted in the primaries for district leaders, and a slate consistently favorable to the machine had always elected a member of the "club." A small cadre of voters who held political jobs could be counted on to vote for the machine's slate, and usually that was enough. Like the voters of Lake County, Indiana, the residents of Newark have legitimate reason to be cynical about government. Newark's recent, notorious history is pockmarked with graft and open collusion between the "mob" and city officials. Gibson has begun to complicate life for the bookmakers and petty white-collar criminals, but Newark still is a beehive of illegitimate activities.

Adubuto knew that in order to wrest the chairmanship from the old pols he had to overcome voter apathy. He had to convince the numerous people who detested Newark's corrupt politics that it was in their power to defeat the machine. This required developing his own network of political activists who could run for district-leader posts. He spent long hours in rap sessions with potential supporters, and while mustering his forces in the Italian American sections of the Ward he made a move he had been contemplating for some time.

In the past the machine had won so handily that it had written off the black voters. Yet these "disfranchised" voters now comprise 20 percent of the North Ward's population. Adubato circulated through the black neighborhoods, conferring with uncounted people. In this fashion he identified leaders in the black community who were potential candidates. Reggie Thomas and his wife first met Steve immediately after he had been informed that Mrs. Thomas, a community activist, was a good prospect for his talent hunt. Reggie said that Steve's straightforward manner impressed his wife, and she agreed to run for district leader in her neighborhood. Adubato, who had developed rapport with the black community over the years, found other blacks who were eager to run on his slate. Nor did his opponents' accusation that he "kept a nigger in his attic" hurt him with his black allies. But the blacks informed him that "if he expected to win their votes, he better move the brother down into the living room." Adubato: "Right off the bat I won 20 percent of the votes necessary for election to the chairmanship."

The black community's support, however, would not give him sufficient votes for victory. He had to build support among the community's Italian Americans.

Adubato collared his friends, neighbors, and fellow teachers and persuaded them to join him in forging a new political movement in the North Ward. Their initial reaction bordered on disbelief. "Get into politics! You crazy? It's crooked, it's not for me." That also was the reaction of his cousin Tony George, an employee at Prudential Insurance, when Steve first approached him. But Adubato's persistence and idealism broke through Tony's apathy. He grudgingly gave in to his cousin's pressure and ran against an opponent who had controlled his district for forty years. The old pol, by delivering a small group of loyalists, beat Tony two to one. His competitive spirit aroused, Tony—who had been a high school football star—tried again the following year; this time, as customary, he chose a woman for his running mate. Several days before the election petitions were to be delivered, he received a call from her. She apologized and told him she had to drop out. Her son worked for a construction firm that was in tight with City Hall, and he had been told that if his mother went through with the election, his job would be jeopardized. Tony said he understood. The first substitute who came to mind was his wife; she agreed to run with him.

Some 1,200 voters lived in their district, and the Georges spoke with most of them. Tony said many of the people did not know who their present district leader was, and few had ever voted in a primary. Tony, a soft-spoken but determined man, won his neighbors' trust. Besides, they were impressed that he took the trouble to elicit their votes. The Georges defeated their opponents by a two-to-one margin.

Adubato turned on other "Tony Georges"—housewives, blue-collar workers, and schoolteachers. Given his length of service in the Newark school system, and through his activities in the teachers' union, he knew all the Italian American teachers who lived in the North Ward. The schoolteachers became his largest reservoir of political activism. Born and reared in the Ward, these men and women in their mid-twenties and early thirties were sensitive to its problems. They were an indigenous cadre of dedicated people, on intimate terms with the voters of the area. Besides, they were socially less insular than most of their neighbors.

These young activists had acquired political savvy in their union and had come to reject the machine's paternalism. While many of them were "militant Italians," they resented the crass exploitation of ethnic loyalties and petty political payoffs, which robbed the people of the opportunity to take part in matters germane to the well-being of their neighborhoods. The old pols delivered jobs and such favors as fixing tickets or taking care of more serious indiscretions. But they ignored the voters' needs concerning such neighborhood matters as street lights and signs and truck traffic—things the "boys" had been taking care of in the past when they were getting started.

Their young opponents discussed matters of real concern to the voters. These sons and daughters of factory workers, truck drivers, and day laborers had little trouble relating to the blue-collar residents who live in the Ward. People who had never considered voting in the primaries were "turned on." Racial moderates, they were not emasculated by the guilt that prevents many middle-class liberals from effectively relating to blacks. They understood that the "black problem" was symptomatic of a larger problem—the failure of our society to allocate resources and deal effectively with urban blight. When they talked about WASPS, they meant the corporate establishment and those institutions and interests that command the resources enabling them to do something about Newark's plight but refuse to act.

In 1969 Adubato was prepared to do battle with the Addonizio machine which, not yet stricken by scandal, conspired to defeat the "nut" who dared to take them on.

When it became apparent that Adubato, by now a skilled political tactician, had built an effective network of energetic activists, the opposition was dumbfounded—and wondering what kind of payoff Adubato intended to offer all "his people." As election day drew near, they resorted to threats and verbal abuse to frighten away the young dissenters. But Adubato's supporters didn't scare easily. One of the strengths of his slate was that the schoolteachers, businessmen, housewives, and blue-collar workers who supported him did not hold political jobs and felt able to secure employment under their own power. They were committed to a new style of politics and were willing to pay a price for that commitment, if need be.

Adubato's team of reformers (a label they reject because it is associated "with naive do-gooders" who often harbor distaste for the people they help) canvassed the neighborhoods with zeal. They were welcomed by the voters who were struck by their candid discussion of community issues. Many people who never before had cast a ballot in a primary voted for Adubato's slate. With their support, Adubato's team defeated the machine—as, since then, it has in every election.

Reflecting upon his success, Adubato has said, "We were better politicians; we beat them at their own game. We were militant. By that I mean we consistently worked hard to get out the vote." He also has noted a growing sophistication among the electorate. He attributes this to education and exposure to the mass media, especially TV. The people, moreover, realize that the machines that once thrived in every major city in New Jersey are losing their effectiveness, even though they are by no means defunct. The convictions of former Newark Mayor Addonizio and Jersey City's Mayor Whalen suggest that such "enterprising" officials will in the future experience closer surveillance.

Until June 1971 the consensus was that Adubato's stock had risen at a time when the Addonizio machine was ailing; but if he dared to take on Imperiale, he would be resoundingly defeated. The confrontation, a topic of much conversation in the social clubs that abound in the North Ward, did take place in the summer of 1971. Imperiale had announced in the spring that he was a candidate for Democratic district leader in his neighborhood (although he was a registered

Republican and could not vote for himself) and would put up a slate of delegates who, he bragged, would elect him party chairman. In private, Tony gleefully predicted that at long last he was going to get "S.A." In a TV interview he said of Adubato: "I don't like Steve; I don't trust him." A few weeks before this interview, a bullet pierced the living-room window of the Adubato home. Adubato said he did not believe that Tony himself would do such a thing.

The thrust of Imperiale's campaign revolved around race and Adubato's reputation as a "nigger lover." While Imperiale's men drove around the community in sound trucks, Adubato's people were quietly setting up the machinery for victory—face-to-face contact with the ward's voters. All of Imperiale's candidates lost, as he did in his race against Joe Ceres, a young teacher who still lives in the house his immigrant grandfather purchased in 1922.

In the June 1971 primary election, when Adubato won over Imperiale in his district, two symbols were presented to the people. They chose the one representing decency and respect for their intelligence. In the 1971 election for the Assembly two seats were up for grabs in the district. Adubato's candidate won, but so did Imperiale.

Since fall 1970 Adubato has been working as a "community specialist" for Rutgers University in the North Ward. He is the first man the university has hired to work in a white working-class community. Adubato has found that the working people in the Ward, including the black workers, have been ignored by local, state, and federal housing, by manpower and educational programs. Through the nonpartisan North Ward Educational and Cultural Center, which he has helped form, he hopes to develop appropriate programs in these areas for the blue-collar residents of the North Ward.

During the eleven-week school strike that erupted in January 1971, Adubato supported the striking schoolteachers. The teachers, he argues, did not wish to strike. "They were prepared to settle without a raise." The real issue was that some elements in the black community wanted to destroy the power of the union. The strike was less a conflict between the black community and the white teachers—Carol Graves, the president of the union, is black, as are many of its most active members—than a reflection of a power struggle taking place within the black community.

One aspect of the strike that disturbed Adubato, though ignored by the media, is that the Italian American teachers believe they are being treated as pawns. They recognize that the black man in America has been abused and that the black community desperately needs help; but they feel they are being asked to pay the debt American society owes to its nonwhite citizens. Teaching school, in the eyes of many youngsters from blue-collar families, is an escape from the factories, in which their parents toil, into the "professions." Today qualified Italian American teachers, as a result of time in service, expect to be promoted to better jobs as administrators and principals; but racial quotas are effectively restricting them to their present positions.

Adubato asserts that the Italian Americans who remain in the center city with their nonwhite neighbors should not be treated as expendable citizens. He recognizes, however, that they will be relegated to this demeaning position if they do not organize and mobilize their power in protest. Not in protest against the blacks, but against the forces in our society that inadvertently or by design are playing off the have-nots against the have-littles.

Despite Adubato's militant defense of the Italian Americans in the North Ward, he remains on good terms with the city's black spokesmen. This includes Imamu Baraka, the mayor, and the more traditional moderate leadership. If an alliance for change in the urban North is ever to develop between blue-collar whites and their black neighbors, it will be forged with the help of indigenous community spokesmen like Adubato.

In the past, European immigrants helped forge labor unions that provided working people with the means to bargain effectively with management. Today, a small but growing number of their descendants are organizing to deal with the multitude of problems in white working-class communities. The old "intermediate agencies" that once took care of their demands — the political machine, the church, and the patronage system — are fading from the scene or no longer work effectively.

The Calumet Community Congress was organized around issues germane to residents of a predominantly working-class area. Jim Wright did not exploit ethnic loyalties in organizing CCC; yet he was aware that to ignore ethnic distinctions would have jeopardized CCC's success. And it is unlikely that anyone but an Italian American could have created the political organization Steve Adubato built in Newark's North Ward. The Italian American subculture is a persistent fact of life there and discrimination against Italian Americans a real issue. There is a consensus among progressive Italian Americans in Newark that if the whites who remain in the city were Irish, WASPS, or Jews, Trenton would not have dared to wash its hands of the school crisis as it did in early 1971.

The democratic Left has prematurely discounted the persistence of ethnicity and ignored the correlation between ethnicity and class. If middle-class champions of a "new populism" remain insensitive to the cultural chasm that separates the "cosmopolitan Left" from Americans of modest means and education, and if mores, lifestyles, and economic problems rooted in class or ethnicity are not taken into account, the prospects are dim for building a nationwide populist movement.

Educational reform, exposure to the media, and the existential reality of social change have produced a growing self-awareness among working-class white ethnics in the urban North, and young leaders have begun to emerge. They possess a sophisticated understanding of power, and espouse a new style of politics that welcomes the participation of the people and stresses the collective needs of the community. Their fledgling community organizations and reform factions in working-class, white ethnic communities are fertile ground for the democratic Left.

II. Three Cities

Blue Collars in Cicero
Joseph Epstein

Cicero, Illinois, population 69,130, is a town with a sordid past and a troubled future. Cicero adjoins the City of Chicago on its West Side, and during a rare reform administration in Chicago it was the site to which Al Capone retrenched during the 1920s till the heat was off in the city. There in Cicero, just across the city line, Capone set up new headquarters, and it wasn't long before his operation was rolling in earnest. Girls, gambling, bootleg booze, name your action, Cicero had it and in epic proportions. In those days, and through the better part of the '20s, if you wanted anything done in Cicero you went not to City Hall but to the Hawthorne Inn where, behind bullet-proof steel shutters and with armed guards stationed at every entrance and window, Capone held court.

Under Capone's reign, Cicero became known as a center for sensuality—his west suburban whorehouses alone were said to gross more than $4 million annually—and for slaughter. One night at the Hawthorne Inn, Capone feted three fellow gangsters who, he had discovered, were planning to betray him in one of the gang wars of the day. In the Sicilian tradition of hospitality before execution, Capone, after serving up a sumptuous meal, had the three men lashed to their chairs, gagged, and then, baseball bat in hand, he personally shattered

JOSEPH EPSTEIN's work has appeared in Commentary. Harper's, *the* New York Review of Books, *and other magazines. He is now writing a book on divorce in America.*

nearly every bone in their bodies till they slunk forward, dead in their chairs. A family man himself, Capone never lived in Cicero proper but in a house in Chicago with his wife and young son, his mother and brothers installed on the second floor.

Long after Capone's death, Cicero retained the reputation of a wide-open town. As recently as the late 1950s, strip joints lined Cicero Avenue, and in their back booths, between numbers, dancers performed tasks both raw and byzantine. A reputation for being a wide-open town is one thing, but a reputation for being a mean town is quite another. Cicero took on the latter reputation in the summer of 1951, when it became the scene of a race riot, one of the first to take place in the United States after World War II. Harvey Clark, Jr., a Negro bus driver, had rented an apartment in the heart of Cicero, and the immediate consequences of his having moved in his family were the destruction of the building, mob violence, and a general brutalization of the Clarks. The family was forced to vacate, and Ciceroans, or at least a minority of them of a certain temperamental bent, learned a lesson: as a solution to racial problems, violence sometimes works.

In the middle '60s, when Martin Luther King, Jr., brought his campaign of moral suasion up from the South to Chicago, he threatened at one point a protest march in Cicero. Before actually undertaking it, however, the King marchers had been assaulted in a Chicago neighborhood known as Gage Park, where moral susaion was met with spittle, unequivocal language, and bricks hurled through the air. A similar march through Cicero, it was widely believed at the time, would have made the one in Gage Park seem like a stroll down Proust's Guermantes Way. In the end, King backed down on his threat to march through Cicero, and anyone who cared even vaguely for human life breathed easier.

Cicero is a blue-collar town. Although a sprinkling of small business and professional families live there, its population is made up predominantly of workers. Many of Cicero's citizens work in the town itself, for it is rich in industry, ranging in size from the mammoth Hawthorne Works of Western Electric (which employs some twenty thousand workers) down to the Bee & Bee Candy Company. Tool-and-die firms, small print shops, and odd-item manufacturers stand alongside the Hotpoint Division of General Electric and the Cities Service Oil Company. No corporation executive on his way up (or on his way down, for that matter) would contemplate living in Cicero, even though he might work there, so clearly déclassé is the town as an address for such men. Fortunately for them, most workers do not — not yet, at any rate — suffer under the subtle lash of such delicate status problems. Living near one's work is after all an immense advantage:

it means not spending an eighth of one's waking life fighting the free-ways, having the possibility of an occasional lunch at home, and saving a lot of wear and tear on one's car. Living near one's work is one of the requisites for an ideal community set down by Paul and Percival Goodman in *Communitas,* a book of utopian city-planning.

Not that the utopian impulse runs with any strength through Cicero. But, more practically, having all that industry within the town borders has the advantage of giving Cicero an extremely solid tax base—which means, among other things, that residential real-estate taxes are very low while community services are of a fairly high order. No small matter this, especially when one lives on wages and plans later to be living on a pension and social security. Every man has his own notion of utopia.

Cicero is a town of homeowners. Its houses are not distinctive, let alone distinguished, but they are magnificently well cared for. In the main, there are one-story bungalows and two-flat apartment buildings, and even blocks of buildings that look as if they started out to be two-flats but stopped after the first floor—vertical structures of uniform design that simply end in a flat roof after a single story. These homes, bungalows, one- and two-flats alike, are maintained with a scrupulosity not possible under absentee ownership. The lawns, though small, are manicured. The trim everywhere appears freshly painted, the brass on doorplates and knobs shined. Curtains are stretched across many of the basement windows, which usually means that the basements are rented out as apartments, thereby providing extra income. Care of a kind made possible only by the utmost pride has been lavished on these modest dwellings.

Cicero's houses—in many ways they are what their inhabitants' lives are really all about. Modestly priced in today's inflationary market—most still sell for under $30,000—these houses are their owners' deepest aspirations palpably realized. They are not only the biggest investment most of them will ever make, but they also symbolize the leg up on society that they and in many instances their immigrant fathers dreamed about. These houses were bought through sweat and at the price of self-denial.

Considering the fierce attachment of people of Cicero to their homes, one is inclined to think that perhaps nothing provides so great a stay to the revolution of the proletariat Marx dreamed of than does home-ownership. James Q. Wilson once noted much the same point in an essay entitled "A Map of Reagan-Land." How, Wilson asked, account for the fact that Southern California has come to be looked upon as—and frequently behaved politically as if it actually were—the Munich of America? The answer, it turns out, is not so very complicated. Workers and people of the lower middle class, the same people who in the large cities of the East and the Midwest lived in apartments, owned their own homes in Southern California. And to own one's own home, when the maintenance and protection of that home becomes a big event in one's life, is in nine cases out of ten to move politically at least two full notches to the right. In Cicero, for reasons soon to be made clear, the shift to the right is more on the order of five full notches.

Few WASPS, fewer Jews, and most decidedly no Negroes live in Cicero. The town is for the most part a conglomeration of white ethnics—Poles, Italians, Greeks (though not many of these), and Slavs—or, in the new and demeaning shorthand, PIGS. Michael Novak, a young writer of white ethnic background, has recently written:

> I am born of PIGS—those Poles, Italians, Greeks, and Slavs, non-English-speaking immigrants, numbered so heavily among the workingmen of this nation. Not particularly liberal, nor radical, born into a history not white Anglo-Saxon and not Jewish—born outside what in America is considered the intellectual mainstream. And thus privy to neither power nor status nor intellectual voice.*

This may seem to smack of a resentment out of proportion with all reality—the country, after all, has a Vice-President who is a Greek and a Democratic presidential candidate who is a Pole—yet there can be little question that, culturally speaking, the white ethnics have taken a beating in recent years. To be black is to be beautiful, to be Jewish is to be (somehow or other) intellectual, to be Spanish is to be special, but to be Polish, Italian, Greek, or Slavic is to be the butt of jokes. Question: What is an Italian with an IQ of 160? Answer: A Jew. Question: What did the Honky do with his first 50¢ piece? Answer: He married her. One-liner: Did you hear about the two flamingos who bought a house in Cicero and decorated their front lawn with two plastic Polacks? And so it goes. . . .

More important than the put-downs explicit in such jokes, the white ethnics, in Cicero and elsewhere, have over the past decade or so experienced a thunderous assault on their most cherished values. In the eyes of, say, a sixty-year-old, Czech-born, Cicero homeowner, a wage worker and a union man, America must seem a place recently gone quite mad—and become quite threatening. My God, such a man feels, is nothing any longer valued in this country—not family, not church, not hard work, not the law, nothing! Easing himself into a

---

* "White Ethic," *Harper's*, September 1971, p. 44.

chair before his television set or unfurling his newspaper, he has in recent years seen and read about universities aflame; children pumping their bodies full of drugs whose effect nobody knows much about; women, blacks, homosexuals making strident demands in abusive language. It is more than enough to heighten the man's normally cautious outlook into a blinding paranoia.

Yet however mad the world may seem to have gone, Cicero has clearly remained much the same; the town has proved remarkably resistant to change. But for the newer-model cars parked along its curbs, walking or driving down Cicero's streets you might think yourself somewhere in the late 1940s. The simple absence of long hair, beards, and Zapata mustaches among men and boys is notable; nor are you likely to find girls got up in hot pants, pantsuits, or the midi. In Cicero, what fashion magazines have called the Costume Party, far from being over, never began. Over at Morton East, Cicero's high school, football practice is ending for the day, and the thick-legged sons of strong-backed men, in helmets, shoulder pads, shorts, and cleats, round off their workout with a mile jog four times around the field. A handful of men, apart from the regular football coaching staff, stick around to discuss the team's prospects for the coming year. In the near distance a power mower whirrs away in someone's backyard.

Cermak Road runs up the middle of Cicero. It is named after Anton J. Cermak, the Chicago mayor who was the first local politician to win a mayoral election by putting together an ethnic political coalition. (Cermak was killed in an assassination attempt on Franklin Roosevelt, though some people believe it was all along a Syndicate killing.) Cermak Road is a wide-berthed street, which runs for blocks and blocks unscarred by chain-store shopping. (E. J. Korvette is two towns away in North Riverside.) Kobzinga Furniture, Novak Sporting Goods, Old Prague Restaurant, Richard J. Talsky: Doctor of Chiropractic, Hruska Bakery, Local 1806 IBEW AFL–CIO, S&H Food Mart, Greek-Italian Imports and Liquors, Law Offices: Mlede & Kucera, Sparta ABA Soccer Club, Pavlicek Drugs, E. Kavin Floral Shop, Klaus Restaurant: Bohemian-American Food — Cermak Road's storefronts offer as useful an index to Cicero's demography, interests, and character as is perhaps to be had anywhere.

"Smile," says the billboard, "You're in Mid-America Federal Country." Mid-America Federal Savings and Loan Association, that is, assets over $185 million. Mid-America Federal Savings, Clyde Federal Savings, Olympic Federal Savings, Hawthorne Federal Savings — savings-and-loan banks, housed in buildings both garish and grand, dot almost every thoroughfare in Cicero. In Illinois a savings-and-loan bank is allowed to pay a half percentage point or so more interest on a savings account than a regular bank, and in Cicero, especially on Friday evenings or Saturday mornings after paydays, the town's savings-and-loans hum with action. By and large the people of Cicero are great savers, a habit that perhaps derives from having had nothing when they or their parents first came to this country, and expecting nothing in the way of help from anyone outside their immediate families in the future. Such is the frenzy of saving that goes on in Cicero that the earlier joke stands in need of substantial revision. Question: What did the Honky do with his first 50¢ piece? Answer: He saved 49¢ of it. Not the least bit funny, but more on the order of the truth.

Neighborhoods within Cicero tend to divide into ethnic concentrations; like Chicago to its east, Cicero is a pot whose human contents have never really quite melted. Certain sections of the town are heavily Polish, others Italian, still others Czech. In part, this is a consequence of the sense of family feeling and ethnic community that still obtains in Cicero, however it may be beginning to break down elsewhere. It is not unusual, for example, to find two brothers who, after marriage, buy houses a block or so away from that on which their parents have a home; or a father and a son or son-in-law sharing a two-flat, and possibly renting out the basement apartment to a cousin.

As with its demography, so with its politics, Cicero tends to be a mini-version of Chicago. The Cicero Democrats do not have the stranglehold on politics that their confreres in Chicago do, nor does Cicero have a figure remotely comparable to Richard J. Daley, but the prevailing politics is the same elaborate chain of favors, clout, and due bills that traditionally goes by the name of ward-heeling. Not long after you move into Cicero, or change your residence within the town, you are likely to get separate visits from the precinct captains of both local political parties. Their gist is to make clear that if you have any complaints (garbage collection not what it should be), or require help with any special little problems (cutting through the red tape of acquiring a building permit to make certain home improvements), your precinct captain is at your disposal. Election day, should you not be noticed at the polls, you can expect a telephone call inquiring if you've voted as yet and reminding you of the time that the polls close. Since precinct captains and aldermen do not work so hard at their jobs out of mere Samaritan impulse, a certain amount of low-level corruption is assumed and, indeed, tolerated. A politician who made too great a show of turning up his nose at lagniappe would in fact be suspect.

Yet there is a considerable difference in political tone between Cicero and Chicago. Cicero's political tone is comprised of roughly equal parts of conservatism, resentment, and xenophobia. The town's conservatism derives from its stake in its homes, its strong family and ethnic feeling, and its generally cautious, savings-and-loan approach to life. Its resentment derives from the way the world is thought to be going against its, Cicero's, grain: with inflation eating into savings, wages, and pensions; with the priority given to welfare and other kinds of government spending in which the town will not share but which will cause an increase in federal taxes; and with the questioning that has been going on in recent years of such core concerns as the correctness of the Cold War (many Ciceroans have relatives still living in Eastern Europe), the extent of dissent a country ought to allow, and patriotism itself.

The roots of Cicero's xenophobia sink deep. As part of the Capone legacy, it was once thought that to live in Cicero one had to be a gangster, or at least in some peripheral way connected with the Mob; then, later, it was thought that to live in Cicero one had to be a racist. The town seems always to have been a patsy for journalists — for the facile generalization, for the ready analogy of Cicero with Mississippi, or Alabama, or South Africa. So much so that it began to be believed that "outsiders" had a stake in misunderstanding Cicero and thereby in judging it in the worst of all possible terms. A town grows tired of always being told how dreary it is. Hearing only bad news about itself from outside, it eventually could accommodate only good news from within.

Not surprisingly, then, Cicero's institutions turn out to be highly supportive of what is felt to be its way of life. The *Cicero Life,* one of a chain of west-suburban newspapers, can surely never be accused of attempting to direct opinion in Cicero. Instead, it echoes what opinion already exists in the community, and in the process reinforces it. For the great part comprised of those minuscule news items — "Cookie Sale Planned," "Viet Hero Returns Home on Furlough" — that are the staples of most suburban newspapers, the *Cicero Life*'s editorials never go against the town's core values.

Nor does any serious attempt to alter the tone of Cicero come from the clergy. Cicero is very much a churchgoing town, but a priest or minister would need to command a rare courage to try to liberalize his parish or congregation in any substantive way. The position of a minister is altogether too vulnerable — funds can be cut off, attendance can drop, resignations can be requested — to steer a congregation into a direction it doesn't wish to take. Few clergymen in Cicero try. In the mid-60s, in fact, there was great animosity toward Archbishop (now Cardinal) John Cody, who had a reputation as an integrationist, to the point where a small movement was underway among Cicero Catholics to cease supporting their churches till Cody cooled it on the subject of race.

During this same period, when there was a clearer consensus than exists now about the value of integration both in education and in housing, Cicero was made to feel uncomfortable about its lily-white status. The pressure came partially from within as well. A Presbyterian minister and his wife, a couple of exceptional courage and intellectual resources named George and Shirley DeHority, founded an organization called the Cicero-Berwyn Council on Human Relations. (Reverend DeHority's church was located in Berwyn, a town adjoining Cicero to the immediate west and one sharing many ethnic and political affinities with it.) The Cicero-Berwyn Council on Human Relations never exceeded forty members in its ripest days nor did it actually come out for integration in the two towns of Cicero and Berwyn, but it was not, in principle, opposed to talking about preparing for the possibility.

Mere talk, however, was sufficient to incite deep passions. Countering the Cicero-Berwyn Council on Human Relations, the Concerned Citizens of Cicero and Berwyn, an organization led by many of the same people opposed to Cardinal Cody, propelled itself into action. Suddenly the letters column of the *Cicero Life* was filled with missives of high indignation against the plot of the Cicero-Berwyn Council on Human Relations to integrate the two towns. A public meeting sponsored by the latter organization, held in Berwyn, with a large contingent of police in attendance, was disrupted at several points by jeering and rowdiness. Some time not long after this meeting, Reverend DeHority woke to find a bomb—a dud, it turned out—planted on his front lawn, à la Ku Klux Klan.

With the notion of black power, which soon engendered talk about black separatism, much of the fire was taken out of the issue of integration, and things in Cicero cooled down. Reverend DeHority left the area. But the simple point that had been underlined during this time was that in a period of crisis or even pseudo-crisis, the worst elements in Cicero tend to prevail. They prevail not because Cicero has more racists, bigots, and other nutty right-wingers per square block than are anywhere else in the country, but largely by default. They prevail, too, because racial fear in Cicero turns out not to be totally unwarranted.

If you drive your car to Cicero neither by the Eisenhower nor the Stevenson expressways but instead through the center of Chicago up Roosevelt Avenue, you get a clear picture of what it is that haunts the hearts, beclouds the future, and scares the hell out of the people of

Cicero. It is a Chicago neighborhood directly to the east of Cicero known as Lawndale. Lawndale is the ghetto—and the ghetto, physically decaying and humanly demeaning, at its cruelest. Decrepit buildings, boarded-up windows, kids and dogs running loose over shattered glass and garbage, street gangs, the stink of poverty—does the ghetto require still another description, still another plodding (if perfectly true) explanation of its origin in human disregard and exploitation? Probably not. There is even a kind of idiot truth in Spiro Agnew's remark to the effect that if one has seen one ghetto one has seen them all.

Viewed from Cicero, the Lawndale ghetto seems the maximum threat, like a knife, aloft and twirling end-over-end, coming at one's heart. Chicago has two large ghettos, the South Side and the West Side. The West Side ghetto has expanded extensively over the years, with Lawndale being its westernmost point to date. Of Chicago's two ghettos, the West Side one is the less organized, the more intensely festering with chaos, rage, and the potential for desultory destruction. It was the West Side ghetto in Chicago that broke into a binge of rioting, looting, arson, and death after the assassination of Martin Luther King, Jr.

The days of that riot were uneasy ones all over Chicago, but perhaps nowhere more so than in Cicero. There, with fires roaring only a few blocks away in the ghetto, shopkeepers along Roosevelt Road in Cicero expected the worst—and prepared for it. Cicero grocers kept pistols under their aprons, tavern owners nestled shotguns beneath their bars.

If Cicero is afraid of the ghetto, the ghetto is also afraid of Cicero. As no one in Cicero of sound mind would dare walk the streets of the ghetto at night, neither would any Negro dare walk Cicero's streets in the dark. The two communities have lived in a state of open if undeclared cold war, with, thankfully, few violent incidents so far.

The true sadness of this state of affairs is that it admits of no easy solution. It isn't as if the problem is altogether traceable to Cicero's lack of liberality. The fact is, the cards of neglect, discrimination, and obtuse social policy have been shuffled for more than a half-century, and Cicero has been dealt a bad hand. All predictive real-estate studies, for example, call for the West Side ghetto to continue its expansion westward, on into Cicero and beyond. Other places—suburban villages on Chicago's North Shore, neighborhoods within the city itself—have been able to achieve a certain minimal integration, and achieved it peaceably. But Cicero is not threatened so much with integration as it is by that more devastating phenomenon known as inundation. Because of its strategic position in the path of the West

Side ghetto, once the dike of Cicero's segregated status is broken—after the usual dreary cycle of panic, blockbusting, and other shoddy real-estate practice has run its course—the town of Cicero figures to be all black. The fate that has visited Lawndale awaits Cicero, and nobody knows this better than the workingman of Cicero who has slaved and saved over the years to acquire his own home.

Faced with this prospect, a community can go one of two ways. It can deal with it legally and aboveboard, letting history run its course—and perhaps, as a result, go under in the process. Or it can deal with it by other than legal means, its realtors either not showing homes to Negroes or discouraging them in ways subtle and varied, while the town itself makes clear that for any Negro family that cares to move in the way will not be made easy. This last is the approach Cicero has chosen, and it has worked all these years. In fact, so strong is the threat—even if unvoiced—of violence that would attend any attempt by a black family to move into Cicero, that none is soon likely to try. Anyone who did would require courage of a kind that would make James Meredith by comparison seem shy and fumbling.

(There is a third way a community can go when confronted with the situation that confronts Cicero, but it, too, is as of the moment illegal. This third way involves the idea of defusing the explosive pressure of the ghetto by parceling out its population to various surrounding towns, suburbs, and neighborhoods. This would be done under government supervision, with the aid of government funds, and under a strict quota system. Advocates of this approach, among them Anthony Downes of the Chicago Real Estate Research Corporation, feel that it is an idea whose time has nearly come; they see a groundwork of precedent for it being laid by recent Supreme Court decisions on busing and other manipulative devices to affix quotas for integration in education.)

It is as homeowners that the people of Cicero—and not without reason—feel threatened. As workers, they apparently feel no such threat.

The Hawthorne Works of Western Electric is located on Cicero Avenue, and its red brick structures stretch southward from Cermak Road for roughly four city blocks. Fortresslike in appearance, it would be equally convincing as a prison or a state insane asylum or in fact what it is—a factory employing approximately twenty thousand people in the manufacture of telephone parts and cable. Across the street from the Western Electric plant the setting is emblematically Ciceroan: along with a few storefronts, there are two bars, another with a sign reading "Exotic Entertainment—All Girl Revue," the Unemployment

Office, a couple of workingmen's hotels, and the Hawthorne Savings and Loan. Parking lots reserved for Western Electric employees also dot the street, and from the look of the cars in them—lots of recent Fords and Chevvies, but no scarcity of Pontiacs, Oldsmobiles, and Buicks—both the company and their unions have done decently by the workers.

There are two security guards stationed at Western Electric's Gate No. 1, one white and the other black. Within the plant itself somewhere between 25 and 30 percent of the employees are either Negro or Spanish (specifically, Puerto Rican, Mexican, and Cuban). Many of the blacks at Western Electric live in Lawndale, many of the whites live in Cicero. At Western Electric and at other plants in Cicero, blacks and whites work side by side, belong to the same locals, take breaks and lunches together. By day they get along well enough, at night they go their separate ways.

As the largest single employer in the immediate area, Western Electric has a stake not merely in Cicero but in Lawndale as well. Perhaps if the company had to do it over again, it would have located its enormous plant elsewhere and in less troubled terrain. With its tremendous investment in physical plant, however, it is not about to move, and so Western Electric has stood its ground and attempts to do what it can to stabilize things. It has an elaborate program of community relations, ranging from working with the merchants and civic leaders of Cicero on a project to take the best commercial advantage of a new freeway that is supposed to cut through the town, all the way down to aiding local Boy Scout programs. In recent years, too, Western Electric has run a program on the order of "sensitivity training" for its own foremen and supervisors as well as for those in supervisory jobs in other plants in the area to enable them to deal better with the day-to-day tug of personal relations in the shop between various ethnic groups.

Whatever the value of "sensitivity training," whatever the quality of relations between ethnic groups in Cicero's various plants—however useful the first, however fine the second—the issue in Cicero is the question of property. Those Cicero homes, those carefully tended bungalows and two-flats, are felt to be threatened by blacks, and no amount of "sensitivity training" can undo that fact. Next to the question of property, class and race seem peripheral issues in Cicero. That class is of less than paramount importance has been made plain by the fact that, in its southeast sector, near Sportsman's Park racetrack, Cicero has in recent years experienced a small ingress of Appalachian whites. It would take a very fine social Geiger counter to distinguish the differences in class gradation between the way blacks and Appalachians are viewed by their countrymen as a class, yet the latter have moved into Cicero without the slightest stir. As for race, who is to say whether Cicero holds blacks in greater contempt than do the people of dozens of other communities around America? How anyone in Cicero would feel if his sister or daughter married a Negro is open to question; how the same person would feel if his neighbor sold his house to a Negro is not.

The leaders of the union locals in Cicero, though integrationist on the matter of employment, sedulously avoid speaking out on the matter of Cicero's segregated residential status. No local president in Cicero cares to be quoted by name on the subject, and most of them seem, if not exactly to stand for, at least prepared to live with, the status quo. "Things have been this way since the 1940s," they will tell you, and they see no good reason why they cannot go on being the same for the indefinite future. When you ask a Cicero union local president what, if any, position his union takes on the question of race in Cicero, the man is likely to respond, friendly but slightly tense, by saying: "Well, you know, we try to stay out of that ball game."

The line, then, has been drawn—specifically, at Cicero Avenue, with blacks to the east and the blue-collar workers of Cicero to the west. There things stand, and have stood for some years now, and may well stand for years to come. But, most assuredly, at a price.

The price is paid in the coin of a continually deepening sense of insularity. Cicero has come to be—and thinks of itself as—an island, its ideas and ideals landlocked in a sea of change. How, for example, does the town replenish itself? People die and new people move in, but in Cicero the new people often bring with them an even heavier fund of resentment than now obtains in Cicero. Many of the people who have moved in in recent years are those who have already been dispossessed by the spread of the ghetto elsewhere. Many whites, forced to vacate Lawndale, for instance, have moved to Cicero. Determined not to be done in again, they came to Cicero, many of them to make what is in effect a last stand. Their overall impact on the town has been to push up its political temperature still another degree or two.

The people of Cicero pay still another toll—that of conformity. Cicero is not a pleasant place to live in, whatever its other conveniences, if one's thoughts go against the reigning ethos of the community. In Cicero, to dissent is unthinkable, merely to express disagreement on basic issues a form of betrayal. Perhaps this is not so stiff a penalty, after all, since most people who live in Cicero live there in large part because they think and feel precisely the way they do—which is to say, in consonance with the town itself. The problem with so total a consensus, however, is that it tends to preclude further discussion; on most questions and issues of the day, the books in Cicero are quite simply closed. The consequence is that a certain rigidity sets in that is limiting, and not only intellectually so. What, hypothetically, if a quota system on residential integration became the law of the land, and Cicero, along with other all-white communities, were required to make room for a black population constituting, say, 15 percent of the town? How would Cicero react? Could the matter even be reasonably discussed? The answer is by no means clear. As things stand currently, if one lives in Cicero and one's thoughts run counter to the town's, one has but two alternatives: shut up or leave.

Can any portent for change be found in Cicero? What, for example, about the young? Does any greening of Cicero seem likely to come from that quarter? Do the tensions of the celebrated generation gap make themselves felt in the town?

The answer is, not noticeably. Even the most cursory glimpse of Cicero's young leads one to believe that the generation gap is a phenomenon originated and anchored in the middle class. Kids in Cicero as a general rule do not have as much, neither in material goods nor psychological attention, lavished on them as do the kids of the more affluent middle class. Nor is there likely to be so considerable a confusion of values in the home. Kids in Cicero do not suffer under parents who make pretense to being more hip, with-it, and attuned to the modern scene than they themselves are. Instead they suffer, as kids have always suffered, under their parents' (not wholly unfounded) belief that they know more about the world than their children do. So the gap that exists between them and their parents is the one that has always existed between parents and children, and, with luck, always will. Unlike the children of the modern middle class, they do not have to run to extremes to find room to breathe.

Which perhaps explains why drugs have been less of a problem at Cicero's Morton East High School than they have been, for example, at Evanston Township High School across the city and in the northern suburbs, where last year, at the height of the drug craze, a security officer was assigned full-time to surveillance of the drug traffic. Not that some of the kids at Morton East haven't been on pot, or that others haven't screwed the gauge of experimentation up higher with speed or acid, but for the most part drug use is not a regular part of teen-age life in Cicero. The kids of Cicero work without the net beneath them the kids of the middle class have—that net, of course, being parents standing by with tolerance and money, ready to pick up any of the pieces generated by a fall. Nor, given their backgrounds, have they had the full opportunity to become jaded by the material aspects of life that children of richer parents have had.

The vast majority of parents in Cicero did not go to college — nor will all the kids now in Morton East. Many of them, like their parents, will go into the trades. Some will take up white-collar jobs in the plants around Cicero. Only the more talented and industrious will go off to colleges. But almost all of the kids of Cicero, excepting only the unregenerate screw-offs, are future-oriented. They want good jobs and the things that good jobs bring: cars, houses of their own, vacations, security. Success in life is still a vivid notion for most of them, and the conquest of boredom not yet a full-time occupation. They are the children of working-class parents, and though the American working class may in several respects be better off than their counterparts in other countries, there is no good reason why their children should be satisfied with what their parents have. As children of the working class, the kids of Cicero, or at least the majority of them, see the climb as still ahead and the abyss — not some vague existential "abyss" but the pit of simple failure — not all that far behind.

The sadness, if not for the kids themselves but for Cicero, is that the best of the town's kids, those who make it in the world, will leave Cicero behind them, much as the most talented young people of the South have over the years left the small towns in which they were raised. And when they do, even as they have begun to now, they will leave behind a town caught in a social dilemma — the ghetto — that represents a responsibility an entire nation has shirked. So Cicero stands today, perched on the edge of chaos, grown sullen in its own implacable sense of self-righteousness, and not quite able to believe in its own future.

Breakdown in Newark
Thomas R. Brooks

Carmine Casciano, a personable, young junior-high school teacher, acts as my guide to Newark's "predominantly white" North Ward. He is a district leader and president of the North Ward Young Democrats—immersed in the politics of his time and place. We first pass through tree-lined streets, a neighborhood of substantial homes and lawns, and this year's cars parked in the driveways. "The strength of the Republican party is here in Forest Hills," Casciano tells me. "The other parts of the ward are Democratic." But not altogether; as Casciano noses his car into a narrow, brick-paved street, he says, "Now we're in Imperiale City, basically a Republican area." This is a neighborhood of short blocks, tiny plots, and small frame houses— "$6,000- to $7,000-a-year people." "Imperiale City" is named for State Assemblyman Anthony Imperiale, elected in November 1971 on an Independent ticket. Imperiale first gained national attention by winning a seat on the Newark City Council in a white backlash that followed the 1967 riots. He once described his followers as "the good guys" and likened Newark to "a town of the old West. The good guys are prepared to shoot to kill to keep the peace if Negroes come to burn our homes." During the tense aftermath of the riot, Imperiale sat at one end of a "hot line" while Imamu Baraka (LeRoi Jones) sat at the other—and neither had reconciliation in mind. Imperiale's is

THOMAS R. BROOKS, a contributor to Dissent *and other publications, is the author of* Toil and Trouble: A History of Labor.

a politics of resentment; his presence on the City Council served to inflame the passions of Newark, not to calm them. I discussed Imperiale with Don Malafronte, one of the most knowledgeable men about Newark and a former mayoral aide, both to Hugh J. Addonizio and later to Kenneth A. Gibson. "You've got to remember," said Malafronte, "that many whites want peace, and Imperiale means trouble." Imperiale lost his 1970 bid for the mayoralty and, although he ran well ahead in his own ward, lost in June 1971 a sortie aimed at the North Ward's Democratic party leadership. (Imperiale was a Republican, which may explain the failure of his 1971 invasion. For other reasons, see Richard Krickus's essay earlier in this book.) In the 1971 fall elections, Imperiale made a comeback, winning an assembly seat in the state legislature as an Independent. The ambulance he drives, as a service to his neighborhood and for part of his living, was parked outside the storefront that houses his Karate Club and the headquarters of the North Ward Citizens' Association. Imperiale's home, I am told by Casciano, is in the North Ward's black neighborhood.

There are some 100,000 residents in the North Ward, a broad rise of land west of the Passaic River and roughly four miles from downtown Newark. The population is an estimated 70 to 75 percent white, with a sizable black and Spanish-speaking minority. Puerto Ricans are the largest single group moving into the ward but, I am told, "a lot of the home-buying is done by Cubans."

"We're basically Italian with a few Irish and mixed," Casciano explains as we drive through a neighborhood of the comfortably well-off — of "judges, lawyers, doctors, professionals" — and on to another with modest, asphalt-sided, single-family houses — of "mostly factory workers." There is a "project," with its load of welfare cases; the privately owned Colonnades where "the minimum rent is in the $200-a-month bracket"; and Academy Spires, "all black, and most of them vote Democratic." We pass a modest, modern structure, the Church of the Immaculate Conception, called "the little Italian Church"; further on, we see Our Lady of Good Council, larger and older, and "the Irish Church." The Catholic high school lets out as we drive by, and a quick look at young faces confirms Casciano's observation, "It's mostly white." Barringer, a prestigious public high school located in the North Ward, is "mixed," and a local junior high seems so, too. There are not as many For Sale signs, as I was led to expect by newspaper and downtown accounts. "People want to sell," Casciano tells me, "but they can't get a decent price." We do see some signs and he points to one: "If you see that sign [put up by the firm Jordan-Barish], you know they want to sell to blacks." There are American flags out in front of the houses, and flag decals decorate automobile windows. There also are some Italian flags and decals. "That's new."

When I ask about reactions to Gibson's election, Casciano says, "People were frightened, afraid that all whites would suffer. During the school strike, it seemed as if their fears were coming true. Things are really polarized now. The way it's around here," he added, Republican and Democrat don't mean much any more; now it's Italian and black." There's a "White Newark" and a "Black Newark" — the pressure of polarization showed in the captions of two photographs illustrating Fred J. Cook's article on Newark and Mayor Gibson in the July 25, 1971, *New York Times Magazine.* One photo showed Broad Street with the new, gleaming Prudential Insurance Company headquarters in the background. The caption quoted Cook: "Bamberger's still there; Ohrbach's still there. Business Newark does $3.5 billion worth of retail trade annually. . . . But to the west and south it is a different story." Well, it's a different story in the North Ward, too, and there white Newark is hardly Business Newark. Another photograph showed fire-gutted tenements along Springfield Avenue, assumed to be "remnants of the 1967 riots." The caption identified this as Black Newark with "the highest crime rate in the nation. . . ." etc.

Black Newark, in truth, is a world of great variety. To give but one illustration: the parents, most non-Catholic and nearly all black, of the children at St. Charles Borromeo parochial school, in the predominantly black South Ward, last summer raised $4,000 at a card party, $20-a-week at school parking lot barbecues, and $111,000 from other sources in a drive to keep the school from closing for financial reasons.*

Newark, with 375,000 souls, is the first American city, after Washinnton, D.C., to attain a black majority. The Census Bureau gave the city's black population in 1970 as 54.2 percent; Harry L. Wheeler, Newark's director of manpower, estimates that 62 percent of Newark

---

* These pictures are much more apposite than the *Times* captions allow. Two years ago I was walking through the blocks off Springfield Avenue, heart of the 1967 riot scene. I asked my companion, George Fontaine — director of the Newark office of the Workers' Defense League — A. Philip Randolph Joint Apprenticeship Program — if a near-block-long, gutted row of brick houses had been burned out in the riot. Fontaine smiled and told me. "No, it wasn't the riot, just fire." Some dwellings were burned in 1967, mostly incidental to the destruction of business establishments. Those vacated buildings one sees in profusion throughout the heart of the Central Ward were emptied by fire. As Fontaine put it, "Fire insurance gets canceled and that's it, baby." Prudential, as the major insurance company in Newark, therefore bears some responsibility for boarded-up housing.

is black and 11 percent of Spanish background, leaving 27 to 35 percent of the city white. Though a recent study notes that immigrants from Europe, "mainly Portuguese and some Italian," still come to the city, there's scarcely a trace left of the 1938 Newark, with its 23,400 Irish, 36,900 Germans, 35,600 Poles, 65,000 Jews, and 85,300 Italians. With the exception of the Italians, the remaining whites in the city are by and large elderly. Their children and grandchildren presumably live in the middle- and working-class suburbs outside Newark.* No one, as far as I know, has recorded the ethnic migration out of Newark nor located exactly those who stayed, but a report of the Newark office of the American Jewish Committee estimates that "approximately 6,000 Jews are left" in the city. The majority live in the South Ward (Weequahic Section) and the balance in the West Ward (Ivy Hill section).

The city's predominant remaining white group is Italian American. In *Beyond the Melting Pot,* their study of New York City, Nathan Glazer and Patrick Moynihan found that Italian neighborhoods were more likely to have a range of generations living in the same brownstone or city block than old Irish, Jewish, or other ethnic neighborhoods. *Street Corner Society,* W. F. Whyte's earlier study, remarked on the propensity of some Italians to become Republicans in reaction to the Irish domination of city politics.

In the North Ward, as in other Italian neighborhoods in American cities, Italian backyards are often devoted to a small patch of tomatoes, peppers, perhaps a few zucchini, and a grape arbor. There are some sixty-odd clubs where the men eat, drink, and watch sports on TV; but none I visited had expresso machines, which still dominate similar clubs in the Little Italys of Boston and New York.

As I described earlier, the North Ward is made up of a series of neighborhoods consisting largely of one- or two-family homes, presumably owner-occupied. Yet, Newark is not a city of homeowners; 74 percent ot its white and 87 percent of its black families live in rental housing. The median income of white households in Newark in 1966 was $6,752.† Roughly 75 percent of white families in the city earned under $10,000 a year. Thirteen percent of its white

---

* Blacks, too, move out as their incomes rise. Nonwhite families with annual incomes of $3,000 or less constitute 27 percent of nonwhite families in Newark, but only 13 percent in suburban East Orange. The black head of Newark's Urban Coalition lives in Maplewood. As a black Newarkian told me, "Once they get to the doctor/lawyer class, they usually move out." Newark, incidentally, is losing population: in 1950 it stood at 438,776; in 1960 at 405,220; in 1970 at 375,000.

† These and subsequent data are from Jack Chernick, Bernard P. Indik, and George Sternlieb, "Newark, New Jersey: Population and Labor Force, Spring 1967," a report published by the Rutgers Institute of Management and Labor Relations.

families are below the poverty line ($3,000 a year). A majority of white males(61.7 percent) work in the city, while nearly 40 percent travel outside to jobs. Of the female residents, 78.2 percent work in Newark and 21.8 percent outside the city.

Nearly half of the whites (44.5 percent), according to the Rutgers study, have always resided in Newark, while 19.5 percent come from other New Jersey points, and 16 percent from New York, Pennsylvania, or New England. 15.6 percent are immigrants. The study estimated that there are 92 white males for every 100 white females in the population. Slightly over one-quarter of Newark's whites are fifty-five years of age or older; about 37 percent are in the age bracket twenty-five to fifty-four, roughly 13 percent sixteen to twenty-four years old, and 22 percent fifteen or under.

Half the white males over twenty-five have not completed high school, but 25.2 percent of employed white males over sixteen have "some college or more." Of the men, 46.1 percent are blue-collar workers — 19.6 percent craftsmen, foremen, etc.; 17.8 percent are operatives and the like, and 8.7 percent are nonfarm laborers. Most working women — 62.5 percent — are white-collar and 41 percent of these clerical — with 5.8 percent in sales, 7.3 percent working as managers, officials, and proprietors; 8.4 percent are professional, technical, and kindred workers. White male workers (43.4 percent) are more evenly distributed among the white-collar occupations, with 16.3 percent working as managers, etc., 11.6 percent as professionals and technicians, 9.6 percent as clerical workers, and 5.9 percent in sales. Of Newark's working white females and white males, 9 and 11 percent, respectively, are in service occupations.

Many of Newark's white workers are found in durable-goods manufacturing (19.6 percent) and in the wholesale-retail trades (16 percent). More women than men are in the professions (18.1 percent female against 12.7 percent male), and more women than men are in finance, real estate, and insurance (14.8 percent female as against 6.2 percent male). Less than 10 percent of all white workers in Newark are in construction (5.6 percent), transportation, communications, public utilities (8 percent), and government (7 percent). The unemployment rate in Newark, as of April 1971, was 14.2 percent, with 23,300 jobless out of a work force of 163,800. Newark is not an affluent city, white or black.* Its white residents are

---

* Black Newark is poorer. According to Manpower Director Harry L. Wheeler, the black male unemployment rate of those over sixteen and under twenty-six is 24 to 27 percent, while among the Spanish-speaking it approaches 34 percent. Thirty percent of Newark's population receives some form of welfare assistance. In describing white Newark I have tried to keep black/white comparisons to a minimum. One crucial sta-

far from wealthy, and they do not control the business establishment.

The current discovery of ethnic America is something of a fad, as was that of black America, and it equally obscures the class character of our society. What trade union leaders have been saying all along—"you can't ignore blue- and white-collar workers"—now runs the risk of becoming an academic cliché—"you can't ignore the ethnics"—often without sufficient recognition of class differences.

How does one record the urban litany? Steve Adubato (again, see Krickus's essay), former teacher, now chairman of the North Ward Democratic party, and chairman of Rutgers (Newark) Project Dislocated Ethnic Groups, brought together in April 1971 at St. Paul's Centenary Methodist Church five young women to discuss the aftermath of the Newark teachers' strike for a TV special. Afterwards they kept on talking as the technicians packed up. It was a reporter's nightmare—snatches of conversation in this corner and a good quote heard from the other side of the room. Steve Adubato told the women, "We're the new niggers in our society," and the TV interviewer's face clearly showed that he wished he'd caught that for his show.

Listening to this group, you get a sense of what was bothering these white parents. (They were not all Italian as it happens.) "Our kids are not getting to college." "We're hurting. If there's one language teacher, he goes to the other side of town." "My kid can't walk around [the junior high school] with 74¢ in his pocket." "No white kids fight back." "The things I've taught my children are being torn apart down there [at Barringer High School]." "Poor education is pushing a lot of people out of the city." "There are forty-two children in my son's fourth-grade class." "We've been all year without a remedial reading teacher." "Newark just got the new math last year." Adubato says his boy left the public junior-high to attend a Catholic school because there were no sports; but getting held up for loose change was a factor, too. "At Broadway," says Adubato, "he was a water boy." This, he explained, is because "the black kids are two years older to begin with."

An exchange: The wife of a fireman complains, "When the engines get there [to a fire in the Central Ward], people start shoving and pushing the firemen." "How many times has this happened?" asks one woman. Another states: "I don't understand why colored

---

tistic, however, should be kept in mind: for households headed by a white male, the median income in 1966 was $7,579, and for black males it was $6,892. But black female-headed households had a median income of $3,242 as compared with $5,926 for white female-headed households. What this means shows up in the difference between the black household median income of $3,580 and that of whites at $7,000 a year.

people call firemen. If they want their places burned down, let 'em burn." "Look, there's crazy people all over."

Another exchange: "LeRoi Jones is teaching them to stick with their own people." "Imperiale is just as bad. He's doing the same thing." "My girlfriend can't sell her house fast enough," says a self-possessed matron. "There was a house for sale right next door," a buxom brunette breaks in, and I got at least five phone calls from Jordan-Barish asking, 'Aren't you selling your house?' " "Could people be using their name to start trouble?" someone asks.

A woman in a purple dress announces, "My house is not up for sale." We all turn, and she continues, "We got a call, 'Aren't you afraid of blacks next door?' I said, 'No, it doesn't scare me at all.' Puerto Ricans did buy that house, and you know something? They're the nicest neighbors I ever had. You can't tell what people are going to be like."

As we break up, the wife of the fireman says, "What makes you think I'm blaming them? I don't think it's their fault."

Adubato and I go off for a round of beer. "I want to show you the clubs," he tells me. "They're a feature of our life." At one, I'm introduced to an "old guy," a Sicilian who tells me, "I hate 'em."

We end up at "Klub Rainier," just off Bloomfield Avenue, and find it unlocked and empty. "No *paese* here," Adubato says. The members are younger men, Adubato's generation. We have a bottle of Manhattan Special, a coffee soda Adubato wants me to try. It's all that he says it is: good. We linger outside, and various members of the club drift up. The guys who belong, I am told, are policemen, school-teachers, factory workers, and "one guy who lives here." He is, I gather, the house hippie, and they are quite proud of him. I'm introduced to Steve George, Adubato's cousin. Adubato laughs, "That's how I got elected. I've got a lot of cousins."

Mostly, we talk about the great meal Steve George is going to prepare for Friday. A black youth, conservatively dressed and well mannered, comes up the street, and someone giggles, "Here comes the next president of the club." More remarks in this vein, *sotto voce,* as the youngster passes by. I don't know if he heard, but he walks straight on and keeps looking straight ahead. Someone mentions that "Eddie Hotdog's brother got shot in the hand by a cop (I never did get the details straight), and this reminds a policeman of a shooting the previous night. "I got no respect for them," he tells us, "with all that talk about blacks *and* Puerto Ricans. This kid [a mugger shot by a patrolman] is bleeding in the street while we wait for the ambulance. The crowd gets nasty, you know, muttering about 'pigs' and 'racist cops.' Then someone takes a closer look and when they see he's not black, they all melt away." Aggressive crime is much on people's minds. Horrific rumors circulate widely, with apparent spontaneity and almost instantaneously.

Another young man explains how he has to pick up his mother every night, who works downtown for an insurance company and is afraid of having her handbag snatched or worse. His father drives a garbage truck, and he has an uncle in the fire department. He's thirty-two, been out of work for three months, and is waiting "to get on the fire department." He also wants to get married, which gives bite to his grievance. He has passed the fire examination and is on the list. "They're holding up the list," he tells me, "because of the PRs and the colored. They keep giving the exam and they can't pass." It never enters his head that the holdup might be financial. "They always need firemen, don't they?"

The North Ward feels cut off from the city, even though many of its residents hold city jobs. It is a feeling of some standing. I exaggerate, but not by much, when I say that there are moments, especially talking to older people, when it is not clear whether "them," directed at City Hall, means the blacks or the Irish. Steve Adubato's great-uncle is still something of a hero in the North Ward as the first Italian to get on the police force back around World War I. He was killed collaring a prohibition-era hood in a New York City fleabag. The first Italian was elected, along with four Irish Americans, to the (then five-man) City Council in 1941. It was Ralph Villani, who is currently a councilman-at-large. He later served as mayor from 1949 to 1953, and the Italians have played a key role in city politics ever since. Yet I heard grumblings about the Irish domination of the police and fire departments. And Adubato, in one breath, told me, "I'm like Imperiale, the Church is something we don't knock, but the Irish run the whole show." *

Unhappily, "them" increasingly means the blacks. Paradoxically, despite those sociologists who see the conflict between the almost-haves (or have-nots) and the most recent haves as the most severe, the upwardly mobile blacks of Newark and the recently arrived whites have much in common—the same need for more police protection, for better schools, and other demands—enough to cement a coalition. Adubato is accomplishing just this, admittedly on a small scale, in his North Ward alliance of Italian Americans and middle-class blacks.

---

* From a more analytical source I gather that this may be why the Church has not played a more positive role in Newark. It has, after all, black and white adherents and could conceivably cement brotherhood in a city torn by racism.

To the tensions of race one must add those of class and age. In 1967, according to the Rutgers study, 46.7 percent of Newark's blacks were fifteen years of age and under as against only 23.3 percent of whites. That's a sizable bulge of young blacks coming up through the school system *and* operating out on the streets. As this group moves into its late teens and early twenties, it faces a high rate of unemployment (37.8 percent for those between sixteen and nineteen) and a high rate of crime. A quarter of the city's whites are fifty-five and over, a group that looms large among victims. This creates continuing, crucial tension in the center city. The white demand for more police veers on a call for control of "them"; therefore, blacks who otherwise would join in such a call hold back. So we end up with immobilization where we need resolute action for the sake of everyone's peace and comfort.

The young, too, are at the center, not as a cause but a reason, of the battle for control of the schools and, ultimately, of the city itself. The eleven-week school strike limns Newark's tragic predicament. The strike was not of the teachers' making. Money was not an issue in the bargaining that preceded the strike. The Newark local of the American Federation of Teachers was forced out on strike because the Board of Education refused to renew two key contract provisions, which should have been normal procedure. These provisions were to provide binding arbitration of unresolved grievances, and the teachers' relief from such nonprofessional chores as patrolling of hallways and cafeterias. The four blacks and one Puerto Rican majority on the Board, as against the four whites, held that the teachers' unwillingness to perform these tasks was "insensitive to the needs of black children." * What put the teachers' backs up was an incident in November, when a black parents' group forced the summary transfer of three white teachers who had refused extra-professional chores not covered under the terms of the then existing contract. The arbitration clause, black militants charged, gave union leaders too much power in setting school policy. † "The union must protect its members from the indiscriminate dictates of the so-called community," said Carol Graves, president of the local union, who served forty-one days of a six-month jail sentence for strike activities. "Without binding

---

* The union demand for more aides to relieve teachers of nonprofessional tasks would provide more time for educating the young. Moreover, hallway and cafeteria patrol often places the teacher in a disciplinary role with bad carry-overs to the classroom. Yet freeing the teacher of this burden requires more aides — which cost money.
† There's some irony here, for in classic worker militancy, binding arbitration is often rejected because it gives too much authority to an outsider.

arbitration, a contract with this board is just a worthless piece of paper."

The strike was marked by sporadic violence from the start. On the first day, fifteen teachers were assaulted by a band of black youths. Teachers' car windows were smashed and car tires slashed. Several members of the School Board were threatened, and shots were fired into the home of one member. The strike ended in mid-April on the basis of a compromise fashioned by Mayor Gibson. The settlement called for "no reprisals" and for the reinstatement of 347 teachers who had been suspended by the Board of Education toward the end of the strike; it stipulated that elementary-school teachers were to escort students to the school front door, and that junior-high teachers were to monitor corridors between classes. A three-man panel—a professional arbitrator, a teacher, and a principal—were to arbitrate grievances. The Local was fined a crippling $270,000 by the courts, to be paid by a 10 percent deduction from salaries.*

The strike was widely misinterpreted as solely a black/white confrontation. It was that, of course; but it was also an attack by black nationalists and black wheelers and dealers against black integrationists and moderates. Black militants split on the issue; i.e., the Panthers supported the union. The AFT is one of the few truly integrated organizations of any power or significance in Newark, and some black extremists were out to prove that reason and racial integration cannot work. One of their tactics was a crude attempt to drive white teachers out of the system. White teachers, it was said, did not live in Newark (which is not true—for perhaps even more white teachers do than black teachers). Board President Jesse L. Jacob prolonged the strike—"If this be the year of attrition, then let it be. In the words of the old Negro spiritual, 'Free at last, praise God Almighty, free at last.'" Jacob opposed the settlement, and he attempted to blow up an incident where a handful of black parents sought to prevent the return of white teachers in several schools into a breakdown of tenuously established relations. By the end of the school year, an uneasy peace settled over Newark.

Clearly, there is missing in Newark that old political device, the balanced ticket. Mayor Gibson has said that he is the mayor of all the people, and he has made white appointments—but he has very few Italians on his staff. And there are none in two of the City's key anti-poverty agencies, the United Community Corporation and the Model Cities program.

The mayor has no real political links with the minority white

---

* This last point is still tied up in the courts on appeal.

community, nor, despite gestures in that direction, with the emerging, smaller minority of the city's Spanish-speaking citizens. One would have expected, for example, in view of Steve Adubato's successful insurgency against the Addonizio machine, some overtures from City Hall. But this has not happened as far as I can determine. Mayor Gibson unfortunately also has not developed a working organization. This makes governing the city difficult, and explains why it took the mayor so long to resolve the school strike.

Current conventional wisdom dictates the condemnation of Mayor Hugh J. Addonizio as a racist, old-line, machine politician. And it is true, in the end the sticky fingers of corruption got him. But that is not the whole story. Back in 1962, Addonizio, ex-quarterback and World War II hero, and six-time liberal congressman, pulled together a coalition of dissident Democrats, liberals, labor people, blacks, and Italians to wrest City Hall from another ward-heeling machine. For a time, Addonizio was a good mayor as mayors go. Newark has the largest per capita public housing program in the country. It is fifth in the nation in the amount of federal funds received for urban renewal purposes. Addonizio saw to it that new campuses were built for the Newark College of Engineering (Mayor Gibson is a graduate), for Rutgers in Newark, and for the Essex County Community College. A new medical center has been built. This is a record that most mayors would be proud of.

Addonizio also integrated city departments. He had the support of Irvine Turner, a black city councilman of the Central Ward, elected in 1953, and a power in his own right. Calvin West, an Addonizio-Turner protégé, was the first black elected on a city-wide basis, becoming a City Council member in 1966. West went down with Addonizio in the 1970 election; so did Turner. The latter was defeated by the Rev. Dennis Westbrooks, the youngest city councilman at age thirty-one. Westbrooks, a native of Homestead, Pennsylvania, won his reputation as a militant and a substantial bloc of votes as director of a community action program at the Scudder Houses, a public housing project, where he led a successful rent strike. He had the support of the LeRoi Jones–organized Black and Puerto Rican Convention; so did Mayor Gibson and Coordinator for the United Community Corporation Earl Harris, who unseated West.

Addonizio might have won again if it had not been for his arrest and subsequent conviction on charges involving corruption. We think of Newark as dominantly black. But, in terms of eligible voters, the city is much more evenly divided: *47 percent of the vote is white, 45 percent black.* In the first electoral round of 1970, chiefly because of the corruption issue, Gibson carried all but the North Ward, leading a slate of six candidates. (Imperiale carried the North Ward but trailed third to Addonizio's second.) In the runoff election, Gibson concentrated on the black wards, South and Central, and on rallying the black vote. Addonizio concentrated on the white voters, and so he lost whatever support he might have had among black voters – and Gibson was the winner: 55,097 to 43,086. Despite the polarization in the runoff, Gibson held an estimated 15 percent of the white vote. Imperiale's North Ward vote clearly went to Addonizio, but Gibson raised his vote there from 4,265 in the first, to 7,405 in the second election. In the first election, with a smaller turnout, Gibson received 37,859 votes to Addonizio's 18,212 and Imperiale's 13,978, most of which (7,656) came from the North Ward.

Much has been written about Gibson as the black saviour of Newark, but the City Council is more representative of Newark than Mayor Gibson. The Gibson slate carried along only two of his six running mates. Newark has what the textbooks call a strong mayor/council government; the council, however, controls the purse. It consists of nine members, four elected at-large, and five in the wards. Three of the council members at large are Italian and one is black. Of the ward councilmen, three are Italian and two are black. Six of these were newly elected, including the three black members. Thirty-two-year-old City Council President Louis B. Turco is a holdover from the old days and an Addonizio supporter. He is the leader of a liberal-labor coalition, which includes Joel R. Jacobson of the United Automobile Workers, battling the entrenched Essex County Democratic machine.

City Council elections are nonpartisan, but understandably the Democrats are the power. Nonetheless, the council is torn along racial lines, a rift exacerbated by Mayor Gibson's acceptance – he had little choice – of a tax package approved by a Republican governor and a Republican-dominated state legislature. The black council members sided with the mayor; the whites fought the adoption of a tax package that included a regressive 1 percent sales tax to be added to the state's 5 percent. In the face of a $50 million budget gap a compromise was worked out, but not without bitterness.*

The May night I visited the City Council was the occasion of a racial fallout over the proposed renaming of Belmont Avenue as

---

* Yet the three black members of the City Council refused in November 1971 to support Mayor Gibson's request for two new municipal executive posts and turned down two of his appointments to the Newark Parking Authority. The latter were whites who lived outside Newark, which perhaps explains the black councilmen's opposition. Four white councilmen, incidentally, backed the mayor on the new appointments and the creation of the new posts. This suggests that when it comes to governing a city, politicians, black or white, do not always act along racial lines.

Malcolm X Boulevard. I was intrigued by the apparent unanimity of the council on a range of financial and substantive matters. Hardly a dissenting vote or voice was raised over quite sizable expenditures of money and such questions as an anti-blockbusting ordinance. Then the blow-up over the proposed new Malcolm X Boulevard. There were hidden eddies, even among the black councilmen. Westbrooks, who wears a mod dashiki to council meetings, was an enthusiast, but the other two councilmen seemed to be less so. One even suggested that it was important to find out the sentiments of those who lived on or owned businesses on the Avenue (or new boulevard), a proposition greeted with scorn by a sizable group of young black citizens who were present. The white councilmen, with the exception of Villani, obviously wanted a way out that would save face all around. When the council majority adopted a motion asking the clerk to prepare a report on the feasibility of the name change, it was roundly booed and the youths shouted, "We're going to change it ourselves."

In the course of all this, the council got into one of those parliamentary hassles that is the despair of even the most initiated. I was struck by the ire the young militants vented against the council clerk — a white, elderly, gray-haired, and parliamentarian gentleman; they seemed to feel that *he* was the enemy. And those young militants — followers of LeRoi Jones — obviously believed that their mere presence and superior number in the gallery entitled them to a victory on the issue. The system, to them so clearly represented by the elderly clerk, of course does not work that way nor should it. But for an instant the black Newark of Imamu Baraka faced the Newark of the North Ward and I shuddered.

Whatever hope there is for a rejuvenated Newark lies somewhere in its confused politics. It was expected in 1968 that the city would give George Wallace 15 to 20 percent of its vote. He got slightly less than 10 percent even though his chief supporter, Anthony Imperiale, won a council seat that year with his votes being three times the Wallace total. Humphrey carried the city and the North Ward, though his North Ward total was not greater than the combined Nixon-Wallace vote there. In 1972, Wallace may do much better in the North Ward, as Assemblyman Imperiale's November 1971 election suggests.*

---

* Each assembly district in New Jersey elects two assemblymen. Imperiale led a field of seven candidates in District 11-B, which consists of Newark's North and West wards. He won as an Independent with 13,750 votes. Frank Megaro, the city councilman from the North Ward and a Democrat, won the other seat with 12,604 votes. The losing Democrat came in third with 11,018 votes — as against 8,247 and 7,375 votes for the Republican contestants. Two other Independents polled roughly 3,000 each.

But meanwhile Steve Adubato's group has secured its hold over the Democratic party in the ward. They are now engaged in building their base, after having opened the North Ward Educational and Cultural Center with financial aid from Rutgers and the National Center for Urban Ethnic Affairs in 1971. "We are going to get colleges and corporations to give us special help the way they do for disadvantaged blacks," Adubato says. He also plans to pressure Mayor Gibson into appointing more Italians to city jobs, especially in the anti-poverty agencies.

"The North Ward is restless," Adubato argues, "because there is no delivery system for whites. Blacks have got all these special programs to help them get to college, or to rehabilitate their houses and help them find jobs. We white ethnics don't get any of these things." And, reminiscent of Imamu Baraka, "All we want is equity." He complains that when white liberals talk about the "priority issues" — housing, unemployment, tax inequities, and education — "they automatically focus on blacks. Liberals have programmed a black agenda and have not directed themselves to low-income, first- and second-generation white Americans. Any new agenda must include both groups. We've got to build a coalition whose objective is to build change."

The goodly number of teachers in Adubato's group first gained political experience in the American Federation of Teachers' Newark Local. Yet unions otherwise do not play much of a role in North Ward politics. No one union dominates or looms large on the scene as, say, the UAW does in Detroit. In the Newark area, local unions are organized into a county council rather than into a city council as in New York and other major cities. This bespeaks, it seems, a weakness within the city. A number of the larger unions in Newark — the International Ladies' Garment Workers' Union and the International Union of Electrical Workers, to name two — have large black memberships in the city and comparatively few whites. My guess is that they are not in a position to bridge racial hostilities in Newark, no matter how well they may do so in the plant.

Surprisingly, Adubato has remained aloof from the Turco/Jacobson alliance, reflecting perhaps a temporary expediency. What is more alarming is the erosion of black/white relations within the Democratic party, which is, after all, an important integrated institution. The blacks of Newark want a black congressman, and there is pressure from black activists and politicians elsewhere who want to build up the number of blacks in the U.S. Congress. To get the necessary redistricting, the interested black groups are perfectly willing to work with the Republicans, who are eager for redistricting, which would also probably guarantee a Republican victory in the Essex County suburbs. At present, the two congressional districts—each consisting of suburban and city areas—return to Congress, with unfailing regularity, two liberals who are both Italian and pro-labor.

I don't think I need spell out further the kind of struggle that appears to be in the offing. The Italians of Newark are likely to be again castigated as racists, blue-collar Wallaceites, hard hats, and ethnics. There is talk in the North Ward of separation from Newark, of a petition to recall the present form of government for an at-large councilmanic system on the theory and possibility that this will guarantee a white majority at City Hall at least for a time, and Steve Adubato talks of a tax boycott. "We're looking for an answer that will work," he says. Newark's property tax is the second highest among the country's major cities, and such a boycott aimed at eliciting better services from the city might be popular though unworkable. I take it as evidence of desperation. Newark is two cities, and neither one is a happy one.

Black City, Black Unions?
B. J. Widick

Detroit Experiences a Painful Transition

Detroit in the 1970s is startlingly different from the factory complex associated with the auto industry, the UAW, and Walter Reuther. Auto workers no longer rush to and from huge industrial plants on the east and west sides. Now the major traffic flows are of white suburbanites driving into the downtown commercial center and inching their way out before darkness. The new buildings downtown stick out like shining thumbs amid parking lots, expressways, and vacant land—less than 30 percent of downtown Detroit is used for commercial and industrial purposes. Within the city limits there are large blots of wasteland.

All the auto companies have decentralized production, partly into the vast metropolitan area surrounding the city—an area in which almost half of Michigan's eight million people live—and partly by developing plants in other states. Meanwhile, the deterioration of the city is visible everywhere.

For every new business moving into Detroit, two move out.

B. J. WIDICK, a veteran trade unionist, teaches industrial relations at Columbia University. He is the author of Labor Today *and co-author, with Irving Howe, of* The UAW and Walter Reuther. *This essay is adapted from a chapter in his new book,* Detroit: City of Race and Class Violence, *copyright* © 1972 by B. J. Widick, by permission of the publisher, Quadrangle Books.

There are over seven thousand vacant storefronts in the city.* Thousands of small stores, with their steel fronts, look like tiny military posts under siege. The *Detroit News* building, downtown, is surrounded by a brick wall, reminiscent of a medieval fortress. These are signs of the changes making Detroit into a black city, surrounded by a white-dominated suburban ring like a noose around the city's neck.

The city lacks a rapid-transit system to facilitate spending from suburbanite consumers. Public sensitivity to race tension and a much publicized "high crime rate" keep buyers away. Even during the day the city seldom looks busy. Downtown shoppers are mostly black. At night, only a few whites can be seen in the downtown theaters. Restaurants do a minimum of business at night; many are quietly folding, as are the night clubs.

The city continues to shrink both physically and in population. There has been a net loss in total dwelling supply each year since 1960, when 553,000 units were available. In 1970 there were only 530,770. The Department of Planning and Building Studies of the Detroit Board of Education explains:

> The net loss is the result of demolitions for both public and private purposes. In the public sector there have been 5,000 units removed for freeway construction, 9,700 units for urban renewal programs, 3,300 for school sites, and 1,000 for recreation and other public uses. In the private sector there has been clearance for gasoline stations, parking lots, and some demolitions with no other objective than reducing value for tax assessment purposes.†

A decline in population has offset the decline in dwelling units. Detroit in 1970 was still the fifth largest city in America, though its population of 1,492,507 showed a drop of 190,000 from the 1960 figure. Meanwhile, in the same period the population in the wider metropolitan area of Detroit grew from 3.7 million to 4.2 million.

Even more important is the change in social composition. Another 345,000 whites fled to the suburbs in the 1960s, causing a 29.2 percent decrease in the white population. Blacks now constitute 43.7 percent of the city's population and are on the way to becoming a clear majority. ‡ The city is also left with more than a normal share of old

---

* *Detroit News,* February 13, 1970.
† Merle Henrickson, "Population Trends Which Have Affected School Enrollment," *Studies Report,* Department of Planning and Building, January 14, 1971.
‡ U.S. Bureau of the Census, *1970 Census of Population* (Washington, D.C.: U.S. Department of Commerce, February 1971).

very young, and poor blacks and whites. Since there is little middle- or lower-income housing in downtown Detroit, and upper-income housing is at a premium, the trend toward suburban living continues unchecked.* A survey of the number of blacks living outside the city limits shows an all-white pattern in major suburbs scarcely duplicated anywhere in the United States. Warren, Michigan, has doubled its population to 180,000 in the past decade; it has all of five black families. Dearborn, with over 100,000 people, lists one black family. Grosse Pointe has two, Harpers Woods one, Hazel Park one, Birmingham five.†

Anxieties permeate the life of Detroit. An astonishing number of citizens have armed themselves, in fear and rage, both black and white. Detroiters possess over 500,000 hand guns, more than 400,000 of them unregistered.‡ The city seldom has a moment of respite from racial incidents. In spring 1971, R. Wiley Brownlee, principal of the Willow Run high school, was tarred and feathered by masked men because he was considered an integrationist. In the fall of 1970 there was a shoot-out between black militants and the police, in which a patrolman was killed. Only the brave intervention of a black woman leader, Nadine Brown, who arranged for a peaceful surrender, kept the city from exploding again.

To the whites, the police appear incompetent to handle major troubles. For the black community, there is the legacy of the Algiers Motel killing of three young blacks. No police were convicted in that incident, although two brilliant studies and newspaper accounts exposed the truth. The full horror was revealed in Van Gorden Sauter's and Burleigh Hines's book, *Nightmare in Detroit:*

> The events of the next hour left a stain on the Detroit police department that will not be erased for decades. Pollard, Cooper, and Temple —unarmed and outnumbered—were shotgunned to death. Each was shot more than once at a range of fifteen feet or less by twelve-gauge double-0 buckshot. Temple and Pollard were apparently shot while lying or kneeling.§

Community passions ran high in 1969 when a policeman was killed and another wounded near the New Bethel Baptist Church and police poured gunfire into the church where 143 men, women, and

---

* "UDA Research Project Document DOX-USA-A60 January 1969," Detroit Edison Co. and Doxiadis Associates, with Wayne State University.
† U.S. Bureau of the Census, *1970 Census of Housing* (Washington, D.C.: U.S. Department of Commerce, February 1971).
‡ *Detroit News,* April 11, 1971.
§ Van Gorden Sauter and Burleigh Hines, *Nightmare in Detroit* (Chicago, 1968).

children were meeting. Mass arrests, recriminations, and mutual antagonism between the black community and the police dominated the city for weeks on end. For one year, while Patrick Murphy acted as police commissioner, he provided the city with a breather because of his effective control of the police, but then he returned to Manhattan. Meanwhile, another police scandal broke: Inspector Alex Wierzbicki, three lieutenants, and twelve policemen were indicted in April 1971 on graft charges, confirming what most blacks think about "white police."

The campaign of the *Detroit News* against "crime waves" keeps the city in a state of fear. Perhaps in consequence, an early 1971 survey showed that people of metropolitan Detroit think that crime is their most important problem.* Thus, at a time when one out of eight persons in the city of Detroit was on welfare, unemployment rates were 50 percent among black youth and 25 percent among black adults, and the general city unemployment rate was 14 percent.†

The school system, which a recent high-level study called "a disgrace to the community," ‡ is the victim of the clash of the races. Since the 1967 riot skirmishes between black and white students, turbulent community meetings and hate gatherings occur continually. In March 1971, for example, a meeting of parents of Osborn Heights high school, held to quiet down two days of fighting between students, turned into a hate session. The school has about six hundred black and three thousand white students. As one observer put it, "Whites fear that blacks have too much power and can get away with anything. while blacks fear they are second-class underdogs." § Policy-making in the school system became a shambles after the liberal majority of the Board of Education was recalled in the fall of 1970, victim of the cross currents between black and white groups, Catholic and upstate school interests, the argument over centralization versus decentralization, and the financial crisis.

As a result, the tax base of Detroit is lower and its income level much lower than those of the suburbs (white median income in 1969 was $8,760, black median income $5,290). There is little likelihood that the city can pull itself up by its bootstraps, though Detroit has witnessed two such attempts in recent years. In February 1970 the Central Business Association launched a "Talk Up Detroit" campaign. Edwin O. George, president of the Detroit Edison Company, declared: "Idle chatter which downgrades Detroit hits us all in the pocketbook.

---

* *Detroit News,* March 20, 1971.
† *Detroit Free Press,* March 29, 1971.
‡ *New York Times,* June 25, 1968.
§ *Detroit News,* March 22, 1971.

The entire economy is sagging because the whole town has a chip on its shoulder," *

Somewhat earlier, after the 1967 riot, there had been a more prestigious effort to revitalize the city through the New Detroit Committee. Its director was Joseph L. Hudson, Jr., brilliant executive of the J. L. Hudson department store. Personally involved were James P. Roche, president of General Motors; Henry Ford II; Lynn Townsend, president of Chrysler; Walter Reuther; the editors of Detroit's newspapers; and downtown business interests—the Power Structure. According to its own report, New Detroit's efforts were "hopelessly inadequate." † The Committee failed to get the state legislature to pass an open-housing bill; it failed to get emergency aid for the city's schools. While a recession wracked the city it spent $3 million, largely in gestures aiding "black capitalism."

The challenge to the New Detroit Committee was outlined by J. L. Hudson, Jr.:

> Negroes must be encouraged to play a larger role in determining how their problems are to be solved. The problems which demand immediate solution are primarily in the area of jobs, housing, schools, and public order.
> The riots themselves were clearly and thoroughly wrong. But behind them lie such fundamental causes as high unemployment among Negroes, mistreatment by some policemen, profiteering by some stores and landlords, substandard housing and the frustration of so many of the benefits of American life. . . . ‡

The statement was made in 1967; it remains valid in 1972.

The New Detroit Committee fell apart for another reason: class tensions broke through. In 1970 the UAW began bargaining for a new contract with the Big Three, which led to a nine-week strike at General Motors. Both the auto industry executives and the UAW leadership were too busy with the strike to be able to participate in the New Detroit Committee. It would probably not have mattered if they'd had the time.

Long before the GM strike, both sides recognized the inevitability of a major walkout, given the discontent over shop conditions—there were over 250,000 written grievances at GM in 1969, one for every

---

* *Detroit News,* February 13, 1970.
† "Progress Report of the New Detroit Committee" (pamphlet), April 1968.
‡ *Detroit News,* November 2, 1967.

other worker There was the impact of inflation on real wages, with the UAW members no longer fully covered by an "escalator" clause. And a new source of difficulty had arisen: the emergence of a "new working class" in the industry. Here is how a knowledgeable executive described the new young workers:

Employees in the 1970s are (1) less concerned about losing a job or staying with an employer; (2) less willing to put up with dirty and uncomfortable working condition; ; (3) less likely to accept the unvarying pace and functions on moving lines; and (4) less willing to conform to rules or be amenable to higher authority than ever in the past. The traditional American work ethic — the concept that hard work is a virtue and a duty — will undergo additional erosion.

There are two basic causes for this new situation. We have on the hourly employment rolls more "problem employees." These people almost habitually violate our plant rules. Although some of them do so with an open attitude of defiance, in a great many cases it is just a matter of the problem employee bringing with him into the plant the mores of his own background.

While some of these problem employees have come to us through our efforts to hire the so-called hard-core unemployables, most of them are simply a reflection of the labor market on which we've been drawing for our normal hiring during recent years.

The other cause of our difficulties might be termed a general lowering of employees' frustration tolerance. Many employees, particularly the younger ones, are increasingly reluctant to put up with factory conditions, despite the significant improvements we've made in the physical environment. Because they are unfamiliar with the harsh economic facts of earlier years, they have little regard for the consequences if they take a day or two off.

For many, the traditional motivations of job security, money rewards, and opportunity for personal advancement are proving insufficient. Large numbers find factory life so distasteful they quit after only brief exposure to it. The general increase in real wage levels in our economy has afforded more alternatives for satisfying economic needs.*

How this kind of young work force affects collective bargaining was summarized in a 1970 Ford Foundation report on labor:

As with the young elsewhere, their attitude toward their union and the leaders is characterized by colossal irreverence. Like the blacks, they demand to be heard, to question and challenge the leadership

---

* Off-the-record report by a personnel director of an auto company.

which, not unlike institutional leadership generally, has not been prepared for this wave of disrespect and revolt.*

Because the UAW remains far more democratic than most
unions, and its leaders far more responsive to social moods and
changes, the 1970 GM strike was inevitable. Spending $176 million
in strike benefits and other costs, the UAW did retain the loyalties
of the younger generation, something management seems at a loss to
achieve.

Perhaps the most striking feature of the GM strike was its
failure either to produce class cohesiveness in the shops or to impair
the mutual accommodation between union and company. GM loaned
the UAW about $30 million during the strike so it could make Blue
Cross-Blue Shield payments for the strikers. It was a security-free
loan, in contrast to the Teamsters' Union loan of $25 million, secured
by a mortgage on UAW property and with an 8 percent interest charge.
On the whole, the GM strike turned out to be a form of controllable
social unrest, making little dent on the consciousness of the auto
workers or the people of Detroit.

On three different visits and through intensive interviewing, including
a return to the plant where I spent fifteen years as a plant worker and
UAW official, I learned that both within the plants and in the city, the
big concern was not class strife but hard drugs and race.

The execution of seven young men and women in June 1971,
part of a bloody war between two black gangs seeking to monopolize
the profitable heroin trade, dramatized the city's overall drug problem. Between twenty-five and fifty persons had already been killed,
gangland style, in this dispute. But until the *New York Times* reported
the concern of auto management over the use of hard drugs in the auto
plants, little attention was given to this problem. †

The *Times* report was published about a week after I visited
an auto plant, talking to plant and local union officials, and to one of
the UAW staff members who functions as a "troubleshooter." Sam
Bellomo, vice-president of Chrysler Local 7—he's been elected to
office either in the plant or the large local for almost thirty years—
described the situation this way:

Boredom on the job? The speedup? That's routine. What the workers
fear most is the drug addict in the plant. They worry about safety of

---

* Mitchell Sviridoff, "Ford Foundation Report on Labor," an address delivered in
1970.
† *New York Times,* June 21, 1971.

operations, and they dread knowing that pushers operate in the plants and their victims work there. Drugs are not confined to any one people. It's the young mainly, both black and white. They don't give a damn about anything.*

I checked this with other officials whom I have known for years. They confirm what Bellomo says. Nor could this be attributed to the returning Vietnam veterans, my friends insisted; there weren't that many of them. It was more of a general problem. At a pay rate of $35 a day, an assembly-line worker is far more likely to have the "loot" to buy expensive fixes than is the welfare client. Hard drugs have found a new marketplace, the auto shop, and a new victim, the young worker. The drug scene is so frightening that it is one reason many local union officials, men still in the shops, feel a need to carry guns.

The other obsession has to do with race relations. A decade ago this plant, like many others, had a mixture of workers: about 20 percent black, the rest Polish, Italian, and Southern white. Winning a local union election usually meant getting together the right coalition with each ethnic group represented. It was basically an integrative concept. This has changed drastically. Now 65 percent of the membership is black, and only the skilled trades remain a white work force. In the plant we were told by white workers, "They have taken over. You do your work, keep your mouth shut, and get the hell out when the whistle blows." At best, the black and white workers tolerate each other in the plants. The UAW of class solidarity, as it was once supposed to exist and in part did, is no longer much in evidence. Jesse Cundiff, a local union president for three terms before becoming a staff man, says:

Among skilled workers and the old-timers, the ethnic groups, nothing has changed. They are still anti-. They hate the colored man's guts but can't do anything about it. As for the blacks, they are aggressive and taking over wherever and whenever they can — in many cases long overdue after all they have had to suffer. †

Politics in local union elections generally follows this pattern. Where the blacks are a majority, they take the big spots and give a white a token job. Men like Sam Bellomo are now the exception; he's executive vice-president in a local where all other officers, including the president, William Gilbert, are black. An indication of how black leadership keeps developing through union politics and bargaining is

---

* Personal interview, June 15, 1971.
† Personal interview, June 16, 1971.

that ten years ago Gilbert was going to union classes to become a better chief steward. Now he teaches at the Wayne State labor college besides being president of this large local. Another young steward ten years ago was Quintan McCrae. He used to represent the janitors. When I talked to him in June 1971, he had just finished five local negotiations with Chrysler. How many dozens of such young leaders have been developed in the UAW no one can say. But they are there, and more are coming up all the time.

Where whites are a majority, they keep as much control as possible and have a token black officer. It works strictly as a power relationship based primarily on race — and with little love lost. Election contests are intense. Each year, as the composition of the plants changes, the blacks gain more and more power on the local union levels — and now have a real base in the international union. Eleven local presidents in the Detroit area now are black.

Between the high quit rate among young workers — over 30 percent annually despite the recession — and the new industry policy of hiring blacks, there are now over 250,000 black workers in the auto plants: at GM about 25 percent, at Ford 35 percent, and at Chrysler about 25 percent. In many Detroit plants the blacks are either a majority or about to be, and this has vast significance for the future of black unionism.

Symptomatic of these trends is the impact on management. We asked what happened to a former secretary of Local 7, one of the first blacks elected to that position. It turns out that he is now an assistant labor-relations director for the company. What about the most popular black steward the Local ever had, a self-educated man with a white constituency? Now superintendent of the night shift! There are black foremen throughout the plant, yet it is only ten years ago that the issue of having one black foreman was raised with the corporation. Those were the days when management didn't believe a black man could fill any supervisory position. They have learned better.

For both blacks and whites, this shift in power is a painful process. Violent incidents exacerbate the tensions. A major topic of conversation in the auto plants last June was the acquittal of a black worker who killed a white foreman, a black foreman, and a white skilled worker in the Chrysler Eldon Avenue plant last year — hence, as the men feel, another reason for carrying guns in the shops.

This case attracted much attention, for the black worker was a veteran, James Johnson, Jr., and his attorneys were Kenneth Cockrel of the League of Revolutionary Black Workers, and Justin Ravitz. They claimed that Johnson was temporarily insane — and a jury of eight blacks and four whites agreed. The lawyers argued that he suffered

severe mental illness resulting from his days as a sharecropper in
Mississippi, and that unsafe working conditions coupled with harsh
treatment by Chrysler foremen drove Johnson to a point where he
could not control his impulse to kill. Transferred from his job over his
protest, Johnson went home, got his carbine, and returned to the plant
on a rampage of killing.

The extent to which these events affect in-plant attitudes and
internal union relationships was illustrated by the election at the
Eldon plant in May 1971. A *Detroit Free Press* article described the
situation:

A candidate supported by black militant auto workers was narrowly
defeated Friday in a runoff election for president of UAW Local 961
at the troubled Chrysler Corp. Eldon Ave. gear and axle plant. Jordon
Sims, fired by Chrysler May 1, 1970, for allegedly provoking a wildcat strike, was defeated by Frank McKinnon, chief steward on the
third shift, by a vote of 1,178 to 1,142. Sims planned to protest the
vote and appeal the election results because, he said, armed private
guards patrolled the union hall corridors and intimidated voters.
Sims also said about 250 votes were invalidated and he was unable
to get from election authorities an adequate explanation for the in-
validation.

Local 961 represents 4,000 production workers at the plant,
scene of a triple slaying last summer. The plant has also been plagued
by wildcat strikes, demonstrations and other violence.

McKinnon, who is white, and Sims, who is black, were
pitted in a runoff after leading four candidates in a hotly contested
previous contest earlier this month. Sims, whose opponents identified
him with militants, led the four candidates in the first round of
balloting. He had 806 votes to 739 for McKinnon. Elroy Richardson,
the incumbent president, finished third and was eliminated from the
runoff. McKinnon and Sims became runoff candidates because
neither had a majority as required by union bylaws.

Sims has denied he is a member of any radical group. But
Richardson said Sims was endorsed in leaflets distributed by the
Eldon Revolutionary Union Movement (ELRUM), an affiliate of
the militant League of Revolutionary Black Workers.

The armed guards were hired by the incumbent president
Elroy Richardson. He defended the decision saying that it assured
a fair election. He said the guards prevented "extremists and outsiders from disrupting the election process." *

Like it or not, in Detroit color-consciousness has come to prevail over
class-consciousness, and for this a major cause has been the growth of

---

* *Detroit Free Press,* May 22, 1971.

the black-power movement. Forty years of strikes have failed to make Detroit workers class-conscious; at best, they are union-conscious, and even this loyalty is being strained by the rise of black unionism.

The growing black working class of Detroit had in 1971 an annual income of $7,500 per person, providing a socio-economic base unlike any in the nation. Since many of these workers have to drive out into the suburbs to the new plants and return to the city at night. they have a daily reminder of the restrictions placed on them in metropolitan Detroit.

This concentration of blacks has made the UAW a vanguard in the rise of black unionism. Among the black officials are Nelson "Jack" Edwards, an international vice-president; Marcellius Ivory, a Detroit regional director; and eleven local presidents in the Detroit area. Not to mention the hundreds of black local union officers, shop committeemen, and stewards. Unlike most other unions, the UAW has caucuses, and an influential one is the ad hoc black caucus, chaired by Robert "Buddy" Battle III, with over one hundred members, all of them local union leaders, who used to meet periodically with Walter Reuther and now have a similar relationship with Leonard Woodcock. Battle is also executive vice-president of Ford Local 600, and president of the Trade Union Leadership Council he formed with Horace Sheffield, which led the struggle to get black men elected to top positions in the UAW. Many of these men constitute a new generation of ambitious unionists who have no more in common with, say, the building trades workers than early CIO militants with the fogies of AFL craft unions.

Almost half of Detroit's unionized school-teachers are black; other city unions have a similar composition. Symbolic of the new relationship was the election of Tom Turner, a black steelworker, to the presidency of the AFL–CIO council. Detroit in the 1970s may well be for this kind of unionism what the city was for the CIO in the 1930s: a major forerunner and an example for other black unionists, still chafing under white paternalism. For while there are more than 2.5 million black workers in the AFL–CIO, they are somewhat less than adequately represented in most AFL–CIO unions, to say nothing of the AFL–CIO top leadership.

The expansion of black economic power suggests that new kinds of struggle, with the city as base, are more likely to occur in the near future than are the primitive battles of Detroit's past. But many obstacles remain to both black aspirations and social peace.

Henry Ford II recently announced that he has approved the construction of a $750 million housing-commercial project in all-white

Dearborn. The drain from Detroit is obvious. Even if some token integration were to occur, what remains of the white middle class in Detroit will have another place to run to. Max Fisher, the oil million-aire, is also spending millions in new housing in the suburbs, beyond the reach of the blacks.* Still, it is too soon to accept former Mayor Jerome P. Cavanagh's projection of Detroit's place in the future: "Detroit's twin cities — Nagasaki and Pompey." †

Nor should it be assumed that the city of Detroit is similar to Newark or Chicago. Economically, Newark is far weaker than De-troit. Detroit blue-collar wages make Newark pay scales seem feeble. The unions and the blacks within them are a powerful socio-economic force. A black mayor in Detroit, with all his handicaps, would have an economic base impossible to achieve in Newark, where Mayor Ken-neth Gibson is at the financial mercy of the state and federal govern-ments.

Detroit offers notable possibilities for blacks. It could become a black metropolis with a strong middle class, a stronger working class, and a generation of young leaders bursting out in every institution. Precisely these factors make unlikely any real revolutionary crisis, the kind loudly proclaimed by both the black and white Left.

The sitdowns in the 1930s turned out to be a demand for a voice and a share in the system rather than a prelude to revolution — as antagonists feared and some proponents hoped. Very probably, black radicalism in the '70s will turn out to have played a similar role. Only when radicals work within the framework of viable institutions — unions, parties, community groups — can they maintain any social roots and thereby have some impact on events.

For most blacks in Detroit, the industrial and public-sector unions and the political process offer an effective vehicle for protest, power, and progress. At times, angry voices from the Left spur the leaders of these organizations and unions to greater effort. What is unmistakable, affecting all aspects of city life, is the trend toward blacks coming to have a major stake in Detroit.

Many setbacks lie ahead; Detroit may explode again. The na-tional economic and political climate always affects the city deeply. Certainly, the police, the firemen, the building trades, and other white-dominated and white-based organizations may be expected to con-tinue resisting black power — I use the phrase to describe a visible reality, not an ideological slogan. But essentially this resistance is a rearguard action.

---

* *New York Times*, April 20, 1971.
† *Time*, April 26, 1971.

The most severe strains are likely to continue in the plants, the unions, and political and social institutions where the blacks have had the biggest impact. Only recently a black caucus was formed in the Michigan Democratic party—a sign of power and independence. In the UAW, it is only a matter of time before all four regional directors in Detroit are black. This trend poses an acute challenge to white politicians and white unionists. The challenge is to form a coalition of *equals*—an integrated coalition, otherwise the current rise of separatism may turn out to be more than the detour we hope it is on the road toward an integrated society. A society of fear and racial clashes cannot be reformed by the tepid measures so often prescribed in the past for Detroit. The blacks have too much power to accept "tokenism" a moment longer.

III. Reflection and Analysis

Old Working Class, New Working Class
Michael Harrington

I.

In recent years the American working class has been called conservative, militant, reactionary, progressive, authoritarian, social democratic, and, the unkindest cut of all, nonexistent. Except for the last, all the labels fit. The labor movement — I sharpen the focus on the organized section of the working class — contains more blacks than any other institution in American society, as well as more young whites attracted by the populist racism of George Wallace. Notwithstanding its tendencies toward ethnocentrism and anti-intellectualism, the labor movement has provided a decisive political impetus for whatever democratic planning there is in America. The organized workers are, in short, no one thing; they are a varied, dynamic, contradictory mass whose position in society can drive its members toward a practical social idealism, an anti-social corporatism, or any one of the complicated variants between those extremes.

I believe that the American workers have been a crucial force behind every social gain of the past two generations, and in domestic politics their unions constitute an American kind of de facto social democracy. Perhaps the exigencies of the future will deepen the best impulses within the labor movement, and I am on the side of those within it who are fighting for such a development. But my partisanship

MICHAEL HARRINGTON is best known for his book The Other America: Poverty in the United States. *He has also written* Toward a Democratic Left *and* The Accidental Century.

does not make me an apologist. Precisely because I am concerned and involved, I cannot afford to gloss over tendencies that run counter to my hopes. I must try to understand the past and present of the working class with as much candor as possible if I am to help those struggling to create its future. In these pages I will try to do that by way of a broad overview of the organized and organizable working class. Insofar as I deal with history, it will be in order to understand the current position of the unions and the various futures it could make possible. But before that can be attempted, I must define a vexing term: the working class. There are serious scholars who argue that it no longer exists in America. My conclusion, however, will be that there is not simply one working class in America but two—an old working class still quite vital and a new working class being created by political and economic evolution.

It is an extraordinary thing that those who argue there is no working class in the United States can be found at the most disparate points of the political spectrum. Herbert Marcuse, who had a notable influence on the New Left youth of the 1960s, writes that "'the people,' previously the ferment of social change, have 'moved up' to become the ferment of social cohesion." * Paul Sweezy and the late Paul Baran, sympathizers first with Russian, then with Chinese, communism, argued that the organized workers in the United States have been "integrated into the system as consumers and ideologically conditioned members of the society." Arthur Schlesinger, Jr., an activist liberal, says that

> the lines of division in our politics have fundamentally altered. The issues are no longer social or economic so much as they are cultural and moral. It is no longer the common men against the boss as much as it is the rational against the indignant, the planner against the spoiler, the humanist against the uneducated, the young against the old.

Perhaps the most emphatic statement of the theme comes from Clark Kerr, a brilliant, pragmatic technocrat. He holds that "the working class not only tends to disappear as a class-conscious and recognizable element in society; it needs to disappear if modern industrial society is to operate with full effectiveness." High technology, he continues, requires consensus and cooperation and therefore cannot tolerate class conflict over basic principles. So even though there are obvious differences between industrialists and file clerks, there are not "any clear class lines to divide them—only infinite gradations."

---

* Sources for all references within each section are grouped in a bibliographical note at the end of this essay.

I disagree with those, from the authoritarian Left to the democratic Center, who think that the American working class does not exist (the Right, which I will not consider here, tends to have a vulgar Marxist, or paranoid, version of the power of organized labor). To use Marx's famous distinction, the working class in this country is not simply a class "in itself"—a mass sharing "a common situation and common interests"—but it is a class "for itself" and the "interests which it defends . . . [are] class interests."

II.

First of all, consider the "old" working class: the primarily blue-collar workers who do physical labor in the industrial economy. It has renewed itself in the last quarter of a century and become a greater force in American politics than at any time in the nation's history.

The total nonagricultural labor force in 1969 numbered 77.902 million men and women. Of these, 48.993 million were "production and nonsupervisory workers on private payrolls," with the 14.647 million in manufacturing the largest single component. Another 12.591 million were employed by federal, state, and local government, and many of them held down such blue-collar and organizable jobs as sanitation man or postman. There were 20.210 million union members, mainly concentrated in machinery, transportation equipment, contract construction, and transportation services.

Among the unorganized one would find the working poor, who numbered close to four million in 1969 according to the government's optimistic definition of poverty. An almost equal number of the "near poor" (who include more whites and tend more to live in families headed by a male than do the poor themselves) were largely outside the unions. Those neither poor nor union members are most numerous in wholesale and retail trade, in finance, insurance, real estate, and the service industries. A good number of these are, of course, white-collar workers, and not a few of them receive wage increases from anti-union employers whenever organized labor in the industry, or the area, makes a gain.

This working class, both organized and unorganized, has a "common situation and common interests," experienced first and foremost in the reality that it does not have enough money. In 1969 the Bureau of Labor Statistics computed a "modest" budget for an urban family of four at $9,076, an amount in excess of the income of well over half the families in the United States. The trade unionists, most of whom are among the better-off members of the "old" working class, do not achieve this standard: they are neither poor nor affluent but in-between and distinctly deprived. In September 1969 the "average production worker" took home $102.44 for a full week's work, and manufacturing workers, most of whom were organized, received only $106.75. Moreover, since these figures were computed, the cost of living has gone up by almost 20 percent and the real wage of the workers has slightly decreased.

Even if one upgrades all of these numbers because of the enormous increase in the number of working wives — eighteen million of them in 1969, double the figure for 1950 — who add an average of 25 percent to their family income, the total still falls short of the government's modest budget. The "modest" standard, it must be emphasized, lives up to its name: it allows for a two-year-old used car and a new suit every four years. In addition to this deficiency in income, most of the union members are employed in manufacturing, construction, and transportation, i.e., in jobs with little intrinsic interest and, in the case of an assembly line in an auto plant, a dehumanizing routine. They are paid not as individuals but as members of a class: after the age of twenty-five, the worker's income does not normally vary with increasing experience, as does that of professional and managerial employees, but usually rises as part of a negotiated group settlement. Indeed, the very fact of being paid a wage by the hour emphasizes another determinant of working-class existence, the vulnerability of the job to the vagaries of the business cycle, the ever-present possibility of being laid off.

Every governmental projection indicates a substantial increase during the next decade in the number of Americans who live under such conditions. The only category of industrial workers that will be in both absolute and relative decline over that period is that of the nonfarm laborers, which is supposed to fall from 3.6 million to 3.5 million. But the number of operatives and craftsmen will increase, and the unions that were created because of the common interest of this great mass are certain to grow in the foreseeable future into the largest membership organizations in the society. In 1980, then, the "old" working class will be larger than ever before in American history.

How is it that such a massive social phenomenon and such obvious trends have been ignored, or declared nonexistent, by many observers? In part, as Penn Kemble has argued, the vantage point of intellectual perception has changed radically during the past thirty years. The social critics of the 1960s and early '70s are relatively affluent compared to the marginality and even joblessness they had experienced during the depression. This change in their own class position may have made them less sensitive to the daily struggles of less-favored people. At the crudest this indifference could be rationalized by confusing the relative decline in manufacturing jobs—they accounted for 39.3 percent of nonagricultural employment in 1919 and for only 28.8 percent in 1969—with an absolute decrease in the number of workers and a consequent loss of political and social power. This error was sometimes abetted by a failure to explore the fine print in the governmental difinitions in which, to take one pertinent example, laundry workers, garage repairmen, and dishwashers in the service industries are not classified as blue collar.

Somewhat more subtly, there were those who acknowledged the existence of the tradiÆional working class but argued that it had become co-opted by the society and therefore lost its distinctive character. But that, as we have just seen, is a misleading simplification. It may be that the workers, as Sweezy and Baran argue, want to be "integrated into the society as consumers," but it is surely of greater moment that the structure of injustice will not allow them, as a rule, even a "modest" income.

Still, the most sophisticated revision of the idea of the working class is based upon a very real, and momentous, shift in class structure (a shift that is also, as will be seen, the key to the emergence of a "new" working class). It is argued that economic classes defined by property relationships—entrepreneurs owning factories, shopkeepers their little businesses, farmers and peasants their plots of land, and workers possessing only their labor power to sell—have become obsolete. The joint stock company, Ralf Dahrendorf holds, separated ownership and control and thereby obviated a theory of class determined by property or the lack of it. He concludes that in the advanced economics authority, not ownership, is central to the formation of social class. And Alain Touraine writes, "It is anachronistic to depict social armies confronting each other. As we pass from societies of accumulation to programmed societies, relationships of power become increasingly more important than opposition between social groups."

These theories are usually developed with the comment that Marx, fixated as he was upon a primitive model of capitalism, was unaware of such changes. I will deal with this historical error in a footnote, since it is not central to the main line of this analysis.* For even

---

* In *The Communist Manifesto,* Marx unquestionably thought society was polarizing into a giant working class and a tiny bourgeoisie and held to a rather simplistic, property-determined theory of social class. But as early as 1856, Marx, whom Dahrendorf charges with not having understood the importance of the joint stock company, wrote, "It cannot be denied that the application of the joint stock company to industry characterizes a new epoch in the economic life of modern nations." (Marx-Engels, *Werke* [hereafter *MEW*], Dietz Verlag, Berlin, 1953, XII, 33.) In a famous letter to Engels in 1858 in

granting that there have been profound transformations in the structure of the advanced economies, some of them unforeseen by even so
perspicacious a thinker as Marx, what is it that makes the workers I
have just described more likely to join unions than any group in society? What predisposes them toward a certain political point of
view? The answer, I believe, is embarrassingly old-fashioned. These
workers derive their livelihoods almost exclusively from the sale of
their labor power in an anonymous, and uncertain, labor market, and
it is quite easy to distinguish them from their "fellow employees"
who are corporation presidents or managers. There is a social chasm
between these groups, not the infinite gradations postulated by Clark
Kerr.

To begin with, in the upper reaches of the society property is
not quite so passé as the notion of a clear-cut "separation" of ownership and control suggests. A 1967 *Fortune* survey revealed that 30
percent of the five hundred largest industrial concerns "are clearly
controlled by identifiable individuals or by family groups." And, as
that survey pointed out, absolute numbers can be more revealing than
percentages when one deals with the holdings of the executive officer
of a multi-billion-dollar corporation. The board chairman of General
Motors at that time "only" owned 0.017 percent of the enterprise
over which he presided—but that little fraction was worth $3.917
million. The chairman of Chrysler, with a mere 0.117 percent of his
company's stock, had a $2.380 million interest in the business.

More generally, the nonowning managers at the top of the
society accumulate wealth. They often enjoy special stock deals and
other arrangements: in 1971 the *Wall Street Journal* reported that

which he outlined *Das Kapital*, he indicated that the culmination of his analysis—which
was never written—would deal with "stock capital as the most developed form [of
capitalism] with all its contradictions." (*MEW*, XXIX, 312.) In the third volume of *Das
Kapital*, Marx did refer briefly to the separation of ownership and control, and Engels
added a note when he published the volume after Marx's death saying that this trend had
become even more important. In the revised edition of his famous popularization of
Marxism, *Anti-Duhring*, Engels was even more emphatic on this count. (*MEW*, XX,
617.) Moreover, in the posthumously published *Theories of Surplus Value*, Marx not
only discussed the appearance of new middle strata linked to the phenomenon of the
corporation but saw them as an inevitable outcome of the capitalist dynamic itself.
(*MEW*, XXVI: Pt. 1, 190.) Why, then, did Marx fail to include this material in his
own theory of class? The answer is found on the last page of Volume III of *Das Kapital*.
It constitutes only the second page of Marx's discussion of classes and it concludes:
"Here the manuscript breaks off." But even though death prevented Marx from formally
and systematically revising the simplifications and errors of the *Manifesto*, it is clear
that he understood that the class structure of his own time was being profoundly modified by the separation of ownership and control. Much of what Dahrendorf, and others,
present as a critique of Marx is thus only Marxian common sense.

the biggest part of executive pay in the auto industry was a bonus based on the size of profits. So it is that these managers must be counted among the golden elite, the 6.5 percent of the American consumer units which, in December 1962 (there has been no downward redistribution since), had incomes of $50,000 a year or more and owned 57 percent of the wealth of the society. At stake here is not simply the annual pay but, in Herman Miller's definition of wealth, "the sum total of equity in a home or business, liquid assets, investment assets, the value of automobiles owned and miscellaneous assets held in trust, loans to individuals, oil royalties, etc." By that standard, the "nonowning" managers own quite a bit.

The middle levels of management, particularly in the modern corporations, are not so easy to define and will be discussed at greater length in the section on the "new" working class. Now it is enough to note that this labor market is not anonymous, its salaries are not determined on a class basis, as in the case of workers, and it is less subject to the ups and downs of the business cycle. Some of the halcyon notions of the security of these strata were rudely dispelled by the recent Nixon recession, yet no one should have any trouble in distinguishing it from the lot of the wage workers.

So there is a distinct and identifiable universe of the working class even after one has taken into account the tremendous changes in class structure since Marx. The pay is better now, the boom-and-bust rhythm has been attenuated, the famous built-in stabilizers, such as unemployment insurance, are at work. Yet there are crucial elements of working class life — relative deprivation, the impersonality of the work process, greater susceptibility to layoffs than that experienced by other groups in the society, group wages — which remain and are the objective determinants of the class itself. Perhaps one of the best statements of this reality was made in the study of the English affluent worker carried out under the direction of John H. Goldthorpe and David Lockwood.

This project subjected the thesis of the *embourgeoisement* of the working class in that country to a careful empirical examination. It concluded that in England this co-optation simply had not taken place:

> A factory worker can double his living standards and still remain a man who sells his labour to an employer in return for wages; he can work at a control panel rather than on an assembly line without changing his subordinate position in the organization of production; he can live in his own house in a "middle class" estate or suburb and still remain little involved in white collar social worlds.

English data cannot, of course, merely be imported to America and applied to the quite different variant of capitalism that exists here. Yet the objective indices show that in the United States as in England the worker is not an integrated participant in affluence but a member of a quite distinct stratum. And this stratum, for the most part, is neither poor nor modestly well off, indeed is better off than ever before — yet still quite deprived. But these statistics are of little political and intellectual significance if they simply describe unrelated facts about an inert mass. One has to come to the second part of Marx's famous distinction: Is the "old" working class a class "for itself," does it act collectively from a consciousness of its position in society?

III.

A preliminary warning: If one looks for a "European"-type class-consciousness in the United States — something like the attitude of that Frenchman, who, when T. S. Eliot accidentally jostled him, responded, "Me, I am a proletarian exploited by the capitalist class" — it cannot be found. It is not even necessary for my purposes that a majority of the workers used the term "working class" to describe their position in society. (When asked to locate themselves on a three-class scale of upper, middle, and lower, the overwhelming majority of Americans, including the members of the AFL–CIO, will say that they are middle-class; but on a five-class scale, on which the working class is in between the poor and the middle class, many more will identify themselves as working class.) I am not in search of a rhetoric but want to describe how workers behave politically in order to maximize goals which go beyond their immediate self-interest, or even the narrow advantage of their craft and skill, and which have to do with the needs of the entire class and through it of the nation itself.

There are two major lines of argument, sometimes convergent, which hold that, even though there may be objective determinants of class in America, there has either never been or cannot now be any significant mass consciousness of that fact, moving workers to political or social action. On the one hand, it is said that the exceptional historical character of the national experience prevented the development of such a consciousness. On the other hand, it is claimed that the recent evolution of the American economy has produced a consensus in which interest groups compete over the details of the distribution of wealth but classes no longer contest more basic questions of the very mode of allocation itself.

The theory that America has always been immune from the

class struggle is the generalization of a profound half-truth.* A country without a feudal past, possessing a vast continent to be settled once genocide had been committed against the Indians, and populated by successive waves of immigrants from the most varied European backgrounds, must differ in a number of crucial ways from the nation-states of the Old World where capitalism first emerged. Lenin wrote of America (and Britain) that there were "exceptionally favorable conditions, in comparison with other countries, for the deep-going and widespread development of capitalism."

Morris Hilquit, theorist of American socialism in the first third of the century, also talked of the "exceptional position" of America with its vast land mass, its prosperous agriculture, its tendency to make wage labor seem only a "temporary condition." But once we grant the apparent uniqueness of American capitalism, is it indeed true that class-consciousness failed to play an important, much less a decisive, role in the nation's history? I think not. The conditions we describe as "American exceptionalism" slowed the emergence of that consciousness and even made its anti-capitalism seem formally procapitalist. It did not, however, stop social class from becoming the most important single determinant in our political life.

Moreover, the chief factor inhibiting and distorting working-class self-consciousness was not, as is widely thought, the wealth of the society. Werner Sombart's famous remark that socialism in America ran aground "on shoals of roast beef and apple pie" was made in 1906 and has survived as a myth until this day. But, in a history of American labor (edited by that patriarch of the nonclass interpretation, J. R. Commons), Don Lescohier described as follows the two decades prior to World War I:

> Undergoing the vicissitudes of repeated periods of unemployment, experiencing in many occupations a less rapid rise of wages than living costs, [the wage earners] could see that while some groups, like the building mechanics, had made distinct progress, other groups, like the iron and steel workers, employees in meat packing plants, cotton mills, saw mills, tobacco and clothing factories had not held their own against the rapidly rising cost of living.

Indeed, if one compares Germany and the United States between 1890 and 1914, the workers experienced steadily a relative rise in their living standards in the country that produced a mass social democratic movement rather than in the one that did not. But if it

---

* What follows is a summary of a much more detailed, and documented, analysis to be found in my *Socialism* (New York, 1972).

was not prosperity that prevented the development of a socialist class-consciousness in America, what was it? Selig Perlman provided part of the answer in his seminal *Theory of the Labor Movement:*

> American labor remains the most heterogeneous laboring class in existence—ethnically, religiously and culturally, With a working class of such composition, to make socialism or communism the official "ism" of the movement would mean, even if other conditions permitted it, deliberately driving the Catholics, who are perhaps a majority in the American Federation of Labor, out of the labor movement, since with them an irreconcilable opposition to socialism is a matter of religious principle. Consequently, the only acceptable "consciousness" for American labor as a whole is "job consciousness" with a limited objective of "wage and job control" . . . .

Perlman was right: heterogeneity made it impossible to organize the great mass of the newly arriving European workers until the '30s and acted, in a thousand different ways, to impede consciousness of membership in a single and united class. Yet Perlman was wrong: even in the '20s when he wrote, and much more so later on, the workers were constantly forced by the exigencies of their class situation to go beyond "wage and job control" and raise class issues about the organization of the entire society. Strangely enough, many scholars failed to take note of this significant phenomenon. For they had adopted, even when they were anti-socialist, the criteria of the left wing of the Socialist party: that class-consciousness must necessarily and exclusively take the form of allegiance to a socialist or worker's party. That party alliance did not come about; class-consciousness did.

So by the early 1920s the majority of the AFL rebelled against Gompers' hostility to social legislation, adopted an approach very much like the one embodied in the socialist proposals that had been rejected during the 1890s, and embarked upon a course that led to an alliance with the Socialist party in the Conference for Progressive Political Action and support for the La Follette campaign in 1924. In 1920 the AFL was in favor of public ownership of the utilities, organization of cooperatives, and workmen's compensation. The railroad men were for the nationalization of their industry, and the Chicago Federation of Labor was in favor of a labor party. The AFL, as Phillip Taft has written of the period, "found itself, against its wishes, propelled into more active political participation." These developments did not, for the reasons Perlman described among others, take place in the guise of a socialist class-consciousness. But they were a clear indication that workers were being driven to consider not simply their jobs but the society as a whole.

The class-conscious movement of the '20s did not succeed and in the latter half of the decade there was a reversion to Gompers' "voluntarist" philosophy. But the reason for this reversal involved a trend that was to prepare the way for the great explosion of working-class militancy in the '30s. With immigration severely restricted after World War I, the expanding economy of the mid-1920s recruited its new workers from the farm and thus tipped the national demographic balance from rural to urban. The initial impact of this progressive turn of events was conservative. Ordinarily, one would have expected the unions to have grown and bettered their wages and working conditions during prosperity, but the influx of farmers, who could be satisfied by cheap wages and were suspicious of group action, depressed the labor market. The war and postwar militancy had driven the average weekly wage in manufacture up to $26.30 in 1920, but in 1921 wages dropped to $22.18 and in 1929 they had only reached $25.03, more than a dollar below the level of 1920.

Still, two momentous events had taken place in the '20s. The American working class was no longer a port of entry for millions of the foreign-born and was becoming, for the first time in its history, homogeneous; and labor was now part of a new urban majority. Once the discrepancy between low wages and high productivity in the '20s helped bring about the Great Depression, these developments were of enormous importance. They helped promote the organization of industrial workers in the CIO and were a major reason why a vast political movement based on class became a crucial feature of politics in the '30s. Richard Hofstadter, one of the few scholars to recognize the importance of this fact, wrote, "The demands of a large and powerful labor movement, combined with the interests of the unemployed, gave the New Deal a social democratic tinge that had never before been present in American reform movements."

IV.

For all the dramatic struggles of the 1930s, it is clear in retrospect that the working class was not in a revolutionary mood. This point must be stressed because many scholarly critics of the notion of a class struggle in the U.S. have unwittingly adopted not simply a Marxian definition of the concept but a "romantic" Marxian definition. For Raymond Aron, a seminal theorist of the notion of "industrial society" (i.e., of consensus capitalism), the class struggle exists only where there is a "fight to the death" between workers and capitalists which eventuates in violence.

Such an idea can indeed be found in *The Communist Manifesto,* for it is a corollary of Marx's youthful error of supposing that society was fast polarizing into only two classes. But the mature Marx did not hold this view and defined the class struggle in a far more subtle and complex fashion which can also serve as an excellent guide to the reality of the American 1930s—and '70s. In his famous Inaugural Address to the International Workingmen's Association, Marx spoke of a campaign to restrict the working day to ten hours in England as "a struggle between the blind rule of supply and demand, which is the political economy of the middle class, and the social control of production through intelligence and foresight, which is the political economy of the working class." *

The kind of class struggle envisioned in *The Manifesto* did not emerge in the America of the 1930s or since; the kind analyzed in the Inaugural Address has. Given the obvious exigencies of the situation, the workers were committed as a class—and, with the elections of 1936, organized as a class—to win full-employment policies requiring that the government manage the economy. But if the American workers thus committed themselves to "the social control of production through intelligence and foresight, which is the political economy of the working class," they did not call this policy "socialist." It was not simply that the historic factors identified by Perlman were at work. Beyond that, as Leon Samson has argued in a fascinating book, Americanism had become a kind of "substitutive socialism." In this country, as distinct from Europe, bourgeois ideology itself stressed equality, classlessness, and the opportunity to share in wealth.

So in the '30s there emerged a mass political movement based upon class institutions (the unions) which demanded not simply narrow legislation related to the needs of this or that trade or craft, but a

---

* Those who wish to downgrade this speech usually argue that Marx was making pragmatic political concessions to the British trade unionists who were so important to him in the First International. But, as I document at length in my book *Socialism,* the tactic of the Inaugural was central to the politics of Marx and Engels from the late '50s to the time of their respective deaths. There was a brief period during and after the Paris Commune when responding to Bakuninist critics on their left and the vilifiers of the Commune on their right, they seemed to turn back to the language and mood of the *Manifesto.* But that was only an episode. It is, however, important to note that there is one basic oversimplification in the Inaugural. As early as the mid-1850s, in his analysis of the "imperial socialism" of Napoleon III, Marx had understood that the conservatives and reactionaries could use collectivist methods to serve their own purposes. (*MEW,* XII, 24, 27, 33.) This notion was deepened, particularly by Engels, in response to Bismarckian "socialism" and led to the theory of "state socialism" in which government intervenes on behalf of the bourgeoisie. So a more comprehensive Marxian development of the formulation in the Inaugural would emphasize that the "intelligence and foresight" would have to be exercised by and for the workers, not by and for Bonapartists, Bismarckians, fascists, Stalinists, Maoists, etc.

mode of planned social organization that would give priority to the value of full employment. Since it involved significant modifications of capitalist society as it had existed until then in the United States, this idea met with violent resistance, both physical and ideological, from most employers. They recognized that, even though the worker insisted upon his loyalty to the American ideal, he was reading it in terms of his own class needs.

Thus I would argue that, for all of its truly exceptional characteristics, American capitalism eventually forced its working class to become conscious of itself and to act as a major factor in political life. The theorists of industrial, or post-industrial, society might even grant this historical case. And they would add that in the period after World War II, changes in capitalist society led to the virtual disappearance of that class struggle.

V.

Raymond Aron was an early advocate of this view. Economic conflicts over wages and hours, he said, are quite real.

> It is pure hypocrisy to think that they are always resolved in an equitable fashion, pure hypocrisy to deny a struggle over the division of the national income. But it does not thereby happen that, on the strictly economic plane, the group of workers and the group of capitalists oppose one another in a fight to the death, each one having an *essential* interest opposed to the other. The common interest of both, within the framework of the system [*cadre du régime*] is the prosperity of the enterprise and of the economy; it is growth whose necessary conditions correspond simultaneously to the interests of the managers and the employees.

Daniel Bell transposed Aron's thesis for America. There was, he said in the 1950s, an end of ideology. At certain points in his writing that phrase referred to the disappearance of grandiose simplifications about society, a happy event from any point of view. But at other points it announced a controversial trend: the disappearance from Western political life of debate and conflict over fundamental questions, a fading away of the very notion that there should or could be alternative forms of social organization. There was, Bell said,

> a rough consensus among intellectuals on political issues: the acceptance of the Welfare State; the desirability of decentralized power; a system of mixed economy and of political pluralism. . . . [And] the workers, whose grievances were once the driving energy for social

change, are more satisfied with the society than the intellectuals. The workers have not achieved utopia but their expectations were less than those of the intellectuals and their gains correspondingly larger.

In a much more recent statement of this theme, Bell wrote that the secret of Western society was "productivity." "Economic life could be a non zero-sum game; everyone could end up a winner, though with differential gains." But hardly had the end of ideology been proclaimed than the most tumultuous ideological decade in recent history began—the 1960s. There was a veritable explosion of ideology in the institutions of mass higher education in the advanced economies. And the workers, most dramatically in France and Italy, but in America, too, kept challenging the differential distribution of gains in strike after strike.

Was this merely a case of groups struggling bitterly over the terms of a consensus? Or, to take Aron's criterion of the most crucial precondition for the existence of a social class, was there a consciousness on the part of those American workers that "their class has a unique destiny and that it cannot fulfill its vocation except by transforming the totality [ensemble] of the social organization"? If the question is posed in this way, so reminiscent of both the early Marx and the early Lukacs, then there was no class struggle in America. Yet it can be demonstrated that American labor was by now more than a mere interest group. Its class-consciousness lies somewhere between the polar extremes of revolutionary transformation and interest politics.

There is, for instance, no question that the intrapersonal culture of the working class has been largely subverted by such changes in class structure as the movement of workers to the suburbs or the achievement of limited access to the consumption-oriented (and rigged) society. As Bennett Berger has documented, it is only in the old working-class neighborhoods, usually ethnic in character, that one finds a face-to-face and daily sense of a common class plight. The old coal-mining towns of Appalachia would be the most obvious example of the vanishing conditions under which social class pervades all aspects of life. But even in looking back, it is wrong to romanticize such working-class neighborhoods or to attribute to them, in Serge Mallet's phrase, a "pseudo-globalness." For instance, the Italian workers who were jammed together in New York before and after World War I were more loyal to their village in the old country, and to the *padroni* who exploited them here, than to their class.

Still, it seems obvious today, in contrast to a generation or two ago, that the worker does not enter a class community when he leaves the factory but rather participates more and more in the nonclass world of consumption. That has its positive side, as Herbert Gans discovered in his study of Levittown. The suburbanized worker, he learned, was not homogenized by the experience as much as critics of the '50s had thought. He became less localistic and suspicious, more inclined to participate in civic and political life. But, I would add, in becoming more of a "citizen" he became less of a worker.

Yet even as there were trends making the impact of classlessness pervasive in the daily life of the individual worker, the labor movement was moving into politics in a much more profound way than in the 1930s. By the end of the '60s, the AFL–CIO, the Auto Workers, and the Teamsters all supported an ongoing political apparatus which, in terms of money, lobbying, campaign workers, and the like, was a major factor in the United States. As David Greenstone documents in his book *Labor in American Politics,* "The emergence of organized labor as a major, nationwide electoral organization of the national Democratic Party was the most important change in the *structure* of the American party system during the last quarter of a century."

This signified the organization of a class, not merely an interest group. An interest group, as Greenstone points out, has very specific demands and avoids committing itself to a single party or a broad social program out of fear that it will compromise its narrow goals. Big corporations, which tend to be Republican, usually maintain a "Democratic" Vice-President to insure access to the White House no matter what. But the unions increasingly have become an organized component of the Democratic party. As Greenstone points out, they could have made a classic interest-group deal in the '60s. If the AFL–CIO had agreed to let Everett Dirksen's congressional override of the Supreme Court's one man/one vote rule go through, Dirksen would have permitted the repeal of the federal enabling clause for state "right to work" laws. Such action on the latter issue would have meant the successful culmination of a trade-union campaign of more than two decades' duration. Yet labor maximized its long-range political program by standing fast on one man/one vote rather than giving priority to its short-range organizational goals.

The unions thus became a class political force, even if in a fairly undramatic way. There was little rhetoric of class war. Yet the very appearance of national health insurance as a political issue is primarily the result of a campaign waged for years by George Meany and Walter Reuther. Even in the area of race, where so many observers tend to pit blacks against the unions, labor is the most integrated single institution in U.S. society and has done more to raise the living standards of black Americans than any force except the federal government. Part of the confusion over this momentous trend stems from a reliance on polling data in most academic accounts of the labor movement. It is precisely the characteristic of an opinion poll that it reaches a man or woman as he or she is isolated and poses questions in a kind of political and social vacuum. It is therefore admirably suited to reflect the privatized area of a worker's mind but what it omits – as elections do not – is the effect of his participation in a workaday world, his membership in a class.

It is a failure to confront this complex reality that makes Derek Bok and John T. Dunlop miss the significance of trade-union political action in their study of *Labor and the American Community*. They point out that, as recorded in the opinion polls, the workers have been giving decreasing support to union political action, and that their unions have become more and more political. The polls, I would suggest, do capture some private elements of workers' responses which in recent years have become more marked. But the elections reveal the much more significant fact that by and large those same workers vote massively in national elections for the Democratic candidates endorsed by their union. What Bok and Dunlop miss, then, is the class political attitude of the workers which is not at all the same as, and sometimes even contradicts, the sum totals of their private views. In 1968, for instance, the polls indicated significant support for George Wallace among young white workers in the North during the early fall. Yet when election day came, most of those same workers voted for Hubert Humphrey, Most of them had not changed their personal prejudices in the process, but they had understood that the exigencies of their class situation demanded they vote for a full-employment economy rather than against blacks – i.e., for Humphrey, not Wallace.

This kind of collectivism is far from the romantic Marxian consciousness as defined by Aron, but it is distinctive and clearly goes beyond narrow organizational interests. Moreover, there are a good many indications that the unions will be forced to be even more political in the coming period.

It is now apparent, even to its sophisticated devotees, that the free market is utterly incapable of allocating the resources of a technological society in a rational fashion. In 1971 Daniel Bell, who only a decade earlier had talked of the end of ideology, wrote,

It seems clear to me that, today, we in America are moving away from a society based on a private enterprise market system toward one in which the most important economic decisions will be made at the political level, in terms of consciously defined "goals" and "priorities." In the past there was an unspoken consensus and the public philosophy did not need to be articulated. And this was a strength, for articulation often invites trials for force when implicit differences are made manifest. Today, however, there is a visible change from market to non-market political decision making.

This marks, Bell concludes, "a movement away from governance by political economy to governance by political philosophy."

It is on the basis of this analysis that Bell has been writing about a "post-industrial" society in which the decisive "new men" are the

scientists, the mathematicians, the economists and the engineers of the new computer technology. . . . The leadership of the new society will rest, not with business or corporations as we have known them (for a good deal of production will be routinized), but with the research corporation, the industrial laboratories, the experimental stations and the universities.

But which values will determine the priorities of these new men? Bell and John Kenneth Galbraith, whose "educational-scientific estate" is another name for the "new men," assume that these educated and generally liberal administrators of power will be able to pursue their own goals. That hope has been around for years and was brilliantly formulated by Thorstein Veblen in his essay collection *The Engineers and the Price System,* which dates back to 1919. The problem is that, from Veblen's day to this, the corporations have been profit-maximizers — more and more sophisticated in their definition of profit, to be sure — and have placed their own interests above those of the society or of the engineers who work for them. The automobile companies, to take a dramatic recent example, have been fighting auto safety and pollution controls for years.

It is at this point that the politics of the American working class become crucial. For if it is indeed true that economic decisions will be increasingly made by a political rather than a market process; if the question is how to manage the economy rather than whether to do so, then what mass force is there in society to fight for social values? Some "new men" might join a progressive political coalition in their off-duty hours but, under present conditions, their working lives will be dominated by corporate values that oppose, or at least would severely limit, any restrictions on the company's freedom of action. Moreover, the corporations tend to favor reactionary Keynesianism, in which the economy is stimulated by incentives to capital rather than through the meeting of human needs, which is social Keynesianism. The largest and most effective force in the society with a commitment to that kind of progressive Keynesianism is the trade-union movement.

In August 1971, when Richard Nixon tacitly admitted the bankruptcy of *laissez-faire* ideas which had created an ingenious recession-inflation, labor reacted in characteristic fashion. Nixon had proposed a federal job cut and a retreat from welfare reform, strict wage controls, vague price controls, and no limit on profits, dividends, and other forms of upper-class compensation. He further proposed an investment tax credit on machinery produced by American companies, a measure that might give business a $5 billion benefit (which would have to be added to the better than $3 billion a year earlier offered by the President in the form of accelerated depreciation for the corporations).

The AFL–CIO Executive Council responded:

> Instead of extending the helping hand of the federal government to the poor, the unemployed, the financially strapped states and cities, and to the inflation-plagued consumer, the President decided to further enrich big corporations and banks. . . . Mr. Nixon's program is based on the infamous "trickle down" theory. It would give huge sums of money belonging to the people of the United States to big corporations. He would do this at the expense of the poor, the state and local governments and their employees and wage and salary earners.

The AFL–CIO was here articulating what Marx called "the political economy of the working class" as it applies in a post-Keynesian society. This response is rooted in the class position of the members of the labor movement. They stand to gain from redistributionist federal policies favoring those either subaffluent or poor; they are opposed to a management of the economy that maximizes the interests of corporations. The difference between these two versions of Keynesianism is, I would suggest, both profound and systematic. Which one of them prevails will determine much about the shape of the future.

When Irving Louis Horowitz asks skeptically why the "interest-determined demands of the working class are somehow instinctively and intuitively more progressive than those of other sectors," he overlooks the union's stand on such an issue. It is the result, not of instinct or intuition, but of class position. For there is a working class "for itself" with a political consciousness that goes far beyond "job consciousness" and expresses itself in social reformism toward the society as a whole. This class consciousness is not revolutionary but, in practical and programmatic terms, it is remarkably similar to that found among the social democrats of Europe—even when it is sometimes couched in an antisocialist rhetoric. It is not based on that "world apart" of intrapersonal class values which existed at an earlier stage of capitalism. It might be more accurately described, to use a term employed by the British students of the affluent worker, as an "instrumental collectivism."

VI.

This working class, very different from the one studied by Marx, is at the moment going through a new mutation—one that has given rise to theories about a "new" working class.

There is no question that a momentous transformation of the American class structure is taking place. In 1980, according to the projections of the Department of Labor, there will be 15.5 million professional and technical workers and 15.4 million operatives (assemblers, truck drivers, bus drivers). That obviously describes a profound shift away from the industrial proletariat of semiskilled workers. In the decade of the '70s government statisticians expect the labor force to grow by about 25 percent. The categories exceeding that rate are professional and technical workers (50 percent), service workers (45 percent), clerical workers (35 percent), and sales workers (30 percent). Those which will lag behind the national average are managers, officials, and proprietors (22 percent); craftsmen and foremen (22 percent); private household workers (15 percent); operatives (10 percent); nonfarm laborers (−2 percent) and farm workers (−33 percent).

In part, the new patterns of education in the United States are a reflection of these changes in class. In 1940, only 37.8 percent of Americans between twenty-five and twenty-nine years of age had completed four years of high school or more; in 1970 that percentage had jumped to 75.4 percent. In 1940, 5.8 percent of the twenty-five to twenty-nine age group had four years of college or more, in 1970, 16.4 percent (the latter figure underestimates the recent increase in college degrees since it omits those between twenty-one and twenty-five in 1970, i.e., the age group with the highest percentage of graduates). These figures mean, among other things, that many children of the working class are now going to college. In 1969, only 23.7 percent of the family heads of students in college had themselves received a degree, which means they lacked a crucial precondition for middle-class status. The rich were, to be sure, disproportionately represented in higher education: 66 percent of the families with incomes of over $15,000 a year had a child in college in 1969, but only 16.4 percent of those with incomes under $3,000.

Yet when one turns to families with incomes in the general AFL–CIO range, the magnitude of the present social change becomes even more evident. Almost a third of the units in the $5,000-$7,499 group had a child in college, 41.8 percent of those in the $7,499-$9,999 group, and 49.0 percent of those with a $10,000-$15,000 annual income. And since, as Brendan and Patricia Sexton have pointed out, the average trade unionist of today is getting younger, these percentages can be expected to go up as the children of those now youthful workers reach college age.

These trends are likely to continue, and deepen, in the future. Yet there were some specific circumstances in the '60s that might have made these trends seem even more vigorous than they actually are. The tremendous growth in professional and technical employment was, in part at least, caused by federal outlays in space, defense, and education, all of which were cut back in the late '60s. It is sobering to realize that Bell's "new men" and Galbraith's "educational and scientific estate" may have loomed somewhat larger than life because of the impact of such federal policies. Certainly when Washington's cutbacks coincided, not accidentally, with the Nixon recession of the early '70s, there were extremely high rates of unemployment among the educated, including Ph.D.s with scientific and engineering degrees.

The liberal arts component of this surge was unplanned and, in some ways, irrational. As a significant number of such students, or graduates, realized that their education had no functional relationship to the society they were supposed to enter, they dropped out or sought alternative life-styles. One suspects that their plight was a consequence of America's refusal to face up to the revolutionary character of its technology, and disguising what would have been middle-class unemployment as middle-class education. In any case, college spending per student will not continue to increase faster than the Gross National Product, as it did in 1950–1970.

But even with these qualifications, it is clear that the new technology is calling into life a new class structure. The analytic problem arises when one tries to make statements about the political and social behavior of the new strata. In *Toward a Democratic Left* I spoke of these people as a "new class" rather than a "new working class" because I wanted to stress the discontinuities signaled by their appearance. In the present context my focus will be upon those factors which drive such professionals, technicians, and others in a trade-union direction—toward collective bargaining on the job and political pressure for full-employment policies outside the job. So I speak of a new working class. The choice of terms is not crucial; the careful delineation of a new social reality is.

The new strata are not the old middle class, nor the "new middle class" as it was recognized around the turn of the century. The old middle class was composed of men and women of property and income on a small scale. The "new middle class" was an educated salariat, and it was noted by Karl Kautsky as early as the 1890s. When William English Walling popularized Kautsky's views in 1912, he spoke of the possibility of winning the professional classes, the salaried corporation employees, and a large part of the office workers to socialism. But that stratum does not concern us here. The new stratum on which we focus is not based upon property or employment in the private corporation. Its members work, for the most part, in public, or semipublic sectors—education, health, social services, defense and defense-related industries, aerospace—and they are therefore dependent on federal political decisions for their economic well-being. They also tend to be employed by large organizations and often, for all their educational attainments, they are subordinate participants in a hierarchical system.

Let me be more specific.

First, there are those directly engaged in the development of technology, most of them classed as professional and technical workers. One of the most important subcategories of this group includes engineers and scientific technicians. In 1980, according to federal projections, there will be 1.4 million of them, an increase of 50 percent over the 1966 total, and a percentage that will be rising twice as fast as the national labor-force average. Of these, about 40 percent are technicians who will not have been to college but will have received post-high school training or have acquired sophisticated skills on the job. As the aerospace layoffs in 1970 and 1971 demonstrated, many of these workers are exceptionally vulnerable to policy shifts in Washington. Therefore—and in this they are typical of most of the people in the new strata—they offer a political base for a narrow, corporatist kind of lobbying, designed to protect particular jobs without reference to social cost or utility; or they could respond to a movement for democratic and social planning.

Second, there are the educated workers in the service industry, a category that will expand at much better than the average rate (45 percent as against 25 percent) for the decade. There are already two million of them, including schoolteachers in the National Education

Association, nurses who belong to associations carrying out "job actions," people who belong to what Bok and Dunlop call "near unions." These groups engage in collective bargaining and political action but refuse, often for reasons of status, to affiliate with the AFL–CIO. But the service category also includes the members of the American Federation of Teachers (which, with more than 200,000 dues payers, is becoming an important union within the AFL–CIO) and the staff members of the Museum of Modern Art who, in September 1971, won a strike as members of a union local.

The trade unionists and the "near unionists" in the service sector tend to be employed, or financed, by the public in education, health care, and the like. There is every reason to expect that they will continue their present tendencies toward job organization and political involvement. Related to them, but not a part of the new strata, are the blue-collar workers in the public sector: policemen, firemen, hospital attendants, sanitation men. Their family backgrounds, education, and income make them a part of the traditional working class. But, like the professional and educated personnel in this area, they also are highly motivated to become active in politics. And by 1980 they will number in the millions.

Third, there are a number of more nebulous categories. In recent years most of the liberal arts students have looked toward teaching as a career. In *Fortune* magazine's 1968 survey of the college campus, 40 percent of the "forerunners" — the two-fifths of the student body who had rejected the vocational-school notion of the college — said that they were interested in teaching. But of the rest only 8 percent were thinking about going into business. Among the 50 percent not accounted for by those two choices will be found dropouts, life-style pioneers, artists, workers in communications, etc. They are not as easy to identify as the other groupings, yet they often have served as a cultural vanguard, and their presence should be noted.

Finally, there are deep-going changes taking place in traditional professions. In both the law and medical schools of the late '60s and early '70s there was a demand for more relevant education, and resistance to such established professional organizations as the American Bar Association and the American Medical Association. These trends are much too recent to survey in any but the most superficial of fashions, yet it is likely that the possibilities for legal and medical practice among the poor and the minorities, so important to these students and the young graduates, will depend upon federal decisions with regard to the fight against poverty and for national health care.

We are dealing then with social categories in change, particularly when one talks of the liberal arts students and the radicals in the traditional professions. And it is obvious that in many aspects of their life, above all in their education and income, most of these people more clearly resemble the salaried middle class than the working class. Yet there are important parallels between the new strata and the traditional working class; indeed, they permit one to speak of a "new working class" so long as it is understood that the phrase cannot be taken as a precise definition. Most of the new strata members occupy subordinate positions in large production units, and this is the basis for the unionism and "near unionism" which has already developed among them. Second, almost all of them are in jobs directly dependent upon the political process, and this means that their notion of collective bargaining includes political action from the very outset (indeed, the NEA lobbied long before it began to bargain). At the top of the income scale, particularly among the scientists and the engineers, the new strata shade off into the upper reaches of management; at the bottom, among the scientific technicians without college degrees, they merge with the more skilled members of the traditional working class. But in between those limits there is a large new grouping, numbered in the millions, which, for all its middle-class education and income, is impelled by virtue of its position in society toward collective bargaining and politics.

All of this should not be taken as implying extreme optimism about a future in which a still dynamic old working class will join with the organized new working class to make the good society. There are, as we have seen, status factors that can, and have, kept these groups far apart. There is a tendency toward corporatism in the new strata and in the old working class as well, with an emphasis on a very narrow and self-interested job protection. But there also is at least the possibility that the progressive tendencies in these two working classes, old and new, could provide the basis for a new political coalition in America dedicated to social and democratic — eventually perhaps social democratic — planning.

Bibliographical Note

I. Herbert Marcuse, *One-Dimensional Man* (Boston, 1964), p. 256. Paul Sweezy and Paul Baran, *Monopoly Capital* (New York, 1966), p. 363. Arthur Schlesinger, Jr., "The New Liberal Coalition," the *Progressive*, April 1967, p. 16. Clark Kerr, *Marshall, Marx and Modern Times: The Multi-Dimensional Society* (Cambridge, England, 1969), pp. 36, 83. For Marx on class "in itself" and "for itself," see Proudhon and Marx, *Misère de la Philosophie, Philosophie de la Misère* (Paris, 1964), p. 490.

II. U.S. Bureau of Labor Statistics, *Labor Force Statistics: Handbook of Labor Statistics, 1970* (Washington, D.C.: Government Printing Office, 1970), Table 1,

p. 25; Table 38, p. 80; Table 40, p. 83. See also, "24 Million Americans, Poverty in the United States, 1969," in *Working Poor: U.S. Bureau of the Census, Current Population Report,* series P-60, no. 76 (Washington, D.C.: U.S. Government Printing Office, 1970), Table 11, pp. 54–55. For workers' income, see Brendan Sexton, "Middle-Class Workers and the New Politics," *Dissent,* May-June 1969; Derek C. Bok and John T. Dunlop, *Labor and the American Community* (New York, 1970), p. 43; Rudolph Oswald, "The City Workers Budget," *Federationist,* February 1968. See also *Wall Street Journal,* March 17, 1969; U.S. Department of Labor, *Manpower Projections: U.S. Manpower in the Seventies* (Washington, D.C.: Government Printing Office, 1970). For class income, see S. M. Miller, "Can Workers Transform Society?" in Sar Levitan, ed., *Blue-Collar Workers* (New York, 1971). On the future of occupational categories, see *Manpower Projections: U.S. Manpower in the Seventies.* See also Penn Kemble, "Rediscovering American Labor," *Commentary,* April 1971. On manufacturing jobs, see Bureau of Labor Statistics, *Employment and Earnings, U.S., 1909–1970,* Bulletin 1312-7 (Washington, D.C.: Government Printing Office, 1971), Chart I. See Ralf Dahrendorf, *Class and Class-Consciousness in Industrial Society,* rev. ed. (Stanford, 1966), pp. 31, 92–93. Alain Touraine, *The Post-Industrial Society* (New York, 1971), p. 172. The 1967 *Fortune* study is quoted in Ralph Miliband, *The State and Capitalist Society* (London, 1969), pp. 30, 36, no. 1. On executive bonus, see *Wall Street Journal,* September 1, 1971. On wealth, see Herman P. Miller, *Rich Man, Poor Man,* rev. ed. (New York, 1970), p. 157, Table IX-3. See also John H. Goldthrope, David Lockwood, Frank Bechhofer, and Jennifer Platt, *The Affluent Worker in the Class Structure* (Cambridge, England, 1969), pp. 162–163.

III. V. I. Lenin, *Lenin on the United States* (New York, 1970), p. 24. Morris Hilquit, *History of Socialism in the United States,* rev. ed. (New York, 1965; orig. 1909), pp. 137–139. Sombart, *Warum gibt es in den Vereinigten Staaten keinen Sozialismus?* (Tübingen, 1906), p. 126. Don Lescohier, *History of Labor in the United States, 1886–1932* (New York, 1935), III, p. 60. Selig Perlman, *The Theory of the Labor Movement* (New York, 1949; orig. 1928), pp. 168–169. Philip Taft, *The AF of L in the Time of Gompers* (New York, 1957), p. 476. For Irving Bernstein on the 1920s, see *The Lean Years* (Boston, 1960), p. 55. On wage statistics in the '20s: U.S. Bureau of Labor Statistics, *Historical Statistics of the United States, Colonial Times to 1957* (Washington, D.C.: U.S. Bureau of Labor Statistics, 1960), D626–34, Richard Hofstadter, *The Age of Reform* (New York, 1955), p. 308.

IV. Raymond Aron, *La Lutte des Classes* (Paris, 1964), pp. 106–107, 119–120. For Marx's Inaugural to IWMA, see *MEW* (Marx and Engels, *Works*), XV, p. 11. For the Employment Act of 1946, see Stephen Kemp Bailey, *Congress Makes a Law* (New York, 1950); Louis Blanc, *Organization du Travail,* 5th ed. (Paris, 1848), *passim.* See Leon Samson, *Toward a United Front for American Workers* (New York, 1933), pp. 3ff, 21.

V. See Raymond Aron, *op. cit.,* pp. 106–107. See Daniel Bell, *The End of Ideology* (New York, rev. ed., 1961), pp. 397–399; Daniel Bell, "The Corporation and the Society in the 1970's," *Public Interest,* Summer 1971, p. 9. For Aron's definition of class, see *op. cit.,* p. 120. See Bennett Berger, *Working-Class Suburb* (Berkeley, 1960). Mallet, *La Nouvelle Classe Ouvrière* (Paris, 1969), p. 49. See Herbert Gans, *The Levittowners* (New York, 1967), p. 195. J. David Greenstone, *Labor in American Politics* (New York, 1969), *passim* and pp. xii–xiv. See Derek C. Bok and John T. Dunlop, *Labor and the American Community* (New York, 1970), chap. 1. Bell, "The Corporation and the Society in the 1970's," *op. cit.,* pp. 31–32. For Bell on new men, see "Notes on the Post-Industrial Society," *Public Interest,* Winter 1967. See John Kenneth Galbraith, *The New Industrial State* (Boston, 1967), p. 282ff. See Thorstein Veblen, *The Engineers and the Price System* (New York, 1933). For instrumental collectivism, see Goldthorpe, Lockwood, *et al., op. cit.,* p. 190.

VI. See *Manpower Projections: U.S. Manpower in the Seventies, op. cit.* For educational statistics, see U.S. Department of Commerce, *Characteristics of American Youth,* series P-23, no. 34 (Washington, D.C.: Government Printing Office, 1971).

Labor in the Post-Industrial Society
Daniel Bell

In the *Communist Manifesto,* which was completed in February 1848, Marx and Engels envisaged a society in which there would be only two classes — capitalist and worker, the few who owned the means of production and the many who lived by selling their labor power — as the last two great antagonistic classes of social history, locked in final conflict. In many ways this was a remarkable prediction, if only because at that time, in Europe and the United States, the vast majority of persons were neither capitalist nor worker but farmer and peasant, and the tenor of life in these countries was overwhelmingly agrarian and artisan.

England was the evident model for industrialization, but despite Manchester, Leeds, Birmingham, and Sheffield, Great Britain at the mid-century mark was not at all industrial, a fact demonstrated in occupational statistics. As David Landes writes:

> The British census of 1851 — for all its inaccuracies — shows a country in which agriculture and domestic service were far and away the most

DANIEL BELL is Professor of Sociology at Harvard University and co-editor of the Public Interest. *His books include* The End of Ideology *and* Marxian Socialism in the United States. *This essay is part of his new book,* The Coming of Post-Industrial Society, *copyright © 1972 by Daniel Bell, and is printed here with the kind permission of the author and publisher, Basic Books.*

important occupations; in which most of the labour force was engaged in industries of the old type: building trades, tailoring, shoemaking, unskilled work of all sorts. Even in the cotton manufacture, with over three-fifths of its working force of over half a million (of a total of almost 16 million) in mills, almost two-thirds of the units making returns employed less than 50 men; the average mill in England employed less than 200; and tens of thousands of hand looms were still at work in rural cottages.*

At mid-century, continental Europe was about a generation behind Britain in industrial development. In Belgium, the most industrialized nation on the continent, about half the labor force was engaged in agriculture (in Britain it was only one-fourth). Germany took another twenty-five years just to reach that 50 percent mark; indeed, as late as 1895 more people in Germany were engaged in agriculture than in industry. In France the number of persons in industry was outnumbered by those in agriculture until World War II! To return to Marx's day, in the Prussia of 1852, which in this respect was representative of all of Germany, 72 percent of the population was classified as rural. As Sir John Clapham comments: "German industry in general could in no sense be called capitalistic; and before 1840 large enterprises of the factory type were extraordinarily rare." In France in 1851, only 10.5 percent of the population lived in towns, and "the number of concerns employing more than a hundred people in 1848," writes Clapham, "was so small that they could not much affect the average for the whole country; outside mining and metallurgy they hardly existed [and] true factory conditions were exceptional in the France of 1848." In the United States in 1850, of a population of 23 million persons, 19.6 million lived in rural territory (in places with under 2,500 persons); of a labor force of 7.7 million, 4.9 were engaged in agriculture, 1.2 in manufacturing and construction combined (it was only in 1870 that the two figures were separated), and almost one million in domestic service. †

Marx's vision of the inexorable rise of industrial society was thus a bold one. But in Western society the most important social

---

* David Landes, *The Unbounded Prometheus: Technological Change and Industrial Development in Western Europe from 1750 to the Present* (Cambridge, England, 1969), pp. 119–120.

† Sources for the above are, Landes, *op. cit.,* p. 187; in J. H. Clapham, *The Economic Development of France and Germany, 1815–1914* (Cambridge, England, 1945; orig. ed. 1921), pp. 54, 70–71, 82, 84; U.S. Bureau of the Census, U.S. Dept. of Commerce, *Historical Statistics of the United States* (Washington, D.C.: U.S. Government Printing Office, 1960), pp. 14, 74.

change of the last hundred years has been not simply the diffusion of industrial work but the concomitant disappearance of the farmer — and in a Ricardian world of diminishing returns in land, the idea that agricultural productivity would be two or three times that of industry (which has been in the U.S. for the past thirty years) was undreamed of.

The transformation of agrarian life (whose habits had marked civilization for four thousand years) has been the signal fact of the time. In beholding the application of steam power to a textile mill, one could venture predictions about the spread of mechanization and the extension of factory work. But who would have made similar predictions with equal confidence following Cyrus McCormick's invention of the reaper in 1832 and its exhibition at the Crystal Palace in London in 1851? Yet in the U.S. today, only 4 percent of the labor force is engaged in agriculture; the work of little more than three million persons (as against more than twice that number two decades ago) feeds 207 million persons, and if all crop restraints were released, they could probably feed fifty million more.

In place of the farmer came the industrial worker. And for the past hundred years or so the vicissitudes of the industrial worker — his claims to dignity and status, his demand for a rising share of industrial returns, his desire for a voice in the conditions affecting his work and conditions of employment — have marked the social struggles of the century. But beyond that, in the utopian visions of Marx and the socialist movement, the working class, made conscious of its fate by the conditions of struggle, was seen as the agency not only of industrial but of human emancipation. The last great brakes on production and abundance would be removed when the working class took over control of the means of production and ushered in the socialist millennium.

Yet if one takes the industrial worker as the instrument of the future, or, more specifically, the factory worker as the symbol of the proletariat, this vision is warped. For, paradoxically, as one goes along the trajectory of industrialization — the increasing replacement of men by machines — one logically comes to the erosion of the industrial worker himself.* By the end of the century the proportion

---

* In Marx's writings there are many contradictory views of this situation. In the *Grundrisse,* the outline sketch for the master work which preceded *Capital,* and which was never published by Marx, he envisaged a time when almost all work would be replaced by the machine and when science, not labor power, would be considered the main productive force. In *Capital,* when he is working out the logic of the changing organic composition of capital, Marx describes a dual process resulting, on the one hand, in an increasing concentration of firms, and, on the other, in an increase in the "industrial

of factory workers in the labor force may be as small as the proportion of farmers today; indeed, the entire area of blue-collar work may by then have diminished so greatly that the term will lose its sociological meaning as new categories, more appropriate to the divisions of the new labor force, are established. Instead of the industrial worker, we see the dominance of the professional and technical class in the labor force — so much so that by 1980 it will be the second largest occupational group in the society, and by the end of the century the largest. This is the new dual revolution taking place in the structure of occupations and, to the extent that occupation determines other modes of behavior (but this, too, is diminishing), it is a revolution in the class structure of society as well. This change in the character of production and of occupations is one aspect of the emergence of the "post-industrial" society.

The concept of a post-industrial society gains meaning by comparing its attributes with those of an industrial and a pre-industrial society.

In pre-industrial societies — still the condition of most of the world today — the labor force is engaged mainly in the extractive industries: mining, fishing, forestry, agriculture. Life is primarily a game against nature. One works with raw muscle power, in inherited ways, and one's sense of the world is conditioned by dependence on the elements — the seasons, the nature of the soil, the amount of water. The rhythm of life is shaped by these contingencies. The sense of time is one of *durée*, of long and short moments, and the pace of work varies with the seasons and the storms. Because it is a game against nature, productivity is low, and the economy is subject to the vicissitudes of tangible nature and to capricious fluctuations of raw-material prices in the world economy. The unit of social life is the extended household. Welfare consists of taking in the extra mouths when necessary — which is almost always. Because of low productivity and large population, there is a high percentage of underemployment, which is usually distributed throughout the agricultural and domestic-service sectors. Thus there is a high service component, of the personal or household sort. Since individuals often seek only enough to feed themselves, domestic service is cheap and plentiful. (In England, up to the mid-Vic-

---

reserve army," i.e., the unemployed. Yet Marx could never escape the power of his own rhetoric, and in the penultimate chapter of *Capital*, when he is describing, nay sounding, the death-knell of capitalism, he writes: "Along with the constantly diminishing number of the magnates of capital . . . grows the revolt of the working class, a class always increasing in numbers. . . . Centralization of the means of production and socialization of labor at last reach a point where they become incompatible with their capitalist integument. This integument is burst asunder." *Capital,* I (Chicago, 1906), p. 837.

torian period, the single largest occupational class in the society was the domestic servant. In *Vanity Fair,* Becky Sharp and Captain Rawdon Crawley are penniless, but they have a servant; Karl Marx and his large family lived in two rooms in Soho in the 1850s and were sometimes evicted for failing to pay rent, but they had a faithful servant, Lenchen.) Pre-industrial societies are agrarian societies, structured in traditional ways of routine and authority.

Industrial societies—principally those around the North Atlantic littoral, plus the Soviet Union and Japan—are goods-producing societies. Life is a game against fabricated nature. The world has become technical and rationalized. The machine predominates, and the rhythms of life are mechanically paced: time is chronological, methodical, evenly spaced. Energy has replaced raw muscle and provides the power that is the basis of productivity—the art of making more with less—and is responsible for the mass output of goods, which characterizes industrial society. Energy and machines transform the nature of work. Skills are broken down into simpler components, and the artisan of the past is replaced by two new figures: the engineer, who is responsible for the layout and flow of work, and the semi-skilled worker, the human cog between machines—until the technical ingenuity of the engineer creates a new machine that replaces him as well. It is a world of coordination in which men, materials, and markets are dovetailed for the production and distribution of goods—a world of scheduling and programming, in which the components of goods are brought together at the right time and in the right proportions so as to speed the flow of goods. It is a world of organization—of hierarchy and bureaucracy—in which men are treated as "things" because one can more easily coordinate things than men. Thus a necessary distinction is introduced between the role and the person, and this is formalized on the organization chart of the enterprise. Organizations deal with the requirements of roles, not persons. The criterion of *techne* is efficiency, and the mode of life is modeled on economics: how does one extract the greatest amount of energy from a given unit of embedded nature (coal, oil, gas, water power) with the best machine at what comparative price? The watchwords are maximization and optimization, in a cosmology derived from utility and the felicific calculus of Jeremy Bentham. The unit is the individual, and the free society is the sum total of individual decisions as aggregated by the demands registered, eventually, in a market. In actual fact, life is never as "one-dimensional" as those who convert every tendency into an ontological absolute make it out to be. Traditional elements remain. Work groups intervene to impose their own rhythms and "bogeys" (or output restrictions) when they can. Waste runs high. Particularism and politics abound. These soften the unrelenting quality of industrial life. Yet the essential, technical features remain.

A post-industrial society is based on services. Hence it is a game between persons. What counts is not raw muscle power, or energy, but information. The central person is the professional, for he is equipped, by his education and training, to provide the kinds of skills increasingly in demand in the post-industrial society. If an industrial society is defined by the quantity of goods that mark a standard of living, the post-industrial society is defined by the quality of life as measured by the services and amenities—health, education, recreation, and the arts—which are now deemed desirable and possible for everyone.

The word "services" disguises different things, and in the transformation of industrial to post-industrial society there are several different stages. First, in the very development of industry there is a necessary expansion of transportation and of public utilities as auxiliary services in the movement of goods and the increasing use of energy, and an increase in the nonmanufacturing but still blue-collar force. Second, in the mass consumption of goods and the growth of populations there is an increase in distribution (wholesale and retail), finance, real estate, and insurance, the traditional centers of white-collar employment. Third, as national incomes rise one finds, as in the theorem of Christian Engels (a German statistician of the latter half of the nineteenth century), that the proportion of money devoted to food at home begins to drop, and the marginal increments are used first for durables (clothing, housing, automobiles) and then for luxury items, such as recreation. Thus, a third sector, that of personal services, begins to grow—restaurants, hotels, auto services, travel, entertainment, sports—as people's horizons expand and new wants and tastes develop. But here a new consciousness begins to intervene. The claims to the good life which the society has promised become centered on the two areas fundamental to that life—health and education. The elimination of disease and the increasing numbers of people who can live out a full life, plus the efforts to expand the span of life, make health services a crucial feature of modern society; and the growth of technical requirements and professional skills makes education, and access to higher education, the condition of entry into the post-industrial society. So we have here the growth of a new intelligentsia, particularly of teachers. Finally, the claims for more services and the inadequacy of the market in meeting people's needs for a decent environment as well as for better health and education lead to the growth of government, particularly at the state and local levels, where such needs have to be met.

The post-industrial society, thus, is also a "communal" society in which the social unit is the community rather than the individual, and one has to achieve a "social decision" as against, simply, the sum total of individual decisions which, when aggregated, end up as nightmares, on the model of the individual automobile and collective traffic congestion. But cooperation between men is more difficult to achieve than the management of things. Participation becomes a condition of community, but when many different groups want too many different things and are not prepared for bargaining or trade-off, then increased conflict or deadlocks result. Either there is a politics of consensus or a politics of stymie.

As a game between persons, social life becomes more difficult because political claims and social rights multiply, the rapidity of social change and shifting cultural fashion bewilders the old, and the orientation to the future erodes the traditional guides and moralities of the past. Information becomes a central resource, and within organizations a source of power. Professionalism thus becomes a criterion of position, but also clashes with the populism that is generated by the claims for more rights and greater participation in the society. If the struggle between capitalist and worker, in the locus of the factory, was the hallmark of industrial society, the clash between the professional and the populace, in the organization and in the community, is the hallmark of conflict in the post-industrial society.

This, then, is the sociological canvas of the scheme of social development leading to the post-industrial society.* To identify its structural lineaments and trend lines more directly, let me turn now to the distribution of jobs by economic sector and to the changing profile of occupations in the American economy.

II. The Sectors of Work and Occupations

Shortly after the turn of the century, only three in every ten workers in the country were employed in service industries, and seven out of ten were engaged in the production of goods. By 1950, these proportions were more evenly balanced. By 1968, the proportions had shifted so that six out of every ten were in services. By 1980, with the rising predominance of services, close to seven in every ten workers will be in service industries. (See Tables 1–3.) Between 1900 and 1980, in

---

* I have omitted here the larger theoretical questions of the nature of class power and the stratification system. These are dealt with in my essay "The Post-Industrial Society: Technocracy and Politics," *Survey* (London), Winter 1971.

TABLE 1

SECTOR DISTRIBUTION OF EMPLOYMENT BY GOODS AND SERVICES 1870–1940
(in thousands)

Year	1870	1900	1920	1940
Total	12,900	29,000	41,600	49,860
Goods-Producing Total	10,630	19,620	23,600	25,610
Agriculture, Forestry, & Fisheries	7,450	10,900	11,400	9,100
Manufacturing	2,250	6,300	10,800	11,900
Mining	180	760	1,230	1,100
Construction	750	1,660	2,170	3,510
Service-Producing Total	2,990	9,020	15,490	24,250
Trade, Finance, & Real Estate	830	2,760	4,800	8,700
Transportation & Utilities	640	2,100	4,190	4,150
Professional Service	230	1,150	2,250	4,000
Domestic & Personal Service	1,190	2,710	3,330	5,710
Government (not elsewhere classified)	100	300	920	1,690

Source: Adapted from *Historical Statistics of the United States: 1820–1940,* Series D57–71, p. 74.

Note: The totals do not always add up because of small numbers not allocated, and rounding of figures.

the exact reversal of the proportions between the sectors, there occurred two structural changes in the American economy.

In historic fact, the shift of employment to services does not represent any sudden departure from previous long-run trends. As Victor Fuchs points out, "For as long as we have records on the industrial distribution of the labor force, we find a secular tendency for the percentage accounted for by the service sector to rise." * From 1870 to 1920, the shift to services could be explained almost entirely by the movement from agricultural to industrial pursuits; employment in industry rose as rapidly as service, and the major increases in services were in the *auxiliary* areas of transportation, utilities, and distribution. This was the historic period of industrialization in American life. After 1920, however, the rates of growth in the nonagricultural sector began to diverge. Industrial employment still increased numerically, but its *share* of total employment tended to decline, as employment in services grew at a faster rate, and from 1968 to 1980, if we take manufacturing as the key to the industrial sector, the growth will be less than half of the whole labor force.

The great divide began in 1947, after World War II, when employment was evenly balanced. But from then on the growth rates began to diverge in new, accelerated fashion. From 1947 to 1968 there was a growth of about 60 percent in employment in services,

* Victor R. Fuchs, *The Service Economy* (New York: National Bureau of Economic Research, distributed by Columbia University, 1968), p. 22.

TABLE 2

SECTOR DISTRIBUTION OF EMPLOYMENT BY GOODS AND SERVICES 1947–1968
PROJECTED TO 1980
(in thousands)

Year	1947	1968	1980	Percentage Change 1947–68	1968–80
Total	51,770	80,780	99,600	56%	23%
Goods-Producing	26,370	28,975	31,600	9.8%	9%
Agriculture, Forestry, & Fisheries	7,890	4,150	3,180	(−48)	(−23)
Mining	955	640	590	(−33)	(−9)
Construction	1,980	4,050	5,480	10	35
Manufacturing	15,540	20,125	22,358	29	11
Durable	8,385	11,850	13,275	41	12
Nondurable	7,160	8,270	9,100	15.5	10
Service-Producing	25,400	51,800	67,980	104%	31%
Transportation & Utilities	4,160	4,500	5,000	8	10
Trade (Wholesale & Retail)	8,950	16,600	20,500	85.5	23
Finance, Insurance, Real Estate	1,750	3,725	4,640	113	24
Services (Personal, Professional, Business)	5,050	11,850	21,000	135	40
Government	5,470	11,850	16,800	117	42
Federal	1,890	2,735	3,000	45	10
State & Local	3,580	9,110	13,800	150	52

Source: The U.S. Economy in 1980, Bulletin 1673, Bureau of Labor Statistics, 1970. The data for 1968 and 1980 are from Table A-16, p. 49. The figures for 1947 are adapted from chart data in Bulletin 1673, by Lawrence B. Krause.

Note 1. The figures for 1980 assume a 3 percent unemployment. At a 4 percent unemployment there would be a drop in the labor force of 1 million (i.e., from 99,600 to 98,600), and this loss is distributed between goods-producing (31,600 to 31,000) and service-producing (67,980 to 67,300) employment.

Note 2. Figures are not always exact because of rounding.

while employment in the goods-producing industries increased less than 10 percent. Despite a steadily rising total output of goods through the 1970s, this tendency will persist. Altogether, the goods-producing industries employed 29 million workers in 1968, and the number is expected to increase to 31.6 million by 1980. However, their share in total employment will drop to less than 32 percent in 1980, from about 36 percent in 1968.*

Within the goods-producing sector, employment in agriculture and mining will continue to decline in absolute terms. The major change—and the impetus to new jobs in that sector—will come in construction. The national housing goals for the 1968–1978 decade call for the building of twenty million new housing units in the private

* All statistical data in this section are from the Bureau of Labor Statistics, U.S. Department of Labor, The U.S. Economy in 1980 (Washington, D.C.: U.S. Government Printing Office, 1970).

TABLE 3

SECTOR DISTRIBUTION OF EMPLOYMENT BY GOODS
AND SERVICES PROJECTED TO 1980
(Distribution by Percentages)

Year	1947	1968	1980
Total	100%	100%	100%
Goods Producing	51.0	35.9	31.7
Agriculture, Forestry, & Fisheries	15.0	5.1	3.2
Mining	2.1	0.8	0.6
Construction	3.9	5.0	5.5
Manufacturing	30.0	24.9	22.4
Durable	16.0	14.7	13.3
Nondurable	14.0	10.2	9.1
Service Producing	49.0	64.1	68.4
Transportation & Utilities	8.0	5.6	5.0
Trade (Wholesale & Retail)	17.0	20.6	20.6
Finance, Insurance, Real Estate	3.0	4.6	4.7
Services (Personal, Professional, Business)	10.0	18.7	21.2
Government	11.0	14.7	16.9
Federal	3.5	3.4	3.0
State & Local	7.5	11.7	13.9

Source: *Ibid.,* conversion of figures into percentages.

market and six million new and rehabilitated units through public subsidy. These goals are now finally being met, and it is expected that employment in construction will rise by 35 percent in this decade.

Manufacturing is still the single largest source of jobs in the economy. It grew at 0.9 percent a year during the 1960s, largely because of increased employment in defense industries—aircraft, missiles, ordnance, communications equipment, and the like—which have higher labor components because the work is more "custom-crafted" than in mass-production industries. But the shift away from defense spending—with its consequent unemployment in aircraft, missiles, and communications—means a slower rate of growth for manufacturing in the future. Any increase will appear largely in the manufacture of building materials for housing construction.

To return to the larger picture, the most important growth area in employment since 1947 has been government. One out of every six American workers today is employed by one of about eighty thousand entities that make up the government of the United States today. In 1929, three million persons worked for the government, or about 6.4 percent of the labor force. Today, twelve million persons work for the government—about 16 percent of the labor force. By 1980 that figure will rise to seventeen million, or 17 percent of the labor force.

Government to most people signifies the federal government.

But state and local agencies actually account for eight out of every ten workers employed by the government. The major reason has been the expansion of schooling, both in numbers of children and amount of schooling, and thus of the number of teachers employed. Today about 85 percent of all pupils complete high school as against 33 percent in 1947. Educational services, the area of fastest growth in the country, comprised 50 percent of state and local governmental activities in 1968 (as measured by employment).

General services were the second fastest growth area for employment between 1947 and 1968, and about 10 percent of employment in general services is in private educational institutions. Thus education as a whole, both public and private, represented 8 percent of total employment in the United States. Within general services, the largest category is medical services, where employment rose from 1.4 million in 1958 to 2.6 million a decade later.

The spread of services, particularly in trade, finance, education, health, and government, conjures up the picture of a white-collar society. But not all services are white collar, since they include transportation workers and auto-repair men. But then, not all manufacturing is blue collar. In 1960 it was estimated that the white-collar component within manufacturing—professional, managerial, clerical, and sales—came to about 28.8 percent of the work force, while 68.5 were blue-collar workers. (By 1975 the white-collar component will reach 33 percent.) And within the blue-collar force there has been a steady and distinct shift from direct production to nonproduction jobs as more and more work becomes automated and blue-collar workers turn to machine-tending, repair, and maintenance, rather than staying "on the line."

In 1980 the total manufacturing labor force will number about twenty-two million, or 22 percent of the whole labor force. But with the continuing spread of major technological developments such as numerical-control machine tools, electronic computers, instrumentation, and automatic controls, the proportion of direct production workers is expected to go down steadily. Automation is a real fact, and the bogey of an accelerated pace has not materialized.* But even

---

* See "Technology and the American Economy," *Report of the President's Committee* on Technology, Automation and Economic Progress (Washington, D.C.: U.S. Government Printing Office, 1966); see also my discussion "The Bogey of Automation," *New York Review of Books,* April 26, 1965.

There are no figures available for industry as a whole on the proportion of direct production to nonproduction workers. On the proportion of white-collar to blue-collar workers in manufacturing for 1960 and projections to 1975, see Bureau of Labor Statistics, U.S. Department of Labor, *Tomorrow's Manpower Needs,* B.L.S. Bulletin 1606, VI (Washington, D.C.: U.S. Government Printing Office), Appendix I.

a steady advance of 2 to 3 percent a year, though it may be manageable economically and socially (people are usually not fired, but jobs are saved through attrition), inevitably takes its toll. The Rand mathematician Richard Bellmann has often been quoted as predicting that by the year 2000 only 2 percent of the labor force will be required to turn out all necessary goods; but the figure is fanciful and inherently unprovable. But if an industrial society is defined as a goods-producing society—if manufacture is central in shaping the character of its labor force—then, clearly, the United States is no longer an industrial society.

The changeover to a post-industrial society is signified not only by the change in sector distribution—the places *where* people work—but in the pattern of occupations, the *kind* of work they do. And here the story is a familiar one. The U.S. has become a white-collar society. From a total of about 5.5 million persons in 1900 (making up about 17.6 percent of the labor force), the white collar group by 1968 came to 35.6 million (46.7 percent) and will rise to 48.3 million in 1980, when it will account for *half* (50.8 percent) of all employed workers. (See Tables 4 and 5.)

Since 1920, the white-collar group has been the fastest-growing occupational group in the society, and this will continue. In 1956, for the first time, this group surpassed the employment of blue-collar workers. By 1980 the ratio will be about 5:3 in favor of the white-collar workers.

Stated in these terms, the change is dramatic, yet somewhat deceptive. For until recently the overwhelming number of white-collar workers have been women, in minor clerical or sales jobs; and in American society, as in most others, family status is still evaluated on the basis of the man's job. But it is at this point—in the changing nature of the male labor force—that a status upheaval has taken place. In 1900 only 15 percent of American men wore white collars (and most of these were independent small businessmen). By 1940 the figure had gone up to 25 percent (and these were largely in administrative jobs). In 1970 almost 42 percent of the male labor force—some twenty million men—held white-collar jobs (as against 23 million who wore blue collars), and of these, almost fifteen million were managerial, professional, or technical—the heart of the upper middle class in the United States.*

---

* For current figures, see U.S. Bureau of the Census, U.S. Department of Labor, *Statistical Abstract of the United States, 1971* (Washington, D.C.: U.S. Government Printing Office), Table 347, "Employed Persons by Major Occupation Group and Sex," p. 222.

TABLE 4

PERCENT DISTRIBUTION BY MAJOR OCCUPATION GROUP
1900–1960

Major Occupation Group	1900	1910	1920	1930	1940	1950	1960
Total	100.0	100.0	100.0	100.0	100.0	100.0	100.0
White-Collar Workers	17.6	21.3	24.9	29.4	31.1	36.6	42.0
Professional & Technical	4.3	4.7	5.4	6.8	7.5	8.6	10.8
Managers, Officials, & Proprietors	5.8	6.6	6.6	7.4	7.3	8.7	10.2
Clerical & Kindred	3.0	5.3	8.0	8.9	9.6	12.3	14.5
Sales Workers	4.5	4.7	4.9	6.3	6.7	7.0	6.5
Manual Workers	35.8	38.2	40.2	39.6	39.8	41.1	37.5
Craftsmen & Foremen	10.5	11.6	13.0	12.8	12.0	14.1	12.9
Operatives	12.8	14.6	15.6	15.8	18.4	20.4	18.6
Laborers, Exc. Farm & Mine	12.5	12.0	11.6	11.0	9.4	6.6	6.0
Service Workers	9.0	9.6	7.8	9.8	11.7	10.5	12.6
Private Household Workers	5.4	5.0	3.3	4.1	4.7	2.6	3.3
Service, Exc. Private Household	3.6	4.6	4.5	5.7	7.1	7.9	9.3
Farm Workers	37.5	30.9	27.0	21.2	17.4	11.8	7.9
Farmers & Farm Managers	19.9	16.5	15.3	12.4	10.4	7.4	4.0
Farm Laborers & Foremen	17.7	14.4	11.7	8.8	7.0	4.4	3.9

Source: Computed from Historical Statistics of the U.S.

TABLE 5

OCCUPATIONAL DISTRIBUTION BY NUMBERS AND PERCENT
1968 (ACTUAL) — 1980 (PROJECTED)

Occupational Group	1968		1980	
	Numbers	Percent	Numbers	Percent
Total	76,000	100.0	95,000	100.0
White-Collar Workers	35,600	46.7	48,300	50.8
Professional & Technical	10,300	13.6	15,500	16.3
Managers & Officials	7,800	10.0	9,500	10.0
Clerical	12,800	16.9	17,300	18.2
Sales	4,600	6.0	6,000	6.0
Blue-Collar Workers	27,500	36.3	31,100	32.7
Craftsmen & Foremen	10,000	13.1	12,200	12.8
Operatives	14,000	18.4	15,400	16.2
Laborers	3,500	4.7	3,500	3.7
Service Workers	9,400	12.4	13,100	13.8
Farm Workers	3,500	4.6	2,600	2.7

Source: Figures computed from Bulletin 1673, U.S. Dept. of Labor.

The blue-collar occupations, which numbered about 12 million men in 1900, rose to 27.5 million in 1968 and will rise at a slower rate to 31.1 million in 1980. In 1900, the blue-collar workers formed about 35 percent of the total labor force, a figure which reached 40 percent in 1920 and again, after World War II, in 1950; but by 1968 it was down to about 36.3 percent of the total labor force, and by 1980 it will reach a historic low of 32.7 percent.

The most striking change, of course, has been in the farm population. In 1900 farming was still the single largest occupation in the United States, comprising 12.5 million workers and about 37.5 percent of the labor force. Until about 1930, the absolute number of farmers and farm workers continued to rise, though their share of employment began to decline. In 1940, because of the extraordinary agricultural revolution which shot productivity to spectacular heights, the number of farm laborers began its rapid decline. In 1968, employment on the farms numbered 3.5 million, and this will decline to 2.6 million in 1980; from 4.6 percent of the work force in 1968 it will fall to 2.7 percent in 1980.

The service occupations continue to expand steadily. In 1900 there were about 3 million persons in services, and more than half of them domestics. In 1968, almost 9.5 million persons were in services, and only a fourth were domestics. The major rises were in such occupations as garage workers, and hotel and restaurant workers. Through the 1970s, service occupations will increase by two-fifths — a rate one and one-half times the expansion for all occupations combined.

From 1920 on, the category of semiskilled worker (called operatives in the census classifications) was the single largest occupational category in the economy, comprising more workers than any other group. Semi-skilled work is the occupational counterpart of mass production, and it rose with the increased output of goods. But the introduction of sophisticated new technologies has slowed the growth of this group drastically. Total employment will rise from 14 million in 1968 to 15.4 million in 1980, but the rate of increase is half of that projected for all employment.

As a share of total employment, the percentage of semi-skilled will slide downward from 18.4 percent in 1968 to 16.2 percent in 1980. At that time it will be *third* in size ranking, outpaced by clerical, which will be the largest, and by professional and technical workers. The proportion of factory workers among the semiskilled will probably drop, too. In 1968, six out of every ten semiskilled workers were employed as factory operatives. Large numbers of them now work as inspectors, maintenance men, and as operators of such material-moving equipment as powered forklift trucks. Among the nonfactory operatives, drivers of trucks, buses, and taxicabs make up the largest group.

Today the professional and technical occupational category is the central one in the society. Its growth has outdistanced that of all other major occupational groups in recent decades. From less than a million in 1890, the number of these workers had grown to 10.3 million in 1968. Within this category, teachers were the largest group (more than 2 million); the second largest were professional health workers (about 2 million), scientists and engineers (about 1.4 million), and engineering and science technicians (about 900,000). Despite the momentary slowdown in the demand for education, and the immediate unemployment in engineering because of the shift away from defense work in 1970–1971, requirements in this category continue to lead all others, increasing half again in size (about twice the employment increase among all occupations combined) between 1968 and 1980. With 15.5 million workers in 1980, this will comprise 16.3 percent of total employment as against 13.6 percent in 1968.

These historic shifts pose a serious problem for the trade-union movement, which in the United States has historically been a blue-collar phenomenon. On the record, the trade-union movement (AFL–CIO plus the major independents) is stronger than it has ever been since the beginning of mass organizing in 1935. In 1970, the total American membership rose to 19.381 million, its all-time high. In the 1960s it gained 2.3 million members, though the major increase came in the mid-years of the decade, and the gains of the last two years were only half those of the major periods of increase from 1964–1966.*

Yet this is a superficial way of looking at the problem, for the extraordinary fact is that, as a percentage of the total labor force, the number of members today is *exactly the same* as in 1947; and as a percentage of workers in nonagricultural establishments, the sector where most members are found and most organizing efforts are made, the percentage of union members is *less today* than in 1947. In effect, trade unionism in the United States has made no real advance in nearly a quarter of a century. (See Table 6.)

After the Wagner Act was passed in 1935, and until the end of World War II, union membership made a fourfold gain. In subsequent years, the membership became stabilized. In 1953–1954, I wrote a series of studies for *Fortune* and other journals predicting that the labor movement would stop growing, and describing the kind of plateau it would reach.† My reasoning was based on the argument that unionism had come to the saturation point in manufacturing and

---

TABLE 6

UNION MEMBERSHIP AS A PROPORTION OF THE LABOR FORCE 1947–1970

Year	Total Union Membership	Total Labor Force		Employees in Nonagricultural Establ.	
		Number	Percent Union Members	Number	Percent Union Members
1947	13,782	60,168	22.9	43,438	31.7
1952	15,805	62,966	23.7	48,306	30.9
1956	17,490	69,409	25.2	52,408	33.4
1960	17,049	72,142	23.6	54,234	31.4
1964	16,841	75,830	22.2	58,332	28.9
1968	18,916	82,272	23.0	67,860	27.9
1970	19,381	85,903	22.6	70,644	27.4

Sources: 1947 and 1952 figures by Leo Troy, Bureau of National Research; 1956–1968 data in Bulletin 1665, Bureau of Labor Statistics; 1970 data in release, B.L.S., September 13, 1971.

Note: In percentage of employees organized, the U.S. ranks among the lowest of Western industrial nations. In Belgium/Luxembourg, more than 65 percent of employees are organized, in Italy more than 55 percent, in Great Britain more than 45 percent, in Holland more than 40 percent, in Germany almost 40 percent, and in France about 20 percent. (Data from European Economic Community, reported in the *Economist*, June 19, 1971, p. 46.)

---

* All statistical data in this section, except when otherwise noted, are from Bureau of Labor Statistics, U.S. Department of Commerce, *Directory of National and International Labor Unions in the United States, 1969,* Bulletin 1665 (Washington, D.C.: U.S. Government Printing Office, 1970), and from preliminary estimates for 1968–1970 in the B.L.S. release, "Labor Union and Employee Association Membership, 1970," of September 13, 1971.

† See "The Next American Labor Movement." *Fortune,* April 1953, and my discussion, "Union Growth," in the *Proceedings of the Seventh Annual Meeting of the Industrial Relations Research Association, December 1954.*

construction simply because it had organized nearly all major companies and found it too costly to tackle small units of under one hundred workers, which thus remained unorganized. There would be an
expansion in the distributive trades (teamsters, retail clerks) since
these were expanding areas of the labor force, but such gains would
be offset by declines in railroad and mining. The unions had shown
themselves incapable of organizing white-collar and technical workers;
the only major area for union growth was government employment,
and this depended on favorable government support.

Union growth in the United States has always been dependent
on favorable government support. While it is clear that the upsurge
of unionism in the 1930s was indigenous, its *institutionalization* was
possible only under the umbrella of the National Labor Relations
Board. The union gains could later be consolidated when the War
Labor Board virtually enacted union-shop clauses in collective-
bargaining contracts during World War II.

The only real growth in American trade unionism in the past
decade has been among government workers, and here the same forces
have been at work. In January 1962, President Kennedy issued Executive Order 10988, which encouraged unionism in the federal service.
This order gave clear and unequivocal support to public unionism,
just as the Wagner Act of 1935 had supported unions and collective
bargaining in private business. It declared that "the efficient administration of the government and the well-being of employees require
that orderly and constructive relationships be maintained between
employee organizations and management." In New York City, in
1961, earlier executive orders by Mayor Robert F. Wagner had
resulted in the "breakthrough" of unionism among 44,000 teachers.
Similar orders were issued in Philadelphia and other cities with evident
results.* The growth of unionism among teachers has been largely
in the public universities, too.

In 1956, when the Bureau of Labor Statistics first started
collecting data on union membership by industry, 915,000 persons,
or 5.1 percent of a total union membership of 18.1 million, were in
government. By the end of 1962, the number had grown to 1.2 million, or to 7 percent of the total membership, and by 1968 union membership had climbed to 2.2 million, or 10.7 percent of the total membership. †

The main push has been in the federal government, where

---

* See Everett M. Kassalow, "Trade Unionism Goes Public," in *Public Interest,* Winter
1969.
† Harry P. Cohany and Lucretia M. Dewey, "Union Membership among Government
Employees," *Monthly Labor Review,* July 1970.

about *half* the employees have been organized. But in the large area of state and local government, less than 10 percent of the employees are unionized. (See Table 7.)

The relatively large advance in government unionism has changed the sector distribution of unionism in the United States. Following the big drive of the CIO, more than half of American unionism was in manufacturing, but in recent years that proportion has slowly begun to change, and we can look for greater shifts in the years ahead. (See Table 8.)

Since 1956, union membership in manufacturing and non-manufacturing has continued to shrink as a proportion of total membership (union membership in manufacturing declined 44,000 between 1968 and 1970), and only membership in the public sector has moved upward. It is estimated that about 60 percent of manufacturing employment is organized, compared to one-quarter in nonmanufacturing and a little less than 20 percent in government employment.

It is the white-collar field, of course, that is crucial for the future of organized labor, and here trade unionism has done poorly. According to reports from 167 unions and estimates for 22, total white-collar membership in 1968 stood at 3.2 million. And this is about 15 percent of all union members. The highest ratio of white-collar union workers, more than 40 percent, was in government service, followed by 22 percent in nonmanufacturing and 4 percent in manufacturing. Sixty-two unions reported a total of 982,000 professional and technical

TABLE 7

PROPORTION OF GOVERNMENT EMPLOYEES ORGANIZED

Year	Government		Federal Government		State and Local	
	Total Employment	Percent Organized	Total Employment	Percent Organized	Total Employment	Percent Organized
1956	7,277	12.6	2,209	——	5,069	——
1960	8,353	12.8	2,270	——	6,083	——
1964	9,596	15.1	2,348	38.2	7,248	7.7
1966	10,792	15.9	2,564	41.8	8,227	7.8
1968	11,846	18.2	2,737	49.4	9,109	8.8

Source: Monthly Labor Review, July 1970.
Note: Dashes indicate data not available.

TABLE 8

UNION MEMBERSHIP BY SECTOR, 1956 AND 1968

Year	Total	Manufacturing		Nonmanufacturing		Government	
		Number	Percent	Number	Percent	Number	Percent
1956	18,104	8,839	48.8	8,350	46.1	915	5.1
1968	20,210	9,218	45.6	8,837	43.7	2,155	10.7

members, but a large proportion of this group consisted of unions exclusively representing such professional employees as actors and artists, musicians, airline pilots, and, of those in government, mainly teachers. The major white-collar areas—in trade, finance, and insurance—remain largely unorganized; so does the entire area of science and engineering technicians and engineers. (See Table 9.)

TABLE 9

WHITE-COLLAR UNIONISM

Year	Number of White-Collar Members	Percent of All Union Members
1956	2,463	13.6
1968	3,176	15.7

III. Some Labor Problems of the Post-Industrial Society

The structural changes I have been delineating pose some crucial, long-run problems for the organized trade-union movement in the United States. But long-run, in this context, means thirty years or so, before these tendencies work themselves out in detail, and numbers or proportions are not always a reliable index of influence. The number of farmers has been dwindling steadily, but the politics of agriculture still plays a major role in the calculations of the political parties, and the influence of the agricultural bloc casts a far longer shadow than its size. Similarly, a movement with about twenty million members, even in a labor force of one hundred million persons, is one that will exercise considerable influence for a long time.

A full-scale analysis of the problems of labor in a post-industrial society would have to include the structure of trade unionism, the problem of bureaucracy and democracy in unions, and the like; but these are outside the scope of this paper. The issues I shall deal with, some of them theoretical in nature, derive largely from the analysis of the changes in composition of the work force, and the nature of the post-industrial society that I have sketched earlier.

1. *Education and Status.* The most striking aspect of the new labor force is the level of formal educational attainment. By 1980, only one in sixteen adult workers (twenty-five years and over)—about 5 million—will have had less than eight years of schooling, while seven in every ten adult workers, about 52 million, will at least have completed four years of high school. In 1968, by contrast, one in ten (about 7 million) had completed less than eight years of schooling and six in

ten (about 37 million) had completed four years of high school or more.

Many will have gone further. Nearly one in six persons, twenty-five years and over (about 13 million) will have completed at least four years of college, as against one in seven, or about 8.5 million, in 1968. Moreover, in 1980 about 9.2 million adults, one in eight, will have had some college training, though less than four years.

Not only is there a much greater degree of educational attainment, but there is also a greater degree of cultural homogeneity. The American labor movement, particularly the blue-collar class, has always had a large component of foreign-born or first-generation workers, many of whom accepted a lower status as a matter of course. In 1950, about 34 percent of the blue-collar labor force (skilled, semiskilled, and unskilled) were either foreign-born or of foreign or mixed parentage. By 1960, this figure had fallen to 26 percent.* It is likely to fall further.

For the first time, therefore, historically speaking, the American blue-collar labor force is approaching the "classical" Marxist image of a relatively well-educated, culturally homogeneous force. To what extent does this change create the basis for a new consciousness or a new militancy? Those entering into plant and factory work today step into conditions far better than those their parents experienced. But, as we all know from generational experiences, the gains of the past count little in the present. The point is that whatever the improvement in wage rates, pension conditions, supervision, and the like, the conditions of work—the control of pacing, the assignments, the design and layout of work—are still outside the worker's control. The trade-union movement, including the UAW, has never really challenged the organization of work itself, though it has modified the arbitrary authority over the workers. It remains to be seen, then, to what extent the entry of a new, young, educated work force creates a very different psychology and new kinds of demands about the character of work.

2. *The Blacks.* In an essay of almost a decade ago, in which I first formulated the theme of the post-industrial society, I wrote:

> Insofar as education is today—and tomorrow—the chief means of
> social mobility, by charting the school dropout rates and matching

---

* These figures are computed from the 1950 Census, Subject Report 3A, Characteristics of the White Population 14 Years Old and Over, and 1960 Census, Subject Report 1A, *Social and Economic Characteristics of the Population 14 Years and Over.* I am indebted to Mrs. Jordy Bell Jacoby for the breakdowns and computations. The figures of 34 and 26 percent are not an averaging: as it turns out, the distribution of native and foreign-born are equal across the skilled, semiskilled, and unskilled classifications.

them against future skill requirements by education one can sketch a rough picture of class society in the United States thirty years from now. . : . By that criterion, thirty years hence, class society in the United States will be predominantly a color society.*

The situation today is not as bleak as it was a dozen years ago. Blacks were 4 percent of the professional and technical group in 1960, but the proportion had almost doubled to 7 percent in 1970. They were 5 percent of the clerical group in 1960, and 8 percent in 1970. Thus, in these key sectors, the pace of gain has been striking. But the total numbers of blacks are still small. Only 22 percent of black males are professional, technical, and clerical, as against 43 percent of white males. (Thirty-six percent of black females are professional, technical, and clerical, as against 64 percent of white females.) Eighteen percent of black males are unskilled laborers as against 6 percent of whites, and 18 percent of black females are domestics as against 3 percent white. †

The single largest group of black workers are semiskilled (28 percent of the black males, as against 19 percent of white males). For this group, the problem of better jobs lies with the trade-union movement which, while formally accepting the principle of help, has been quite slow, particularly in the construction and skilled trades (14 percent of blacks are skilled as against 21 percent of whites) in upgrading black workers. Whether the blacks maintain an alliance with the labor movement, particularly in the political field, depends more on the behavior and response of labor than on that of the blacks. The political independence of the blacks—at least of the top leadership—is one of the realities of the politics of the '70s.

3. *Women.* A service economy is largely a female-centered economy —if one considers clerical, sales, teaching, health technicians, and similar occupations. In 1960, 81 percent of all workers in the goods-producing area were men, and 21 percent women; conversely, in the services sectors only 54 percent of all workers were men and 46 percent women. Looked at along a different axis, 27 percent of all employed females worked in the goods-producing sector, while 73 percent of all women worked in the services sector. ‡

The fact that the service industries are so largely unorganized creates a special problem for the labor movement in its relation to

---

* "The Post-Industrial Society," June 14, 1962 (unpublished).
† All data are from U.S. Bureau of the Census, U.S. Department of Commerce, *The Social and Economic Status of Negroes in the United States, 1970*, Series P–23, no. 38 (Washington, D.C.: U.S. Government Printing Office, 1970).
‡ Victor R. Fuchs, *The Service Economy, op. cit.*, Table 66, p. 185.

women. In 1958, women unionists totaled 3.1 million, or 18.2 percent of total union membership; by 1968, their number had risen to 3.7 million, or 19.5 percent of all members. During these ten years, unions added over 2 million new numbers to their ranks, and women made up 30 percent of that increase; since 1958, 600,000 more women in the United States have joined unions.

During those same ten years, however, the number of women in the labor force grew from 32.7 percent to 37.1 percent. Thus the ratio of women union members to employed women has declined over the decade from 13.8 to 12.5 percent. Moreover, most women are bunched into a few unions. A considerable number of women workers are blue collar and belong to such unions as the International Ladies' Garment Workers, the Amalgamated Clothing, Service Employees (formerly Building Service), the Teamsters, and the Auto Workers. The bulk of the others are in the communication workers', teachers', and government workers' unions.

For a variety of sociological reasons, women have been more difficult to organize than men. Fewer women have thought of their jobs as "permanent," and have been less interested in unions; many female jobs are part-time or "second jobs" for the family, and the turnover of the number of women at work has been much higher than that of men. Since the proportion of women in the labor force is bound to rise — the efforts of women's lib apart — simply because of the expansion of the service industries, the problem for organized trade-union movement in recruiting more union members will be an increasingly difficult one.

4. *The Nonprofit Sector.* The services industries, as I indicated earlier, can be divided into many different kinds: those which are directly auxiliary to industry, such as transportation and utilities; those handling distribution and trade, as well as finance and insurance; those providing professional and business services, such as data-processing; those deriving from leisure demands, such as travel, entertainment, sports, recreation, including the media; and those that deal with communal services, particularly health, education, and government. The latter has been the largest-growing area since the end of World War II.

The growth, in effect, has been taking place in the *nonprofit* sector of society. In 1929, according to estimates of Eli Ginzberg and his associates, the nonprofit sector accounted for 12.5 percent of all goods and services purchased. By 1963 it stood above 27 percent, and it is still rising.* In 1929, 4.465 million persons were employed by

---

* Ginzberg, Hiest, and Reubens, *The Pluralistic Economy* (New York, 1965), p. 86.

government and nonprofit institutions, or about 9.7 percent of the labor force. By 1960, 13.583 million or 20 percent of everyone employed were in the nonprofit sector; at that time, the number employed by government was 8.3 million. Government employment has risen rapidly (at a rate of 4.5 percent a year), reaching 11.8 million in 1968, and an estimated 16.8 million in 1980. (While there are no immediate figures for the rise of the remaining nonprofit sector, principally health, one can assume a substantial rise there, too.)

More important, the nonprofit sector is the major area of net *new* jobs, i.e., actual expansion as against replacement. From 1950 to 1960, the nonprofit sector accounted for a large percentage of new jobs, and in the period 1960–1970, government alone contributed one-third of the *new* jobs in the service areas.

Are there significant differences in the ethos of those engaged in the profit and nonprofit sectors? There have been almost no studies in this field. Yet, since the heart of the nonprofit sector is health, education, and research, which by 1975 will comprise about six million persons,* one can assume here a core of middle-class and upper-middle-class persons who not only form a large market for culture but whose political and social attitudes, in the main, will be more liberal than those of the society as a whole. It is in this area that the greatest pressure for social change will come, and here the wave of radicalism of the '60s will break in the '70s.

5. *The "New" Working Class.* In a recent dialogue, the romantic French Marxist, Régis Debray, tested Chile's President Salvador Allende on his revolutionary purity:

DEBRAY:
... the main question is which sector of society is the motive force behind the process [of revolution], which class is in charge of the administration of the process.

ALLENDE:
The proletariat; that is, the working class.

But the problems for an advanced industrial society are: What is the working class? Is it the "factory worker," the "industrial

---

* Detailed projections by occupations are available only to 1975. *Tomorrow's Manpower Needs,* B.L.S. Bulletin 1606, VI, *op. cit.;* "The National Industry–Occupational Matrix," makes the following estimates (p. 28):

Medical and Health	2,240
Teachers	3,063
Natural Scientists	465
Social Scientists	79
Clergymen	240
Editors and Reporters	128

worker," or, even more widely, the "blue-collar worker"? (For Marx, the proletariat was not identical with the masses of poor working people, and certainly not the *lumpen*-proletariat, who he thought had lost the ability to function in human terms in society. The classical proletariat consisted of factory workers whose class-consciousness was created by the conditions of their work.) But, even at its most comprehensive definition, the blue-collar group is in an increasing minority in advanced or post-industrial society. Is the proletariat, or the working class, *all* those who work for wages and salaries? But that so expands the concept as to distort it beyond recognition. (Are all managers workers? Are supervisors and administrators workers? Are highly paid professors and engineers workers?)

For a long time, Marxist sociologists simply ignored the issue, arguing that the "inevitable" economic crises of capitalism would force a revolutionary conflict in which "the working class" would win. In Germany in the 1920s, where the phenomenon of the new technical and administrative class was first noticed, it was categorized as "the new middle class," and in this sense, too, C. Wright Mills used the idea in his 1951 book, *White Collar.* For the German sociologists, particularly Emil Lederer and Jacob Marschak, who first analyzed the phenomenon in detail, the "new middle class" could not be an autonomous independent class but would eventually have to support either the working class or the business community.* This was also Mills's argument:

> Insofar as political strength rests upon organized economic power, the white-collar workers can only derive their strength from "business" or from "labor." Within the whole structure of power, they are dependent variables. Estimates of their political tendencies, therefore, must rest upon larger predictions of the manner and outcomes of the struggles of business and labor. †

The German sociologists, and Mills, had been writing principally about managerial, administrative, and clerical personnel. But, particularly in the 1950s, it became evident that there was a large-scale transformation in the character of skilled work, with the expansion of engineers and technicians in the advanced technological fields — such as aerospace, computers, oil refining, electronics, optics, and polymers. It was evident that this new occupational stratum was gaining

---

* For an analysis of the history of the idea of new social classes in post-Marxian discussions, see my essay "The Post-Industrial Society: The Evolution of an Idea," *Survey* (London), Spring 1971).

† C. Wright Mills, *White Collar* (New York, 1951), p. 352.

importance and replacing the skilled workers as the crucial group in the industrial process. Now the problem of sociological definition became crucial.

The first Marxist to seek a theoretical formulation fitting this new development was the independent French radical Serge Mallet. In a series of articles in *Les Temps Modernes* and the magazine *La Nef* in 1959, Mallet wrote an analysis of the new industrial processes in France's petit counterpart to IBM, la Compagnie des machines Bull, and in the heavily automated oil refinery, Caltex. These studies, plus a long essay, "Trade Unionism and Industrial Society," were published in France in 1963 under the title *La Nouvelle Classe Ouvrière (The New Working Class)*. Though not translated, the book had a definite influence on some young American radicals, particularly in SDS (after all, they could eat their working-class cake and have it too). For a while "the new working-class tendency," as it was called, seemed to be making its way among independent Marxists until it was swamped, on the one hand, by the revolutionary adventurism of the Weathermen, and, on the other, by the heavyhanded dogmatism of the young Progressive Labor party groups. The breakup of the SDS left the tendency without a home.

The Mallet thesis is quite simple. The engineers and technicians are a "new" working class, in part replacing the old, with a potential for revolutionary leadership and the ability to play a role far beyond their numbers. They are a "new" working class, even though well paid, because their skills are inevitably broken down, compartmentalized, and routinized, and they are unable to realize the professional skills for which they were educated. Thus they are "reduced" to the role of a highly trained working class. The fact that they are better paid does not make them a new "aristocracy of labor," but in fact provides a model for the other workers. As Mallet writes:

> The "new working class" is, in effect, tied to the most highly developed industrial capitalists, and the standard of living which they have is due entirely to the high degree of productivity of these enterprises. It is, however, a situation which could change according to the economic situation and it is a superficial analysis which permits one to assimilate these modern industrial technicians to a "working-class aristocracy." It is true that there exists between them and the masses of workers an appreciable difference in the level of living. But, as we shall see, far from having negative consequences on the behavior of the rest of the working class, the existence of this "avant garde" has, on the contrary, positive effects.*

---

* Serge Mallet, *La Nouvelle Classe Ouvrière* (Paris, 1963), p. 69. (My translation.)

In principle, the idea is not new. It is central, of course, to the writing of Thorstein Veblen (little known to the French), who, in *The Theory of Business Enterprise* (1903), made a fundamental distinction between industry and business—between the engineer, devoted largely to improving the practices of production, and the finance capitalist or manager, who restricts production in order to maintain process and profit. In *The Engineers and the Price System* (1920), Veblen wrote "A Memorandum on a Practicable Soviet of Technicians," which laid out the argument of the revolutionary potential of the production engineer as the indispensable "General Staff of the industrial system."

> Without their immediate and unremitting guidance and correction the industrial system will not work. It is a mechanically organized structure of the technical processes designed, installed and conducted by the production engineers. Without them and their constant attention, the industrial equipment, the mechanical appliances of industry, will foot up to just so much junk.*

Veblen wrote in the first flush of excitement after the Russian Revolution, and he felt that a syndicalist overturn of society was possible—in fact, he thought it could be the only one, since political revolutions in advanced industrial society were passé. For half a century that idea has seemed strange indeed, but its revival by the French writers has been possible because the idea of a professional new class has meshed with the idea of alienation.

Where Mallet, like Veblen, restricted his analysis largely to the technicians, the French social critic André Gorz, an editor of *Les Temps Modernes,* has extended his thesis to the "alienated situation" of the entire professional class. Until now, he argues, the trade-union movement has taken the necessary stand of fighting for "quantitative gains," but this continuing strategy has become increasingly dysfunctional because it has tied the workers into the productivity of the economic system and the consumption society. The new strategy for labor, as well as for all professionals, should be to fight for "qualitative" changes, and in particular for control of production. In Gorz's words:

> . . . technicians, engineers, students, researchers discover that they are wage earners like the others, paid for a piece of work which is "good" only to the degree that it is profitable in the short run. They discover that long-range research, creative work on original prob-

---

* See Thorstein Veblen, *The Engineers and the Price System* (New York, 1963), pp. 4–5.

lems, and the love of workmanship are incompatible with the criteria of capitalist profitability. . . . They discover that they are ruled by the law of capital not only in their work but in all spheres of their life, because those who hold power over big industry also hold power over the State, the society, the region, the city, the university—over each individual's future. . . .

It then becomes immediately evident that the struggle for a meaningful life is the struggle against the power of capital, and that this struggle must proceed without a break in continuity from the company level to the whole social sphere, from the union level to the political realm, from technology to culture. . . . From then on everything is involved: jobs, wages, careers, the city, the regions, science, culture, and the possibility of developing individual creative abilities in the service of humanity. . . . This goal will not be reached merely through nationalization (which risks turning into no more than bureaucratic governmentalization) of the centers of accumulation of capital and credit: it also requires the multiplication of centers of democratic decision-making and their autonomy; that is to say, a complex and coordinated network of regional and local autonomous bodies. This demand, far from being abstract, has or can have all the urgency of imperious necessity . . . because once a certain level of culture has been reached, the need for autonomy, the need to develop one's abilities freely and to give a purpose to one's life is experienced with the same intensity as an unsatisfied physiological necessity.

The impossibility of living which appeared to the proletarians of the last century as the impossibility of reproducing their labor power becomes for the workers of scientific or cultural industries the impossibility of putting their creative abilities to work. Industry in the last century took from the countryside men who were muscles, lungs, stomach: their muscles missed the open spaces, their lungs the fresh air, their stomachs fresh food; their health declined, and the acuteness of their need was but the empty functioning of their organs in a hostile surrounding world. The industry of the second half of the twentieth century increasingly tends to take men from the universities and colleges, men who have been able to acquire the ability to do creative or independent work; who have curiosity, the ability to synthesize, to analyze, to invent, and to assimilate, an ability which spins in a vacuum and runs the risk of perishing for lack of an opportunity to be usefully put to work.*

The most serious efforts to apply Gorz's ideas to the American scene have been made by a group of radical young economists at Harvard, notably Herbert Gintis. Gintis sees a "new emergent social class in

---

* André Gorz, *Strategy for Labor* (Boston, 1967), pp. 104–106. The book was first published in France in 1964 under the title *Stratégie Ouvrière et Néocapitalisme*.

modern capitalism," a new working class which he broadly labels
"educated labor." Drawing upon the standard work of Edward Deni-
son, and of his Harvard colleague Samuel Bowles, Gintis emphasizes
the importance of "educated labor," because, if one compares the
relative contribution of physical capital (machines and technology)
with "human capital" in the economic growth of the United States
between 1929 and 1957, labor is between five and eight times more important than physical capital. But Gintis sees educated labor as pressed
into a mold by the requirements of the capitalist system. A revolutionary outlook emerges because of the alienated desire of educated persons for a full life as producers, as against the fragmentation and
specialization that is their lot in the workaday world. For Gintis, the
student rebellion against the university foreshadows the possible revolt of all "educated labor" against capitalism.

The weakness of this abstract analysis lies, first, in seeing the
students as the model for the revolution of the future. The university,
even with required courses, is not the prototype of the corporate world,
and it is unlikely that even "raised student consciousness" was a
consciousness of "oppression." Universities are a "hothouse" in
which a student lives in a world apart, free largely, especially today,
from the sanctions and reprisals of adult authority for almost any
escapade. After graduation students enter a different, highly differ-
entiated society and begin to take on responsibilities for themselves
and their new families. It is not so surprising, therefore, that whatever
the initial benchmark of radicalism, the college generation, as it
grows older, becomes more conservative.*

A second weakness is the monolithic rhetoric about the requirements of "the system." Paradoxically (and perhaps tongue-in-
cheek), Gintis drew his analysis not from Marcuse but from the functionalist school of sociology, particularly Talcott Parsons, which Marxists have attacked as too simple a view of the "integration" of society.
In any event, both the functionalist and the Marcusian views are too
constricted in their understanding of the diversity and multiplicity
of the society and the culture. And third, Gintis sees bureaucratization as identical with capitalism ("The bureaucratization of work is
a result of the capitalist control of the work process, as bureaucracy

* For a comprehensive review of the evidence for this argument, see S. M. Lipset and
E. C. Ladd, Jr., "College Generations—From the 1930's to the 1960's," *Public Interest,*
Fall 1971. It is also true, as Lipset and Ladd point out, that each succeeding college
generation starts out from a point further left than the preceding one; while they end
up more conservative than when they began, the final resting point may be more liberal
or left than even the starting point of generations a long time ago. To that extent, there
is a basic liberal or left drift among the successive college-educated generations in the
society.

seems to be the sole organizational form compatible with capitalist hegemony"), rather than as a pervasive feature of the historic development of all technological and hierarchical societies, capitalist and communist.* And what he misses, in his abstract conception of bureaucracy, is the large number of changes taking place in organizations which are modifying the classic hierarchical structures of bureaucracy by encouraging committees and participation. While such changes, it is true, do not alter the fundamental character of authority, the modifications often serve to provide the individual with a greater degree of participation than before.

The sources of these critiques are the moral impulses of socialist humanism, but though one can sympathize with their values, it is folly to confuse normative with analytical categories and convert socal tendencies into rhetorical wish-fulfillment, as Gorz and Gintis do. The engineers, for example, fit many of the attributes of the alienated "educated worker." Few of them are allowed to decide how their skills and knowledge will be used; the transition from a defense economy, combined with the drastic slash in research-and-development spending, have made many of them aware, for the first time, of the precariousness of a "career." Yet they do not in the least identify themselves with the "working class." (As *Fortune* found in a recent study of engineers, in June 1971, "Many have moved up into engineering from blue-collar union families and don't want to slip back.") What counts for the engineer is the maintenance of a "professional status." They complain that the word "engineer" is now used to describe everyone from a salesman (a systems engineer at IBM) to a garbage collector (a sanitary engineer, in the Chicago euphemism). The effort to reassert their professional status—through membership in high-prestige associations, through stiffer requirements for professional certification, through changes in school curricula—is an effort at differentiation, not identification. †

This effort to maintain professional status—one aspect of a society in which individual social mobility is still a positive value—

---

* Gintis's major statement is to be found in the essay "The New Working Class and Revolutionary Youth," a supplement to *Continuum,* Spring-Summer 1970. The quotation in the text is from p. 167.

† One sees here, in particular, the sociological differences between English and American life. In England, where engineering has never been considered a true profession, and technical schools until recently never had the status of universities, the Association of Scientific, Technical and Managerial Staffs has grown from 9,000 members in 1947 to 220,000 today. There are a dozen or so engineering unions in the U.S. today, and the independent federation, the Council of Engineers and Scientists Organizations, claims to represent 100,000 members in the U.S. and Canada, but few collective-bargaining contracts in the U.S. cover engineers.

comes into conflict, however, with New Left populism, which dero-
gates professionalism as "elitism." In the schools, in the hospitals,
in the community, the New Left political impulse is to deplore professionalism and hieratic standing as a means of excluding the people
from decisions. Thus one finds today the paradox that "educated
labor" is caught between the extremes of bureaucratization and populism. If it is to resist the "alienation" that threatens its achievement,
it is more likely to assert the traditional professionalism (certainly on
the ideological level) than go in either direction. To this extent, the
phrase "new working class" is simply a radical conceit, and little more.

IV. The Constraints on Change

There is little question, I believe, that in the next few decades we shall
see some striking changes in the structure of occupations and professional work. Within the factories there will be new demands for
control over the decisions of work as the new, younger, and more
educated labor force faces the prospect of long years in a mechanical
harness and finds the monetary rewards (which their forebears struggled to achieve) less important. Within the professions there will be
more social-mindedness as a newer generation comes to the fore and
the structure of professional relationships changes. Within medicine,
for example, one of the central occupations of a post-industrial society,
the inevitable end of the "fee-for-service" relationship, replaced by
some kind of insurance-*cum*-government payment scheme, means
the end of the doctor as an individual entrepreneur and the increasing
centrality of the hospital and group practice. A whole new range of
issues opens up: who is to run the hospitals—the old philanthropic
trustees, the municipal political nominees, the doctors, the "constituencies," or the "community"? How does one balance research and
patient care in the distribution of resources? Should there be more big
teaching hospitals with greater sophisticated facilities or more simple
community medical services? Similarly, within the law, the greater
role of government in welfare, services for the poor, education, consumer standards, and health provides a whole new area of public-
interest law for the lawyer alongside the older areas of business, real
estate, labor law, will, and trusts. The multiplication of junior and
community colleges and the breakup of the standard curricula in most
universities provide an arena for experiment and change.

    And yet, ironically, at a time when many needed reforms seem
to be imminent in the area of work and in the professions—in part
out of the upheavals of the 1960s, in greater part because of the deeper

forces of structural changes of a post-industrial society—there will be stronger objective constraints on such changes (apart from the vested and established interests which are always present) than in the previous several decades of American economic and social development.

¶ There is, first, the constraint of productivity. The simple and obvious fact is that productivity and output grow much faster in goods than in services. (This is crucial in the shift in the relative shares of employment: men can be displaced by machines more readily in goods production than in services.) Productivity in services, because it is a relation between persons, rather than between man and machine, will inevitably be lower than it is in industry.

This is true in almost all services. In retailing, despite self-service, supermarkets, and prepackaging, the rising proportion of the labor force engaged in marketing reaches a ceiling of productivity. In personal services, from barbering to travel arrangements, the nature of the personal relations is fixed by time components. In education—despite programmed learning and television instruction and large lecture classes (which students resent)—the costs have increased from 5 to 7 percent a year. Productivity for all services (including education) has shuffled upward at 1.9 percent a year. In health, despite multi-phasic screens and similar mechanized diagnostic devices—a gain in numbers examined, but a loss in personal care—there is only so much of a physician's time to be distributed among patients. And, at the extreme, there is the example of live musical performances, where, as William J. Baumol is fond of pointing out, the performance of a half-hour quintet calls for the expenditure of two and a half man-hours—and there can be no increase in productivity when the musician's wage goes up.*

This problem comes to a head in the cities, whose budgets have doubled and tripled in the past decades (apart from welfare) because the bulk of municipal expenditures—education, hospitals, police, social services—falls into the nonprogressive sector of the economy, and there are few real economies or gains that can halt these rises. Yet it is productivity that allows the social pie to expand.

¶ The second constraint is an inflation that has been built into the structure of the economy itself by the bilateral actions of strong unions and oligopolistic industries. The inflation that has wracked the American economy since 1968 has been due, in great measure, to the

---

* For a comprehensive scrutiny of technical problems of measurement, see Victor R. Fuchs, ed., *Production and Productivity in the Service Industries*, Studies in Income & Wealth Series, no. 34 (New York: National Bureau of Economic Research, distributed by Columbia University, 1969).

deceptions of President Johnson, who masked the costs of the Vietnam War from the country and was afraid to raise the necessary taxes to finance the war; the bill, inevitably, is paid for in later years. But the Vietnam War apart, inflation has become a structural problem for the economy. The major alarums and noises of collective bargaining in such major industries as steel and auto, electric products and rubber, have been, in reality, mimetic combats in that an unstated but none-theless real accommodation had been worked out between the con-tending parties. The unions receive substantial wage increases, and these increases become the occasion for even more substantial price increases which the industries, with their ability to "administer" prices, are able (until recently) to pass on to the public without protest either from the unions or from government.*

As a result of this system, the unions have been able to force wages up at an average rate of 7 percent annually for the past four years (while in some industries, such as printing and the construction trades, the rate has been 12 percent a year). Meanwhile productivity has been growing at only 3 percent a year. If the economy were only a manufacturing economy, this would be manageable. The labor costs in goods manufacturing are about 30 percent of the total costs. A 10 percent wage increase means, then, only a 3 percent increase in the cost of production, which can be offset by productivity. But in the services sectors, the wage proportion may run 70 percent or more of the total costs of the services; and a parallel 10 percent increase in wages adds 7 percent to the cost of production, while productivity in the services sector averages between 1.2 and 1.9 percent. The gap between these rates is a rough measure of the cost-push factor of inflation that is being built into the system.

When the pattern of steadily rising wages becomes so fixed, one finds an exacerbation in the communal services sector, for the higher "prices" become, necessarily, higher "taxes" — and more po-litical grumbling.† One can extend the urban problem to the society

---

* For a detailed discussion of the origin of this system and how the play was worked out, see my essay "The Subversion of Collective Bargaining," *Commentary*, March 1960.
† For a theoretical model of this problem, see William J. Baumol, "Macroeconomics of Unbalanced Growth: The Anatomy of Urban Crisis," *American Economic Review*, June 1967. As Professor Baumol writes:

> Since there is no reason to anticipate a cessation of capital accumulation or innovation in the progressive sectors of the economy, the upward trend in real costs of municipal services cannot be expected to halt; inexorably and cumula-tively, whether or not there is inflation, budgets will almost certainly continue to mount in the future.... This is a trend for which no man and no group should be blamed, for there is nothing that can be done to stop it. (*Ibid.*, p. 423.)

as a whole. As a larger portion of the labor force shifts into services, there is inevitably a greater drag on productivity and growth, and the costs of services, private and governmental, increase sharply. And yet there is, also inevitably, a greater demand for government activities and government goods to meet the social needs of the populace. But one then faces a painful contradiction, for if the service sectors, especially government, rise without compensating gains in productivity, they become additional claimants on social resources, competing for money with hospitals, schools, libraries, housing, roads, clean water, clean air, etc. This is an intractable problem of all post-industrial society.

¶ A third constraint, more peculiar to the United States, is the evident fact that (from a businessman's point of view) American manufactured goods are pricing themselves out of the world market. From the view of theoretical economics, in the inevitable "product cycle" of goods production a more advanced industrial society finds itself at a price disadvantage when a product becomes standardized, inputs are predictable, price elasticity of demand is higher, and labor costs make a difference, so that less advanced but competing nations can now make the product more cheaply. And this is now happening to American manufacture. In the world economy the United States is now a "mature" nation and in a position to be pushed off the top of the hill by more aggressive countries, as has happened to England at the end of the first quarter of this century.

If one looks at the position of the United States in today's world economy, three facts are evident:

(1) Only in technology-intensive products does the United States have a favorable commercial balance in its trade with the rest of the world. In agricultural products, in minerals, fuels, and other nonmanufactured and nonagricultural products, and in nontechnology-intensive manufactured products, the balance is heavily the other way. In textiles, and in such technological products as transistor radios, typewriters, and electronic calculators, which have now become standardized, the U.S. market has been swept by foreign goods. Even in technology-intensive products (computers, lasers, instruments) there has been a decline: in 1962, the favorable balance was 4:1 (exports of $10.2 billion and imports of $2.5 billion); in 1968, it was 2:1 (exports of $18.4 billion against imports of $9.4 billion). In 1971, the unfavorable balance of trade as a whole was running at a deficit rate of $12 billion when President Nixon moved to force the revaluation of competing currencies and quotas of foreign goods to be sold in the United States.

(2) The reduction in costs of transport, and the differential in wages, has made it increasingly possible for American multi-national corporations to manufacture significant proportions of components abroad and bring them back here for assembly. The Ford Motor Company could only bring out its low-priced Pinto by having most of the components manufactured abroad, and Chrysler has announced that an increasing proportion of the parts for all of its cars will be manufactured abroad rather than in Detroit.

(3) Increasingly the United States is becoming a *rentier* society, in which a substantial and increasing proportion of the balance of trade consists of the return on investments abroad by American corporations, rather than exports.

All of this poses a serious problem for American labor. The area in which it is best organized — manufacture — faces a grave erosion of jobs. In response, American labor, which has traditionally been committed to free trade, is now heavily protectionist. This may save jobs in some sectors (textiles, electronics, steel, automobiles), but at a higher price to the consumer.

In effect, because of the constraints in two major areas — in the changing ratios between goods- and service-producing industries, and in the newly threatened position of American manufactures in the world economy — there may be less margin for social experiment. Thus, at a time when workers may be asking for more control over the conditions of work — which will inevitably increase costs — the squeeze may be greatest because of the changed condition of the economy.

¶ The fourth constraint is the multiplicity of competing demands in the polity itself. A post-industrial society, as I pointed out earlier, is increasingly a communal society wherein public mechanisms rather than the market become the allocators of goods — and public choice, rather than individual demand, becomes the arbiter of services. A communal society by its very nature multiplies the definition of rights — the rights of children, of students, of the poor, of minorities — and translates them into claims of the community. The rise of externalities — the effects of private actions on the commonweal — turns clean air, clean water, and mass transit into public issues and increases the need for social regulations and controls. The demand for higher education and better health necessarily expands greatly the role of government as funder and setter of standards. The need for amenities, the cry for a better quality of life, brings government into the arena of environment, recreation, and culture.

All this involves two problems: we don't really know, given our lack of social-science knowledge, how to do many of these things effectively; equally important, since there may not be enough money to satisfy all or even most of the claims, how do we decide what to do first? In 1960, the Eisenhower Commission of National Goals formulated a set of minimum standards for the quality of life — standards that already seem primitive a decade later — and when the National Planning Association projected these goals to 1975 and sought to cost them out (assuming a 4 percent growth rate, which we have not maintained), it found that we would be $150 billion short in trying to achieve all those goals. So the problem is one of priorities and choice.

But how to achieve this? One of the facts of a communal society is the increased participation of individuals and groups in communal life; in fact, there is probably more participation today, at the city level, than at any other time in American history.* But the very increase in participation leads to a paradox: the greater the number of groups, each seeking diverse or competing ends, the more likelihood that these groups will veto one another's interests, with the consequent sense of frustration and powerlessness as such stalemates incur. This is true not only locally but nationally, where, in the past twenty years, new constituencies have multiplied. The standard entities of interest-group politics used to be corporate, labor, and farm, with the ethnic groups playing a role largely in state and city politics. But in the past two decades we have seen the rise of scientists, educators, the intelligentsia, blacks, youth, and poor — all playing a role in the game of influence and resource allocation. † The old coalitions are no longer decisive. What we have been witnessing in the past decade is the rise of an independent component, committed to neither of the two parties, whose swing vote becomes increasingly important. Thus the problem of how to achieve consensus on political questions will become more difficult. Without consensus there is only conflict, and persistent conflict simply tears a society apart, leaving the way open to repression by one sizable force or another.

Industrial society in the West was marked by three distinctive features: the growth of the large corporation as the prototype of all business enterprise; the imprint of the machine and its rhythms on the character

---

* For an elaboration of this argument, and a documentation of these assertions, see Daniel Bell and Virginia Held, "The Community Revolution," *Public Interest,* Summer 1969.
† Does business always have the disproportionate influence? It depends on the issue. One has to distinguish between the underlying *system* of the society, which is still capitalist, and the actual "ecology of games" wherein, on different issues, there are different coalitions, and even sizable disagreements within the business community on specific political issues.

of work; and labor conflict, as the form of polarized class conflict, which threatened to tear society apart. All three of these elements are markedly changed in the post-industrial society.

The modern business corporation was a social invention, fashioned at the turn of the century, to implement the "economizing mode" that had become the engine of social change in the society.* This device differed markedly from the Army and the Church (the two historic forms of large-scale organization) in its ability to co-ordinate men, materials, and markets for the mass production of goods. In the first half of this century, beginning symbolically with the forma-tion of the first billion-dollar corporation—the U.S. Steel Company in 1901, by J. P. Morgan—the role of the corporation grew steadily, and the economy came to be dominated by such familiar giants as General Motors, General Electric, Standard Oil, and the other monoliths that make up the banner listing of *Fortune*'s 500 industrials. Yet by 1956 the corporation seemed to have reached a plateau in the economy, when incorporated businesses accounted for over 57 percent of the total national income, and since then the proportion has remained stable or has even begun to show signs of decline.

The modern business corporation is marked by large size: of assets, sales, and the number of employees. (General Motors, the largest corporation in the United States, in 1970 had 695,790 employees; Arvin Industries, the 500th largest, had 7,850.) But the distinctive character of the services sector is the small size of unit enterprise. Though one finds giant corporations in the services fields as large as any industrial corporation—in utilities (AT&T), banking (Chase Manhattan), insurance (Metropolitan Life), retail trade (Sears, Roebuck)—most retail-trade firms, personal and professional services, finance and real estate firms, and hospitals employ less than one thousand persons. The word "government" conjures up a picture of a huge bureaucracy, but employment at the local level of government exceeds that of state and federal, and half of this local employment is in governmental units with fewer than five hundred employees. †

Even where unit size is larger, in hospitals and in schools, what is different about these enterprises is the larger degree of au-

---

* For an elaboration of the "economizing mode," see my essay on "The Corporation and the Society in the 1970's," *Public Interest,* Spring 1970.

† The data on unit size of enterprise is woefully inadequate, and even such recent ac-counts as Victor R. Fuchs's *The Service Economy,* are forced to use data a decade old. Fuchs has used a unit size of five hundred employees as the cut-off point in his own cal-culations. Assuming an increase in unit sizes in the decade, I have arbitrarily used one thousand employees as a cut-off point to emphasize the difference in the distribution of employment between the goods-producing and the services sectors. For Fuchs's data see his chap. 8, particularly pp. 190–192.

tonomy of smaller units (the departments in the hospitals and colleges) and the greater degree of professional control. Surely this is an "organizational society" in that the organization rather than the small town is the locus of one's life. But to make this observation, as many sociologists do, is to miss the fact that there now exists a multiplicity of diverse types of organization, and that the received model, the large business corporation, while still pre-eminent, is not pervasive. New forms of small professional firms, research institutes, diverse kinds of government agencies, plus schools and hospitals—all subject to professional and community control—become the locus of life for more and more persons in the society.

The change has come not only in place but also in character of work. In an essay I published fifteen years ago, *Work and Its Discontents,* I wrote: "The image of tens of thousands of workers streaming from the sprawling factories marks indelibly the picture of industrial America, as much as the fringed buckskin and rifle marked the nineteenth-century frontier, or the peruke and lace that of Colonial Virginia. The majority of Americans may not work in factories, as the majority of Americans never were on the frontier, or never lived in Georgian houses; yet the distinctive ethos of each time lies in these archetypes." I argued, further, that while a large variety of occupations and jobs were far removed from the factory, "the factory is archetypal because its rhythms, in subtle fashion, affect the general character of work the way a dye suffuses a cloth." *

The rhythms of mechanization are still pervasive in the United States. The nature of materials handling has been revolutionized by the introduction of mechanized devices. Office work—particularly in large insurance companies, banks, utilities, and industrial corporations—has the same mechanical and dronelike quality, for routing procedures serve the same pacing functions as assembly lines. And yet the distinctive archetype has gone. Charlie Chaplin's *Modern Times* at one time symbolized industrial civilization, but today it is a period piece. The rhythms are no longer that pervasive. The beat has been broken.

Does a new archetype exist today? The fact that in services relations are between persons led C. Wright Mills twenty years ago to declare that the white-collar world had become a "personality market" in which each person "sold himself" in order to impress another and get ahead. Mills's prototype was the salesman and the setting was "the big store." But even at that time his argument was

---

* *Work and Its Discontents* (Boston, 1956). The essay was reprinted in 1971 by the League for Industrial Democracy, with an introduction by Lewis Coser.

not entirely convincing (especially to those who tried to get service in some of those stores), and it is even less so today. New stereotypes abound. An important one – to judge from some of the television commercials – is the researcher or the laboratory technician in a white coat, carrying out an experiment (usually to prove that the sponsor's product is better than the rival's). But this is more an effort to catch the reflected authority of science than the mimesis of a new civilization.

If there are no primary images of work, what is central to the new relationship is talk or communication, and the response of ego to alter, and back – from the irritation of a customer at an airline ticket office to the sympathetic or harassed response of teacher to student. But individuals now talk to other individuals, rather than interact with a machine; and this is the fundamental fact about work in the post-industrial society.

Finally, for more than one hundred years, the "labor issue" dominated Western society. The conflict between worker and boss (whether capitalist or corporate manager) overshadowed all other conflicts and was the axis around which the major social divisions of the society rotated. Marx had assumed, in the logic of commodity production, that in the end both bourgeoisie and worker would be reduced to the abstract economic relation in which all other social attributes would be eliminated so that the two would face each other nakedly – as would all society – in their class roles.*

Two things, however, have gone awry with this prediction.

The first has been the persistent strength of what Max Weber called "status groups" – race, ethnic, linguistic, religious – whose

---

* Marx's view is laid out most starkly in *The Communist Manifesto*. At various points he writes:

> The bourgeoisie cannot exist without incessantly revolutionizing the instruments of production; and, consequently, the relations of production; and, therefore, the totality of social relations. . . . All stable and stereotyped relations, with their attendant train of ancient and venerable prejudices and opinions, are swept away, and the newly formed becomes obsolete before it can petrify. All that has been regarded as solid, crumbles into fragments; all that was looked upon as holy is profaned; at long last, people are compelled to gaze open-eyed at their position in life and their social relations (p. 29). Those who have hitherto belonged to the lower middle class – small manufacturers, small traders, minor recipients of unearned income, handicraftsmen, and peasants – slip down, one and all, into the proletariat (p. 35).
> . . . The development of large-scale industry severs all family ties of proletarians, and . . . proletarian children are transformed into mere articles of commerce and instruments of labor. . . . National distinctions and contrasts are already tending to disappear more and more as the bourgeoisie develops . . . (pp. 48, 50).

loyalties, ties, and emotional identifications have been more powerful and compelling than class at most times, and whose own divisions have overridden class lines. In advanced industrial no less than in tribal societies such as Africa or in communal societies such as India, the "status groups" have generated conflicts that often have torn the society apart more sharply than class issues.

Second, the labor problem has become "encapsulated." An interest conflict and a labor issue—in the sense of disproportionate power between manager and worker over working conditions—remains, but the disproportions have shifted and the methods of negotiation have become institutionalized. Not only has the political tension become encapsulated; there is even the question whether the occupational psychology that Veblen and Dewey made so central to their sociology carries over into other aspects of a man's behavior as well. (A bourgeois was a bourgeois by day and a bourgeois by night; it would be hard to say this about some of the managers who are executives by day and swingers at night.) The crucial fact is that the "labor issue" *qua* labor is no longer central, nor does it have the sociological and cultural weight to polarize all other issues along that axis.

In the next decade, the possible demands for the reorganization of work, the decline in productivity, and the persistent threat of inflation because of the disproportionate productivity in the goods and services sectors, the threats of foreign competition, and other issues such as the recalcitrance of some unions on race, or the bilateral monopolies of unions and builders in the construction trades—all these factors may make labor issues increasingly salient and even rancorous. Some unions may even turn from concern with income and consumption to problems of production and the character of work, and this is all to the good. But it is unlikely that these will become ideological or "class" issues.

The politics of the next decade is more likely to concern itself, on the national level, with such public-interest issues as health, education, and the environment, and, on the local level, crime, municipal services, and costs. These are all communal issues, and on these matters labor may find itself, on the national level, largely liberal, yet, on the local level, divided by the factious issues that split community life.

But all this is a far cry from the vision of *The Communist Manifesto* of 1848 and the student revolutionaries of 1968. In the economy, a labor issue remains. But not in the sociology and culture of the society, and less so in the polity. To that extent, the changes that are summed up in the post-industrial society represent a historic metamorphosis in Western society.

White Workers/Blue Mood
Gus Tyler

"It's us they is always chokin' so that the rich folks can stay fat."
—A twenty-eight-year-old Kentucky miner on the "freeze."
New York Times, *September 24, 1971*

What are the facts about the American workers—especially white workers? Of the 77.902 million gainfully employed in 1969, 28.237 million wore blue collars; that is, 36 percent. But others might as well have worn that collar. Of the 36.844 million "white-collar" workers, about 18 million were in clerical and sales—an added 22 percent of the employed. In addition, there were another 9.528 million engaged in service trades—a category that earned less than the blue-collar, clerical, or sales people. The total in all these blue and bluish jobs comes to 69 percent of the employed.

Who, besides farm workers, is not included? There is the class listed as professional, technical, managerial, as officials and proprietors, who make up about a quarter of the employed. Despite their lofty titles, millions of these are just plain, worried workers. Consider that Italian "professional" who teaches in Franklin K. Lane High School or that Jewish "proprietor" who owns a candy store in Harlem.

The white worker is currently called "middle American," a description that evokes the image of a man and his family at the center of American affluence. But what is the reality?

The white worker is not affluent—not even near-affluent. The median *family* income in 1968 (pre-Nixon) was $8,632, about $1,000

GUS TYLER, *assistant president of the International Ladies' Garment Workers' Union, is the author of* Organized Crime in America, Labor Revolution, *and* The Political Imperative.

short of what the Bureau of Labor Statistics calls a "modest but adequate" income. That this median family cannot meet the American standard of living refutes the mischievous myth that poor means black, and white means affluent. The myth is mischievous because it turns an ethnic difference into a class struggle and implies—and sometimes states—that the way to end poverty is simply to end racism. This myth, as that of "the vanishing American worker," is based upon a truth that when exaggerated becomes an untruth.

While it is true that a much higher percentage of nonwhites than whites is officially poor, it is equally true that in 1968 two-thirds of the poor were white. Nor is this white poverty limited to Appalachia.

Our latest report on who is poor (March 1970) reveals that of the 5.047 million U.S. families listed as living in poverty, 1.363 million or 25 percent are black: only one out of four poor families is black.

TABLE 1

BREAKDOWN OF EMPLOYED PERSONS AGE 16 AND
OVER BY OCCUPATION AND COLOR

(in thousands)	White	Nonwhite
Blue Collar	24,647	3,591
Service	7,289	2,239
Clerical	12,314	1,083
Sales	4,527	166
Professional-Technical	10,074	695
Manager, Officials	7,733	254
Proprietors, Farmers	2,935	356
Total	69,519	8,384

TABLE 2

PERCENTAGE OF THE TOTAL EMPLOYED IN VARIOUS
CATEGORIES OF WHITE LABOR

(percent)	White Percentage of Total Employed of All Races
Blue Collar	32
Service	9.3
Clerical	16
Sales	6
Professional-Technical	13
Managers, Officials	10
Proprietors, Farmers	1.7
Total	88

Whites, then, make up 88 percent of the employed; nonwhites 12 percent. Of the whites, the categories that compose the blue-mooded (exclude farmers and include about half of those in the professional, proprietor, etc., category) make up about 75 percent of the employed.

In the metropolitan areas of America in 1968, there were 2.477 million poor families of which 777,000 were black: less than one-third. In the central cities of these metropoles, there were 748,000 poor families, of which 358,000 were black: less than half.

The poor are not mainly the unemployed. One-third of the family heads listed as officially poor work full weeks at least fifty weeks a year. Others work part years. Most of the poor have jobs – and are white.

While families with incomes under $3,000 are officially poor, those with incomes above $3,000 are not all rich. Twelve percent of the families in America have an income between $3,000 and $5,000. (A recent Labor Department study found that an urban family of four needed at least $5,895 a year to meet its basic needs. If $6,000 a year were used as a cut-off poverty line, then 29.3 percent of the families in America are living in poverty.) A high 52 percent of the families had an income of less than $9,000 a year – a figure still below the official "modest but adequate" income. Seventy-two percent of the families have an income below $12,000 a year – a sum just above what the BLS considers adequate for a family of four in New York City. In round figures, about three out of four families struggle along.

If so many Americans are nonaffluent, who gets the money in this affluent society? Here are some facts on income distribution.

In 1968, the bottom fifth of the nation's families received 5.7 percent of the country's income; the top fifth received 40.6 percent. The middle three-fifths were bunched between 12 and 23 percent. These figures, from the U.S. Department of Commerce publication *Consumer Income* (December 1969), actually understate the great gap between top and bottom. In calculating income the Department of Commerce excludes "money received from the sale of property, such as stocks, bonds, a house, or a car . . . gifts . . . and lump sum inheritances or insurance payments." If these items were included, the income of the top fifth would be appreciably increased – and, by the inclusion of these receipts in the total calculation of income, the percentage of income of the other fifths would be automatically decreased.

Between 1947 and 1968, income shares did not change. The bottom moved from 5 percent to 5.4 percent; the top from 43 percent to 41.2 percent. The change is negligible – and, after allowance for other receipts not counted as income, we find that there has been no meaningful redistribution of income in the quarter-century since the end of World War II.

This iron law of maldistribution applies not only to the nation as a whole but also to the nonwhite families of America, which darkly mirror the class structure of the mother culture. Among nonwhite families in 1968, the lowest fifth got 4.8 percent of the income and the top fifth 43.6 percent; in 1947, the lowest fifth got 4.3 percent and the highest 45.7 percent. In sum, whether we look at white or dark America, in 1947 or 1968, the maldistribution remains almost constant—an economic fact regardless of race, creed, etc.

Recently, a young man at Harvard undertook a study of income distribution reaching all the way back to 1910. Although his findings may be subject to some refinement, his rough conclusions— reached after more than casual digging—tell us a bit more about the rigidities of our class structure. In 1910, he finds, the lowest tenth received 3.5 percent of the income; in 1961, it received a mere 1 percent. The bottom tenth got a smaller share of the GNP in 1961 than it did in 1910. In 1910, the top tenth received 33.9 percent of the income; in 1961, it received 30 percent. Table 3 records the economic truism that the more times change the more they remain the same.

In a recent study by Herman P. Miller and Roger A. Herriott, in which they recalculated income to include some of the factors excluded from the Commerce Department reports, they found that in 1968 the top 1.4 percent of families and individuals drew 11 percent of the nation's income, while the bottom 16 percent drew only 2 percent and the next-from-the-bottom 18 percent drew only 7 percent of the national income. In sum, a top 1.4 percent drew more than the bottom 34 percent.

This maldistribution of income is repeated in a maldistribution of wealth (ownership) which is the major cause of our economic inequities. A study by Robert Lampman points out that although there was less concentration of wealth in the period after World War II than after World War I, a creeping concentration began to set in after 1949. That year, the top 1 percent held 21 percent of the wealth. In 1956, this rose to 26 percent—by 1962, to 33.3 percent. (Data are drawn from statistics provided by the Internal Revenue Service, based

TABLE 3

PERCENTAGE OF NATIONAL PERSONAL INCOME, BEFORE TAXES,
RECEIVED BY EACH INCOME-TENTH *

	Highest Tenth	2nd	3rd	4th	5th	6th	7th	8th	9th	Lowest Tenth
1910	33.9	12.3	10.2	8.8	8.0	7.0	6.0	5.5	4.9	3.4
1960	28.0	16.0	13.0	11.0	9.0	8.0	6.0	5.0	3.0	1.0

* In terms of "recipients" for 1910–1937 and "spending units" for 1941–1959. Data for 1960–1961 were available in rounded form only. Figures for 1910 were taken from National Industrial Conference Board, *Studies in Enterprise and Social Progress* (New York: National Industrial Conference Board, 1939), p. 125; data for 1960–1961 were calculated by the Survey Research Center.

on estate tax returns that offer loopholes for the most affluent. It is therefore not unreasonable to conclude that all of these figures understate the true concentration of wealth in America.) By 1970, if this trend has continued, we were back to 1929, when the top 1 percent held 36.3 percent of the nation's wealth.

If, however, the maldistribution of income is an inequity of ancient origin, whose persistence we have noted for this whole century, why is the white worker turning restless at this particular moment? The reasons: (1) a quantitative erosion of income; (2) a qualitative erosion of living; (3) a frightening erosion of social order.

Although not living in affluence, the white worker was better off in the '60s than at any other time of this century. In the recovery years following the Great Depression of the early 1930s, he and his family were enjoying an ever-rising standard of living. In 1947, the median family income (in constant 1968 dollars) was $4,716; by 1967, it rose to $8,318, an increase of about $4,000—after allowing for inflation.

During the same period, the percentage of families making under $7,000 a year decreased and the percentage making more increased sharply—again in constant dollars. In 1947, 75 percent of the families had an income of less than $7,000, and 25 percent had an income above that figure. In 1967, on the contrary, 63 percent of the families had an income above $7,000 and only 36 percent had an income below that figure.

All this was happening, however, without any basic redistribution of income in America. Per capita income was growing because the total national income was growing at a rate faster than that of the population. There was more available for everybody.

The rise in income was reflected in a life-style based on rising expectations. You mortgaged your life for a home, because you expected to earn more in the days to come. You bought on the installment plan, everything from baby carriage to auto. You planned a future for your kids: a nice neighborhood, a good school, a savings plan to put the kids through one of the better colleges—maybe even Harvard or Vassar. You were out to "make it," no matter how hard you worked, how much you scrimped, how often you borrowed, how late you moonlighted. You had hope!

You didn't even mind paying ever-higher taxes, so long as your take-home pay was bigger. The tax was an investment in the future—a town or a country where things would be better. You would enjoy it tomorrow, and the kids would enjoy it for generations. You were future-minded.

As a result, this numerous class became the mass base of social stability in America. It was not status quo-ish in the sense that it would be happy to have its present frozen forever; it was constantly pushing for change. But it sought change within a system that it felt was yielding more and could continue to yield more. And to keep moving, this class joined unions for economic advance and voted Democratic for socio-economic legislation.

Sometime in the mid-60s, however, this social structure began to fall apart. Almost unnoticed by the media was the decline in the real income of the nonsupervisory employee. Between 1965 and 1969, the buying power of the worker was in steady decline—despite sizable wage increases. The pay envelope was being chewed up by inflation and taxation.

The year 1965 was the first of the escalated involvement in Vietnam, and this imposed a triple burden on the American worker. First, he had to pay a greater tax to help finance the war. Second, he had to pay more for consumer goods because this war, like any other, automatically increases demand without increasing supply. Third, he supplied his sons for the military; the affluent found ways to escape in schools and special occupations, the poor were often too ill or illiterate.

The year 1965 is also the mid-point of a decade in which America began to respond to poverty and discrimination. The Johnson years produced a spate of national legislation to provide income and opportunities for the poor, especially the blacks. Local governments were trying to cope with their crises. At all levels, America began to spend public money to resolve pressing problems.

The American worker supported these social measures through the unions and the Democratic party. He saw these bits and pieces of socio-economic legislation as a spur and parallel to his upward effort.

It was not apparent to this same worker that the upside-down system of taxation in the United States placed the cost of these measures on the shoulders of the huge "middle" sector—the sector neither poor nor rich enough to escape taxes. Although the federal income tax supposedly is graduated so as to make the wealthy pay at a higher rate, this expressed intent is annulled by the many loopholes for those who derive income from sources other than wages or salaries. At the local level, it is the small homeowner who pays the tariff through *ad valorem* property taxes and the small consumer who pays through the nose for city, county, and state sales taxes.

The worker feels that he is paying triple: he pays for his own way; he pays for the poor; he pays for the rich. He is ready to do the first; he resists the others.

Finally, this same worker has been squeezed by a system of private taxation, operated through monopoly pricing. Everything from electricity to eggs is manipulated in closed and increasingly enclosed markets. As buying power goes up (current dollars in income), the response of dominant sectors of the economy is not to *increase* supply but to *limit* production (or distribution) to keep the consumer on the same level while increasing profits for the seller.

To add insult to injury, the worker is advised by the media and, more recently, by the administration, that if prices are going up, it is his own fault: high wages make high prices. If he wants to buy for less, he must work for less. This logic boggles the worker who cannot understand how he can live better by earning less. Once more, he is the victim of a myth. The truth was stated in an editorial by the sober *Wall Street Journal* on August 5, 1968:

> In the past 20 years, there have been three distinct periods in which factory prices climbed substantially over a prolonged interval. In each instance, labor costs per unit of factory output were *declining* when the price climb began—and these costs continued to decline for a considerable period after the price rise was underway. In each case, corporate profits began to increase sharply well before the price climb started.

To keep up with rising prices, workers demand higher wages and salaries—through unions and as individuals. But they never catch up, for in a monopoly-oligopoly conglomerate economy, the man who can fix the prices must always end up winning the game.

The result is that millions of workers feel they are paying more and more for less and less. They are paying for a war—with their sons, their taxes, and their overcharged purchases—only to feel they are losing the war. They are paying more for what they buy—and get more cars doomed to early obsolescence, phones that ring wrong numbers, houses that are jerry-built, doctors who make no home visits. They pay more and more in local taxes—and feel they are subsidizing crime and riot.

Hard work seems to have brought nothing but hard times. After federal taxes are taken out of the pay, after local taxes are paid, and then the rest is used to buy debased goods and services at inflated prices, the worker knows—and his wife knows still better—that he is no longer moving up.

The worker in urban America, however, is the victim not only of income maldistribution but also of population maldistribution, a catastrophe whose impact he cannot stand and whose origin he does not understand. Few city dwellers even suspect that much of their urban crisis started down on the farm.

Since World War II, about a million Americans a year have moved from a rural to an urban culture. This massive shift of about twenty million people in one generation has been described as the most gigantic migration in the history of man. Such a collision of cultures has always meant crowding, crime, and conflict. In the 1960s, history repeated itself—except that the immigrant was invisible because he was an in-migrant.

What set this wave in motion? Two contradictory national policies: to increase agricultural productivity and to restrict its production. Subsidized science found ways to make four stalks grow where one grew before. Subsidies to farmers, then, reversed the process by rewarding growers for nonproduction. The result was less and less need for labor on the soil. Farm workers went jobless; small farm owners went bankrupt or were bought out. Rural Americans were driven from their familiar farms into the unfamiliar cities, from warm earth to cold concrete.

This rural-push–urban-pull has been in motion ever since the turn of the century. But what was once a drift became a flood in the 1960s. The discomfort and disorder that followed set another dynamic in motion: the urban-push–suburban-pull.

If the worker can afford it, he generally flees—to outskirts and suburbs. He does so whether he is black or white. (Between 1964 and 1969, 600,000 blacks fled the central cities for other parts of the metropolitan areas.) Those who cannot flee, stay and get ready for the fight.

A current notion holds that the central cities are black and the suburbs white, dividing metros into separate but unequal societies in geographic separation. Again this is a half-truth which, if it were totally true, might well lessen social conflict. But the truth is that many whites cannot move because they cannot afford to. Typically they are white workers of more recent stock: economically unmonied and geographically immobile. Often their neighborhoods abut black ghettos where—after the flight of the more affluent blacks—there are left, according to James Q. Wilson, "only the most deprived, the least mobile, and the most pathological."

Through the '60s, the crush became a crunch—not simply because there were more bodies in the central cities but also because there were fewer places to put them. By public action, we have torn down about twice as many housing units as we have put up. Private builders have bulldozed slums to erect luxury highrises. Hundreds of thousands of units are abandoned annually by their landlords because the rotting property is all pain and no profit. As decay sets in at the ghetto core, rats and rain and fleas and fire take over to deprive the most deprived of their turf. So these newly dispossessed become the latest in-migrants, driven from their holes into the surrounding neighborhoods, spreading panic in their path.

Under these pressures, the ethnics—white and black—move from economic frustration and personal fear to political fury. The physical stage on which this tragedy is unfolding is a tiny piece of turf. Now 70 percent of the people—our urban population—live on 1.6 percent of the total land area. The American worker—white or black—is the victim of maldistribution—of people as well as income and wealth.

In the 1970s, fury comes easily to the white worker. It's stylish. He sees it everywhere. In the form of common crime—in the subway, on the street, at his doorstop; in the form of riots in the ghettos or the campus or the prison. The present generation of workers has grown up in an age of war: World War II, Korea, Vietnam. For three decades, they have lived with mass violence, directly and vicariously.

Retribalization reawakens ancient feelings. The white worker has always had the sense of belonging to some special group. There were constant reminders of ethnicity in neighborhood names, groceries, bars, funeral parlors, holidays, papers, ward politics, gang leaders, subtle prides and prejudices. But in an America that was devoted to the mythos of the melting pot and in a period dedicated to the ethos of one world, the white worker tucked his ethnicity up his sleeve. Now, in a retribalized world, he displays his ethnicity—as a pennant to carry into battle.

The young among the white workers, like the young everywhere, add their special stridency to the clamor. They are high on expectations and low on boiling point. To a civilizational distemper, they add their hot tempers, turning ethnic salvation into a moral justification for violence.

Our white worker is ready for battle. But he does not quite know against whom to declare war.

As a child of toilers he holds the traditional view of those who labor about those who don't. He feels that those inflated prices, those high taxes, those inadequate wages are all part of a schema for fattening up the fat. While he rarely, if ever, uses the words "establishment" or "system," he instinctively assumes there's an establishment that exploits him through a devilishly devised system.

Part of the system, his experience teaches, is for the rich to use the poorest to keep the once-poor and the possibly-poor as poor as possible. For generations, employers who demanded protection against foreign imports were importing foreigners to depress wages and break strikes. Out of this arose the Know-Nothing party that threatened, within a couple of years, to become a major national movement. In the mid-nineteenth century, Irish workers (themselves recent immigrants) feared that the Emancipation Proclamation, ending chattel slavery for the blacks, would intensify wage slavery for the whites. Out of this fear rose the sadistic Draft Riot of 1863 with its lynching and burning of blacks. In the 1920s, the white worker opted for immigration legislation to stem the flow of cheap hands.

As we move into the '70s, many workers fear that the Brass is using Underclass to undermine the Working Class. They seldom use this language but often feel these sentiments. As they hear it, this is what the rich are saying: "We must fight poverty and discrimination to the last drop of *your* blood. Share *your* job; share *your* neighborhood; pay *your* taxes." These moral exhortations come from the high and mighty, economically ensconced in tax havens far from the madding crowd.

In protest against this establishment, the worker turns to strikes for higher wages and revolt against taxes. But neither remedy works. Wage gains are offset by higher prices. Lower taxes mean lower services—schools, streets, travel, sanitation, police, medical care. What looked like a direct way out turns out to be a maze.

Since our worker does not know how to deal with the system, he tries to do the next best thing: to act within the system to protect his own skin. And in our torn and turbulent cities, it is too often his "skin" that determines his mood.

This mood is generally called "backlash," a reawakening of ancient prejudice directed against blacks because they have dared to raise their heads and voices. But to explain the growing tension simply as "backlash" is once more to create a mischievous myth out of partial truth. To deny that prejudice exists is naive; to ascribe rising racial clash to a simple proliferation of prejudice, equally naive. The white worker feels economically threatened, personally imperiled, politically suckered. His anxieties make him meaner than he means to be. Racial suspicion turns into tribal war when people—no matter their color—are oppressed by their circumstances. Maldistribution of income and people must multiply strife. This strife, ironically, tends not to change but to continue the system that produced the conflict. So long as black battles white and poor battle not-so-poor, the establishment can continue to "divide and rule."

The further irony is the innocence of those on top who are, in a depersonalized way, responsible for the turmoil on the shrinking turf. The upper 1 percent rarely suspects that its incredible wealth is the prime reason the lesser people, without urging, are at one another's throats. As the wealthiest see their role, they are the great creators: investing, employing, making. They are the great givers, turning tax exempt funds to do God's work.

In short, there is no devil: those at the top merely move their money around in a depersonalized way through impersonal channels (corporations) to multiply their money so they may do man's and God's work better; those in the middle merely try to lift their real income so they and their family can live—better; those at the bottom merely want what man needs to stay alive and kicking. Yet somehow they all end up in a fight, with the top acting genteelly through finances, and the lesser people resorting intemperately to fists.

If there is a devil, he is—as he always is—invisible, ubiquitous, and working his evil will through the way of all flesh. In our case, he is the inherent imperative in a culture that has badly distributed its wealth and people: the devil still is the system.

Apathy and Other Axioms
H. W. Benson

Expelling the Union Dissenter From History

When Cesar Chavez came to organize farm workers, his cause was applauded by every labor and liberal group; when Joseph Yablonski stepped forward to lead insurgent miners and was murdered, there was mostly silence. From a few labor leaders came clumsy mutterings lest "labor" be blamed; otherwise, with only few notable exceptions, labor-oriented liberals turned away. The same embarrassed silence followed the 1965 murders of Dow Wilson and Lloyd Green, two leaders of a Painters' Union reform movement in California. All of which sadly illustrates the great paradox of the labor movement: its attitude toward democracy.

The miners' story of underground death, black-lung cancer, impoverished Appalachia, neglected pensioners has been too dramatic to be ignored; but the coaldiggers' struggle for elementary rights within their union has yet to break into the social awareness of labor-oriented intellectuals. What flaw? What failure of sensitivity makes them incapable of responding adequately to *this* labor struggle? There's a question!

"Union democracy is the single most important issue in the campaign for election of a new UMW president," Yablonski wrote to UMW President Tony Boyle late in 1969, "I challenge you to grant

---

H. W. BENSON, as a machinist and toolmaker, was active in several industrial unions. He is now editor of Union Democracy in Action, *a newsletter devoted to civil liberties in the labor movement.*

full democracy to the UMW by removing your autocratic grip on the districts." To protect themselves against all the miseries of their trade, coal miners needed the support of a powerful union; for that, they had to change the UMW officialdom; and, to do that, they needed internal democracy. Yablonski was surely murdered because he led that battle.

Nor is the ferment inside the miners' union some divagation from the norm of labor events. It is the latest evidence of widespread activity among union men who insist upon using their democratic rights to reform their unions, even when it means severe sanctions against them—sometimes danger to their lives.

Late in 1959, the publication *Union Democracy in Action,* of which I am editor, began systematically to chronicle the activities of some of those union reformers. There were reports of struggles for union democracy among

> Machinists in Chicago, St. Louis, and California;
> Painters in New York, California, District of Columbia, and Minnesota;
> Seamen in the National Maritime Union, Marine Engineers Beneficial Association, and Masters', Mates' and Pilots' Union;
> Musicians in New York and New Haven;
> Pulp and Paper workers in two AFL–CIO Internationals;
> Operating Engineers in Detroit, California, Long Island, and New Jersey;
> Building Service Employees in New York;
> United Mine Workers.

All this represents only what could be pieced together by one editor in his spare time.* Yet it is enough to indicate how widespread were the stirrings in labor unions. There were also rebel movements, which I could not report, in many Teamster locals, in Engineers' locals, in the Steelworkers, the Hotel and Restaurant Union, in Carpenters' locals. If some resources had been put behind an effort to keep track of union insurgency in the last fifteen years, such a project would undoubtedly have compiled an astonishing record.

Most writings about the labor movement have neglected this record of insurgency. Something deeper is involved than carelessness or lack of imagination. Labor unions are the principal institutions created by the industrial working class. Union democracy is more than clauses in a constitution; it signifies freedom for workers within

---

* Detailed accounts of reform movements in most of these unions and evidence for assertions made in this article were published in forty numbers of *Union Democracy in Action,* 1960–1971.

the labor movement. Can democracy be sustained by workers in their own organizations?

It is customary these days for friends of the labor movement to insist that intellectuals are overwhelmingly anti-union, even to add morosely that there is no pro-labor current in American intellectual life. Who, then, writes all those hundreds of books, monographs, and studies that are sympathetic to unions and union leaders? While some "left" literary intellectuals may be hostile to unions as they now exist, an army of labor-oriented intellectuals produces an enormous pro-union output, from Harvard, the Fund for the Republic, and some fifty labor-relations centers in the universities. When it comes to union democracy, these labor-oriented intellectuals have trouble not because they are "practitioners" but because they run up against, and do not know how to cope with, the great paradox of the American labor movement — a movement democratic in external impact and often autocratic in internal life.

In society the labor movement is the most effective single force for liberalism. It can exist only in a democracy; it utilizes all the mechanisms of democracy; it is almost always on the side of those who seek progressive social legislation. This truth is a fundamental guide to American politics. But the same labor movement that insists so ardently on democratic rights for itself and for others *in society* too often denies those same rights to its own membership. Any self-respecting union will defend your right to denounce the president of the United States. But criticize your business agent — and it's at your own risk!

Basic civil liberties are protected in unions like the United Auto Workers, the American Federation of Teachers, the Newspaper Guild, where a man can say what's on his mind without fear, organize a caucus, and run opposition candidates. These unions prove that union democracy is possible and that a strong union need not be dictatorial. But they are a minority. By and large, too many top officials of major unions treat their members in an authoritarian way.

Except in those few unions with a functioning review board, trial procedure for union dissidents is a mockery of due process. The officialdom customarily operates internally as policeman, prosecutor, judge, jury, and final appeals court, even though that stark reality may be hidden behind a constitutional curtain. The oppositionist who is convicted on disciplinary charges finds himself in the ludicrous position of appealing for recourse to the very officials he has been combating, or worse, the officials who have been fighting him. Unionists who instigate opposition, especially those who circulate handbills and hold caucus meetings, have been blacklisted, fined, suspended, expelled as disloyal. Officials in power dominate the election process and usually rule on appeals against themselves; in critical instances where there are rival slates, elections are suspect, even stolen. Access to the membership by insurgents can be blocked. The use of mailing lists was denied to oppositionists until the law made them theoretically available to all candidates; even now, practical obstacles are placed in the path of insurgents, which vitiate the law's effectiveness. The union press almost everywhere is monopolized by the administration in power and glorifies the incumbents. None of this offsets the democratizing role of labor in society. But neither does the liberalizing effect of the labor movement upon the country's politics cancel out authoritarian practices within it. The overwhelming impact of unionism is enlightening, civilizing, liberalizing—and all the other social goods; but that doesn't tell us very much about *internal* union democracy.

The paradox of labor and democracy paralyzes the labor-oriented intellectual. Anxious to shield unions from hostile criticism, he guards against providing ammunition to the enemy. That's hard enough; but in addition he knows that if he faced forthrightly the issue of internal democracy, his relations with labor leaders would be poisoned and his ability to influence the course of the labor movement through those leaders hopelessly jeopardized. And for what?

Unions surely command respect and wield influence. In comparison, rank and filers, who must fight hard just to speak up, may appear, at best, like impractical idealists if not mere cranks; their finest efforts seem feeble and futile. Why, comes the nagging question, sacrifice a chance to shape real events in cooperation with strong leaders of a real mass movement just because they bully their members a bit? Compelled to this unhappy choice, the laborite intellectual usually looks outward toward the social conflicts where events are decided rather than inward to mere squabbles over democracy. In the urgency of the moment, that seems justifiable enough. It is not a new idea.

The conception of sacrificing someone else's democracy (reluctantly, of course) to advance a worthier social cause is a familiar one. From quite a different standpoint, such a mood plagues even the American Civil Liberties Union where some spokesmen, vigorously anti-establishment, are ready to diverge from the nonpartisan civil libertarian ACLU traditions to promote their selected social-political aims. In union circles it may seem justifiable to overlook the rights of dissidents in the interests of labor power. In the ACLU a different variety of social actionist finds it permissible to undercut certain rights of the labor movement in the interests of other goals.

The ACLU experience, because it involves civil libertarians, warns that it is not easy to stick to democratic principles when you take sides in social struggles. Granted. And that explains why labor-ite intellectuals are uncomfortable with problems of internal union democracy.

It is these pro-labor intellectuals, not the hostile critics, who create the prevailing aura around the subject of union democracy; for the critic is generally not sufficiently interested in labor to bother with union democracy as such. The attitude of liberal-laborite intel-lectuals toward union democracy is shaped by their attitude toward labor unions, an attitude aptly described by Maurice Neufeld as "sophisticated tolerance." *

"Sophisticated tolerance" does not mean uncritical apologetics —a fact that often confuses labor officials who interpret the absence of adulation as a sign of latent hostility. It does imply a continuing am-bivalence, even equivocation. If there is corruption in unions, the argu-ment goes, there is far more in business—more bank employees are indicted for embezzlement than union officials. If union officials, and members, are sometimes narrow-mindedly out for what they can get, we must blame the acquisitive mores of our business society; why sanctimoniously denounce in labor what we take for granted in society?

Whatever its value in orienting us in an imperfect world, the stance of "sophisticated tolerance" is upset by the dilemma of union democracy. Here the orthodox labor defender faces an unpleasant choice:

1. If unions *ought* to be democratic, surely something should be done, or at least said, about the violation of members' rights where they occur. But in the last twenty years, laborite intellectuals have turned away from that nasty problem. On the other hand. . . .

2. If important segments of the labor movement are not demo-cratic, or need not be, how do such conceptions square with the en-lightened standards liberal intellectuals apply to most other spheres of social life? Have liberals discovered in the labor movement, of all places, one area where the normal standards of democracy do not apply? If so, their position toward the labor movement resembles the pose of totalitarian radicals who demand democracy unlimited in bourgeois society but insist that their own "socialist" states be exempt from these exacting standards.

---

* Maurice F. Neufeld, "The Historical Relationship of Liberals and Intellectuals to Organized Labor in the United States," Cornell Reprint Series, *No. 145,* from *Annals of the American Academy of Political Science,* November 1963, pp. 115–128.

In short, the problem is this: how do we handle violations of democratic principles in our own world?

With a divided soul, laborite intellectuals approach the challenge of internal union democracy. If some unions, happily, are democratic, they see evidence of labor's civilizing role. If, regrettably, other unions appear undemocratic, they caution against exaggerating such "superficial" facts when the labor movement is so profoundly progressive in other respects. In hard cases, like the murder of dissidents in the Miners' or Painters' unions, they often say nothing. Out of these clashing impulses, there follows a compendium of misgivings and notions:

¶ Union leaders, on the average, are more socially responsible and enlightened than the rank and file. If members exercised their democratic rights and had a closer measure of control over their leaders, would we be any better off? Probably worse.

¶ As a rule, workers are not concerned with the lofty issues that entrance idealists. Give them steady jobs at good wages and conditions, and they will truckle to any leadership that brings such blessings; if the officials are crooks and dictators, that may be what they want.

¶ Modern collective bargaining, a delicate art, involves complex and highly technical subjects beyond the grasp of the average unionist. Union administrators are responsible for vast sums in welfare funds and union treasuries and make decisions affecting the lives of thousands. Expertise and experience are indispensable; not every cook and bottle washer can run a union today.

¶ An incumbent administration usually enjoys such advantages in resources, talent, influence, experience, that it can usually convince the membership that insurgents are irresponsible troublemakers.

This list of ineluctable circumstances, it is suggested, constitutes a formidable barrier to union democracy and explains why it is superficial to decry its lack. These are troubles which express the disquietude of serious observers, so that it would be presumptuous to dismiss them as inconsequential. Yet these considerations, however weighty, are not unique to democracy in *unions;* they pertain to democracy in *society.* They are the lasting issues of democracy in government, bearing upon the interrelations between any electorate and their officials. These are the reservations traditionally expressed by those who distrust democracy. It is startling that labor intellectuals, who can cope with such issues when they are raised by conservatives in regard to the philosophy of government, become uncomfortable when these same issues arise in regard to unions.

All the dangers and difficulties of democracy in unions—every one—are there in national life, only on a vaster scale. The intricacies of economic life, for example, can be turned as easily against the labor movement as against the labor rank and file.

America is plagued by poverty and pollution, corruption and crime, racism and violence. The mass of voters is ill-informed, swayed by narrow interests, often manipulated by demagogues. People are ignorant of computers, incapable of comprehending atomic physics, unable to administer modern industry. Vast resources are concentrated in the hands of a few, overwhelming the many with a sense of powerlessness.

What, then, is the "answer"? There is none, if we are looking to whisk away these harsh realities. It is a matter of living and coping with them. The choice is inescapable: either (1) to overcome the weaknesses of democracy by strengthening the hand of a (hopefully) responsible authority, freed from the control of a (presumably) ignorant and irresponsible mass, or (2) to strengthen the effectiveness of democracy by lifting the level of enlightenment through free speech, free press, the right to organize—all the fundamental civil liberties available in a democracy. Faced by that choice in government, liberals and laborites unhesitatingly opt for democracy. In respect to unions, they waver.

Leaders and members share in the benefits of a strong labor movement, but not equally; for their interests are not identical; sometimes they are even sharply antagonistic. Apart from the natural tendency of any official—any person!—to get jaded, careless, and lazy with age, union officials are drawn by a powerful gravitational force away from their obligations to the workers who elect them. Employers can offer gifts, favors, joint business ventures, quick deals, and executive jobs. All of which can induce a man to neglect his constituents. Even without such outside encouragement, a not-too-scrupulous man can find ways to benefit from distributing good jobs, tapping welfare funds, and dispensing favors. These practices are not nice to mention, but they happen often enough. The only guarantee that officials will continue to serve the members at least as well as themselves is through membership control. And that control can be exercised effectively only if the fundamental rights of civil liberties are available. All this is commonplace to the point of tedium in discussions of government; it is often forgotten when union democracy comes up for analysis.

What is to be done? What conclusions flow from the various conceptions of democracy?

In 1958, before he became Secretary of Labor, Arthur Goldberg told a conference of the Fund for the Republic that "there are serious questions about the extent to which it is proper to apply the standards of political democracy to internal union affairs." Comparing unions with governments, which face war and revolution, he said, "The constraints which by common consent we accept temporarily in the political arena when such conditions exist may perhaps explain and justify the existence of similar, although permanent, restraints in the practice of union democracy." Once, while Goldberg was at a podium praising the Steelworkers' Union for its contribution to industrial democracy, Donald Rarick, an opposition leader, was at that very moment being beaten by thugs in the rear of the convention hall. Goldberg's reflections about union democracy skip over such incidents. When he became Secretary of Labor, he was supposed to enforce a federal law that provided for "political democracy" in unions. Not surprisingly, where it depended on him for enforcement, the law was a failure.

In our list of the liberal-laborite's misgivings about union democracy, one has been omitted—one that transcends all the others. It is The Apathy Axiom. Most writers seem convinced that the fundamental defect of union democracy is membership apathy.

The Apathy Axiom makes it unnecessary to dwell on the gritty details of internal repression. If the members don't care, why must we? But let's look more closely at this axiom.

There are at least fifteen million union members in the United States. Is a majority "apathetic"? In one way, probably so. Those millions would rather spend time with their families than busy themselves with union work. Their attitude here resembles that of many more millions toward affairs of state. Our nation's democracy might enter a new golden age if all plunged into politics. On the other hand, such a surge of activity might create an unprecedented crisis. How would society endure? People might be killed in the crush. Admittedly, there is no reason to expect such massive participation in government —just as there is no reason for demanding it in unions. Even with the "apathy" of the electorate, democracy survives in the country; it should be able to survive in unions. The issue is not whether the union majority is apathetic, but whether that putative apathy accounts for the low level of civil liberties in the labor movement.

Let us assume that a majority of American citizens are apathetic to the big political and social issues; can that account for the fluctuating curve of American politics?—McCarthyism succeeded by the civil rights movement; Johnson by Nixon, etc. Any explanation of the course of American society in terms of a constant like citizens' apathy would be worthless. It explains nothing because it "explains" everything. The Apathy Axiom is just such an explanation applied to the labor movement.

Now 75,000 local unions are serviced by executive board members, shop stewards, officers, delegates, committee members — the volunteer or lightly paid part-time activists. Thousands of retired workers donate their time. True, millions may be inactive ("apathetic"), but there *is* an active cadre of hundreds of thousands. That level of union participation rivals anything in the nation. Proportionately, there is probably more sustained involvement by workers in unions than by all the people in politics.

Government involves more than a multitude on one end and ruling officials on the other. In between, there are competing parties and groups; critics and crusaders; oppositions, politicians, muckrakers. Democracy fulfills its function in political life because the majority is regularly shaken out of its lethargy by the provocation of all these agitators. The fate of democracy depends upon the fate of the vociferous minorities. If not, who needs civil liberties? What's missing from most treatises on union democracy is . . . the missing link. They examine the membership; they analyze the leadership; but they ignore the gadflies, the critics. What happens to *them?*

Leave the unions for a moment and get into a neighborhood where there are, say, 100,000 eligible voters; start organizing a political reform movement to oust the dominant machine. You make phone calls, visit homes, pass out handbills, announce a rally. A dozen curiosity seekers show up. The rest remain at home, watch TV and busy themselves with affairs that you, in your newly aroused zeal, known to be trivially personal. Weeks pass, they respond to your efforts with indifference. Respond? They don't know you exist. There it is: apathy.

So far, as a political reformer you're starting out no better than most union reformers, no better, say, than Frank Schonfeld who could assemble all of a half-dozen painters at his first meetings — twenty-five at public "rallies" and one hundred at "mass" meetings to reform the Painters' Union in New York City. And he had a constituency of ten thousand.

Still, you keep at it. More meetings, petitions, handbills, candidates, forums. At a spectacularly successful event, you soar to one hundred. Things are going well; *but where's the majority?* It's that apathy again. Some voters, shaken loose, are beginning to listen; but most people still don't seem to care.

Life goes on. Things come up, like Vietnam, schools, corruption, filthy air, police, garbage, high prices, rents, slums, drugs. The ruling politicians get lazy — that's human nature — neglect their constituents, can't handle the issues. If you keep plugging away and stay with the issues, you may reach that inert majority and with a little luck, throw the other rascals out. Maybe. Maybe not. If you don't succeed at first, you can try and try. Limping and creaking, America survives as a democracy because it guarantees you, and all the other activists, the right to be heard. Sometimes no one seems interested. But that right remains available; and under propitious circumstances, startling things happen. That's how a band of students and a dissident Senator forced a President of the United States to retire.

But notice: while you were deep into that political campaign, your life went on. You and your colleagues could still work and make a living; you enjoyed or endured your family as before. Your kids went to school, played in the street. No problem.

Now let us, hypothetically, change all the rules. The night you held your first insurgent political meeting, suppose a lurking character jotted down the names of those who came and you got a threatening phone call. The next day, four tough-looking guys in a black Cadillac drove up to the playground and stared menacingly at your kids. And you – you were beaten on the head with a lead pipe, and fired from your job to be turned down mysteriously wherever you applied for another, arrested on trumped-up charges and fined, your home and printshop bombed. And suppose when you tried to run for office, you were barred from the ballot, or the votes were stolen, and all this was the experience first of one and then another. The whole neighborhood would soon know about it and your friends might lapse into, say, apathy. You might get a little apathetic yourself.

Imagine, now, that the written record of all these events is lost, assuming there was any record to begin with. An eminent foundation assigns a scholarly political scientist to survey your neighborhood. When his monograph appears, complete with charts and footnotes, it reports the fundamental problem is that the local citizens are apathetic and apparently nothing can be done about it.

Absurd? Yet that absurdity is usually the basis of labor "history" when it comes to recording the story of union democracy.

Can it really be true? The black Cadillac, the lead pipe, the firings, blacklistings, fines, trials, expulsions, phony elections? How often do things like that happen in the labor movement? Often enough, I believe, to implant "apathy." This conclusion follows from what I have learned in ten years of publishing *Union Democracy in Action,* based upon correspondence and conversations with union reformers in many states and upon a study of documents in their cases.

Teamsters tell stories about those cruising black Cadillacs; Jim Morrisey had his skull fractured and was almost killed by a lead pipe outside the NMU hall. Painters, seamen, miners, steelworkers, machinists, operating engineers have all made complaints of serious election malpractices, backed by substantial evidence; in the International Union of Electrical Workers (IUE), the election for International president was crudely stolen; and it required a federal judge to enable Paul Jennings to replace James Carey. Reformers in IAM Lodge 113, Frank Schonfeld and his friends in District Council 9 (Painters), Operating Engineers in New York, New Jersey, and California, Hubert Albertz in the Building Service Employees Union were all blacklisted for insurgent activity. Job discrimination against reformers was so blatant in Local 138, Operating Engineers in Long Island, that for a time the NLRB took over control of the union's hiring hall.

Yet normally intelligent commentators can write about an important union, the Teamsters for example, and not face up to the tragic reality that in some locals a man organizing against the officialdom risks being shot. That single fact reveals more about the state of union democracy than a whole library of Harvard productions.

If you destroy the right of a dissident minority to organize against the regime, the majority can easily be manipulated. What appears as "apathy" in many unions is not the *cause* but often the *result* of a disintegration of democracy, the end product of the suppression of the dissenting spirit that is an essential ingredient of democracy.

The Apathy Axiom passes over the intricate relationship between officials, masses, and dissident oppositions; it ignores the ordeal of the reformer and writes his effort out of history. How do we account for its popularity? For one thing, there is ignorance. A nuclear physicist can win the Nobel prize without ever knowing about work in an African uranium mine. Philip Taft can write the standard work on union government without knowing about men who are blacklisted or receive death threats; they'd never dream of telling him!

Above all, however, the prevailing idea of apathy serves, in labor relations, the same function that the notion of the innate inferiority of black slaves once served in race relations. Civilized men might ponder whether slavery was morally sanctified and disagree like gentlemen. If, however, it was commonly agreed that blacks were indeed inferior, there was no need to do anything drastic. The Apathy Axiom permits that kind of irresponsibility toward insurgents in the labor movement.

Democracy is kept alive by minorities, dissidents and reformers who disapprove, call for changes, and sometimes try to upset a ruling regime. Critics and crusaders were once supplied by the radical groups within the labor movement: Socialists, Communists, Wobblies, assorted progressives. The virtual disappearance of such tendencies from unions is one of the big facts of labor history, noted but not adequately assessed. Dissidence has not disappeared, but its character has been altered. The union insurgent of our day belongs to no radical tendency and is acclaimed in no party press. Yesterday's oppositionist was often part of a larger movement and was sustained by it; today's dissenter is a *lonely* union reformer, unknown and neglected.

In twenty-five years there has been a sharp shift in the intellectuals' attitude toward the labor movement, a change that leaves no room for the dissenter. In the mid-1920s and early '30s, intellectuals identified themselves, as radicals, with the labor movement, wrote with feeling about it, and even joined it. Their association was not with the labor movement as it was, but with what they felt it would become.

The actual labor movement, not the one they anticipated, mocked their dream. The AFL was in wretched shape; factory workers were not organized; the United Mine Workers had come under control of the Lewis machine which wiped out the union's democracy; racketeers swarmed all over. Only a small percentage of the industrial working class was in unions; the masses were outside.

In November 1930, A. J. Muste excoriated the 50th AFL convention for its "tie-up with Hoover, the Republican party, and big business," for failing to organize, and for opposing unemployment insurance. Nevertheless, as leader of the Conference for Progressive Labor Action and editor of its *Labor Age,* Muste considered himself part of the labor movement and had dedicated himself to organizing a progressive wing within it. In that same issue of *Labor Age,* Louis Stanley wrote, "The 'golden' convention of the American Federation of Labor showed that the AFL was reposing securely in the house of American capitalism, happy that it had become a welcome guest. Whether it can be aroused from its contentment depends upon the action of labor progressives."

These harsh words from forty years ago seem very much like the strictures of contemporary radicals who write unions off as contented and corrupt. But those words meant something else in 1930, when labor progressives were confident that a resurgent labor movement would change the world.

Their hopes seemed near fulfillment when the CIO battered down the country's mightiest corporations and helped shift the balance of political power in the United States. While these events captured the imagination of writers, the radical groups dispatched their youth into factories.

In those days union insurgency was inseparable from the broader movement on the outside. The individual radical might be working by himself in some grimy factory; but he was warmed by an inner glow. If he was alone like a moon walker, he felt that the team back home was monitoring his efforts. And often it was.

That was my own experience in the two years during World War II when I worked as a machinist in the Detroit plant of the U.S. Rubber Company. A series of unauthorized strikes by tire builders over piecework rate cuts led to a jurisdictional battle between the United Rubber Workers–CIO and the Mechanics' Educational Society of America–Independent. After the plant was shut down by an MESA-called strike and taken over by the Navy, these events became front-page news in Detroit. One daily newspaper reported the existence in the plant of a "small" group of seventy-five Socialists, which presumably was a factor instigating the crisis. Actually there were three of us. There was me; there was one deeply religious young worker who had just joined out of strong moral convictions only lightly tinged with politics; and there was one probable part-time FBI agent. (It took me a long time to admit that to myself. He was really a great guy, a former militant coal miner who must have gone to the FBI after consulting his conscience and his church. Not to mention a nagging wife.)

We had nothing to do with initiating the strikes; we worked in the toolroom while the battles raged in production. But our modest presence was blown up into a big thing because we were part of an active national movement. In all Detroit there were maybe fifty of us at our best; but we got attention. Nationally, we had friends in the research and educational departments of a few unions. The experience of union insurgents was part of the political experience of a generation of radicals.

In those days, radical intellectuals and radical workers were bound in a fraternity nowhere dreamed of in contemporary talk about a new "alliance." They shared more than common ideals; they often shared membership in the same party or group. Often the student-intellectual became a worker; sometimes the faculty member became a labor leader. Walter Reuther, who combined in his own person the qualities of worker and intellectual, assembled others like himself in the Reuther caucus.

They were all engaged fervently in the labor movement, or around it, in its struggles for recognition, in its internal politics. The union insurgent was spurred on, his self-confidence bolstered by the writers and thinkers who ranked his activities high on their scale of values. The last serious work composed in this spirit was the *UAW and*

Walter Reuther, by Irving Howe and B. J. Widick, which told about union democracy, convincingly, with sympathy. But that was 1949; it was the end of the line.

Around 1950, intellectuals and union dissidents went rocketing off in opposite directions. Intellectuals were becoming "disenchanted" with the labor movement while the old breed of radical rank-and-file insurgent was becoming extinct, to be replaced by a new species of dissenter, not a political radical and not as sophisticated but just as militant, maybe more so.

It is impossible to maintain the posture of friendly critic within the labor movement unless there is some expectation that criticism can affect the course of events; and that expectation was fast disappearing. Some laborite intellectuals remained in unions as part of the full-time staff; others drifted off into the universities; most came to accept the labor movement as it was. They now saw inherent limitations rather than shortcomings. And so, laborite intellectuals made peace with the labor movement, reconciled themselves to its limitations, and stopped nagging for reforms. In that mood of disenchantment, there is often such a resemblance between friends of unions and critics that their positions can seem indistinguishable at a fast glance. The critic writes off the labor movement because, he insists, it has betrayed its original promise; the friend replies, wistfully, that it was self-deluding ever to have expected more.

For intellectuals still in unions, the labor movement became an institution to be served; for those in universities, a subject for sympathetic study. Labor literature proliferated just when intellectuals were losing interest in workers. Meanwhile, the link between radical groups and unions became increasingly tenuous and finally disintegrated.

By the mid-'50s, there were signs that a new kind of rank-and-file insurgent was beginning to speak out. Inside the labor movement and all through the country there came mounting demands that unions become more democratic and honest. Even before the AFL and CIO merged, labor reform was in the air. After public hearings by government investigators on New York waterfront crime and terror, the AFL expelled the International Longshoremen's Association on corruption charges by near-unanimous vote.

When the grim tale of thievery and personal enrichment by officials of some big unions was spread on the public record and played before TV audiences, together with accounts of stolen elections, arbitrary trusteeships, manipulation of much money and many men—after two years and twenty thousand pages of testimony— George Meany admitted he was astonished at the extent of corruption and vowed to act against it. He admonished the rank and file to do its duty and keep their unions clean. Robert Kennedy urged unionists to come forward with evidence. When the AFL and CIO merged, the new federation adopted unprecedented constitutional provisions authorizing disciplinary measures against corrupt affiliates and implemented the new policy by Ethical Practices codes. The Teamsters' Union was expelled, as were other unions. A hundred flowers of democracy were to bloom in the gardens of labor. Who could know that in a few years, brush, brambles, and vines would take over?

The new insurgents were not motivated by ideologies. They wanted their rights; they sought to get rid of crooks; they protested favoritism and demanded fair hiring; they didn't like backdoor deals and sweetheart agreements; they wanted impartial grievance procedure; they expected fair trials.

The reappearance of union dissidence went unmarked by labor writers; it didn't fit old patterns, and there was no longer any interest. If the big hopes had evaporated, who could bother with small ones? If labor was not likely soon to lead the way to a new society, who could be impressed by quarreling little groups squawking over humdrum details?

Most of the new reformers were not radicals. Even those who had been radicals were now taking a new tack. In 1958, leaders of a reform caucus in the IAM Tool and Diemakers Lodge 113, Chicago, joined the Socialist party for a time, but their new affiliation did not dominate their union activity. Paul Jacobs, even while writing a sympathetic account of their battle against Machinists' President A. J. Hayes, missed its significance as an example of a new trend. Jacobs, it should be remembered, was staff director of the Trade Union Project of the Fund for the Republic when his piece appeared in the *Reporter*.

"Ciepley and Rappaport [two expelled reform leaders] are both members of the Socialist party," he wrote; "two of a disappearing breed — the self-educated, skilled, radical worker who, with their insistent cries for industrial justice, were once the leavening agents of the labor movement."

Jacobs noted, nostalgically, only a momentary flash of the good old days, though actually here was something new. Ciepley, for example, had never been touched, even slightly, by radical politics, and joined the SP only while he was active in the reform union battle; when the fight was lost, he left the SP and the labor movement. The IAM reformers said nothing about industrial justice, or any broad social program. They stuck to the issues of democracy and corruption. It was not the rearguard action of an old war but the sign of a new awareness.

As organized radicalism lost contact with the shops and as writers became indifferent, the link of collaboration between union dissenter and intellectual was broken. But dissent has not disappeared from the labor movement, it has only lost its publicists.

In 1952, Peter Batalias helped form a reform caucus in Operating Engineers' Local 138, Long Island. In the years that followed, like others in his group, he was beaten, expelled, blacklisted, and given a dreary run-around in government and in the labor movement. In 1958, the McClellan Committee reported on that local: "The testimony revealed a pattern of continuing intimidation of union members and their subjugation through violence and undemocratic procedures. Members who dared to speak out were faced with expulsion from the union and loss of their jobs."

Local 138 officers were convicted of extortion and sent to prison but continued to dominate the local. In 1959, Batalias testified before the House Labor Committee only to be badgered by liberal congressmen, especially James Roosevelt, who were eager to discredit him. As he left, demoralized, he told the committee:

> I have been a labor man all my life. I have had it up to here. . . . I don't think it is worthwhile for one man to devote too much of his life to correct a situation. I believe it is more important that others get involved. I am completely fed up. When you can no longer seek integrity in the house of labor, you can't get results in Government, I believe that the whole cause is worthless. . . . My first impulse is to go back to New York and try to save what personal belongings I still have.

In 1967, after fifteen years of reform struggle in that same Local 138, William Wilkens wrote to prominent congressmen reminding them of their obligations to the men who had testified on conditions in the local:

> Letters to the esteemed Senator Robert Kennedy fall on deaf ears. At the Senate rackets hearing of 1958, he denounces DeK. [one convicted official]. When running for office of Senator, he comes to Long Island and praises him. My heart is broken when I have meetings of the Reform Group of Local 138.

The experience in Local 138 is typical; the union insurgent now is a lonely reformer. There are union reformers, many of them. Reform groups and individuals, seeded through the labor movement, acting in isolation, cut off from any unifying center, political or intellectual. It helps to know that someone cares; today, mostly, that concern is missing.

In 1935–1937, when insurgents fought on the East Coast against the corrupted officialdom of the International Seamen's Union, their ordeal was chronicled in the radical press and recorded in books. A citizens' committee, set up by Walter Gellhorn and Sterling Spero, held hearings attended by 380 seamen where charges against the officials were aired in public. But for James Morrisey there was no citizens' committee when he was almost killed outside the NMU hall during his campaign against Joe Curran.

If you are fired for organizing a union, you can, naturally, get help in the labor movement; if your civil liberties are violated outside the union, you can count on the American Civil Liberties Union; if you'd like to change the basic character of the social order, one or another party offers a membership card; if you want to fight for civil rights or black separatism, to resist cops, make and plant bombs, skip bail, evade, oppose, or even support the draft, there is always expert advice and practical aid available. But if modestly, even humbly, you try to establish democracy in your union and are whacked over the head, there is a void. You can't even get much help from a civil liberties organization. In 1958, the American Civil Liberties Union adopted an excellent position paper that was never seriously implemented. The ACLU is broadening its concept of civil liberties to take in almost every sphere of human activity (including oceanic oil spills), without ever doing much about union democracy.

So far this must sound rather gloomy, and it is. But some civil libertarians have a capacity for responding to dissenters in trouble. Perhaps a wisp of change is already in the air. There was the murder of Joseph Yablonski, hard to shrug off.

Like raggle-taggle rebels, the coal miners fighting for workers' democracy have never been acknowledged inside the labor movement; but they have broken through the blackout that conceals other union reformers. Joseph Rauh, who became Yablonski's lawyer, is a former ADA chairman, a rapier-sharp attorney with skills finely honed to deal with bureaucrats. When most commentators were skirting the implications of the murder, reporters asked Rauh if he thought the crime was related to the internal union fight. His reply: "Of course."

Ken Hechler, West Virginia congressman, stepped forward as an outspoken defender of the Yablonski movement, even though he earned the hostility of UMW officials in his state. West Virginia doctors, outraged by the indifference of union and government officials to spreading black lung, helped form the Black Lung Association. The Association of Disabled Miners and Widows, founded in 1966, won a federal suit against the UMW on charges that it had mishandled welfare funds. After Yablonski's death, his sons Joseph and Kenneth, both lawyers, went to work for the Miners for Democracy and, with Rauh, prodded the U.S. Labor Department into challenging the UMW election. In Washington, D.C., Thomas Bethell publishes *Appalachia Information and Coal Patrol,* a nonprofit news service on miners' affairs, with sympathies for the insurgents. In January 1971, a group of Charleston, West Virginia, lawyers set up the Coal Miners' Legal Fund to defend miners in conflict with the companies or the union. James Wechsler, in the *New York Post,* suggested the formation of a broad citizens' committee on mine union democracy; but that got nowhere. A man can't get too far ahead of his times.

This is the "cabal" that UMW President Anthony Boyle complains against, an informal collaboration of rank-and-file miners, political leaders, doctors, lawyers, and liberals, which has kept alive the movement for democracy in the United Mine Workers of America, the kind of collaboration that has been lacking elsewhere in the labor movement. (So far, not one labor leader is among them!) The Miners for Democracy are the first of the new labor insurgents to send shock waves of conscience rippling through the world of liberalism. Is it a passing flash or the first sign of changing times?

Liberal Intelligentsia and White Backlash
Richard F. Hamilton

In the world view of liberal intellectuals, those persons who share decent and humane values form a tiny minority standing on the edge of an abyss. They are always standing there, the problem being that there are so few people who share those values and so many potentially powerful and, if aroused, dangerous groups in the society. The best one can hope for is that the threatening groups not be aroused.

The American liberal finds himself in a difficult world; he is sincere, concerned about the pressing problems in the society, willing to see changes made, but he also is trapped by the inexorable dictates of the situation. If these hostile groups were to be aroused (at one time the dangerous lower middle class was the problem, now there is also the dangerous white working class), the liberal minority would be unable to stem the reaction that would follow.

Are the liberals really as threatened as they imagine? Is it true, as John W. Gardner says, that:

> The collision between dissenters and lower middle class opponents
> is exceedingly dangerous. . . . As long as the dissenters are confront-
> ing the top layers of the power structure, they are dealing with people

RICHARD F. HAMILTON teaches sociology at McGill University. He has written on the French working class and on West Germany, and is at work on two books on aspects of the American scene — Class and Politics in the United States *and* Restraining Myths.

who are reasonably secure, often willing to compromise, able to
yield ground without anxiety. [But] when the dissenters collide with
the lower middle class, they confront an unsure opponent, quick to
anger, and not prepared to yield an inch.

Is it true, as Adam Walinsky puts it, that "there are now only
two identifiable ethnic groups—blacks and those who hate them. . . ."?

The white workers, so goes the sedulously repeated lesson,
compete with blacks for jobs and hence are hostile to any moves that
would tend to favor the latter. And a second major source of "strain"
for the white workers appears when blacks move into "their" neighborhoods, the housing areas immediately adjacent to the ghettos. White
working-class communities are broken up, property values suffer,
hard-earned equities disappear or are seriously diminished, problems
develop in the schools, and intense racial hostilities result. Clear,
tangible evidence of this reaction appeared in support for George
Wallace provided by the white working class.

Again one may ask the question, is this true?

In 1963, the National Opinion Research Center (NORC)
asked a representative sample of the American population a question
touching directly on what is presumed to be the central area of the
black-white struggle, the matter of jobs. In all that follows, the attitudes of the white working class and middle class will be contrasted
(or, for the sake of stylistic variation, the white manuals and nonmanuals, the blue-collar and white-collar workers). Since the pattern
differs in the South, we will consider first that three-quarters of the
white population living outside the South and the border states, those
who live in the North, Midwest, and the Western states.

The job question reads as follows: "Do you think Negroes
should have as good a chance as white people to get any kind of job,
or do you think white people should have the first chance at any kind
of job?" Given the impressive agreement in liberal circles on the virtue
of the educated and responsible middle class, it is not surprising to
learn that 91 percent of the white-collar group favor equal treatment. It
may well come as a surprise, however, to learn that approximately the
same percentage, 87 to be exact, of the blue-collar group also say
Negroes should have an equal chance.

One might conclude that this was 1963, before the black revolution took on such aggressive form, before there were any serious
demands made on the available supply of jobs, that is, before the white
working-class *reaction* had occurred. In April 1968, the same organization asked a somewhat different job question, this one reading:
"How do you feel about fair employment laws—that is, laws that make

white people hire qualified Negroes, so that Negroes can get any job they are qualified for – do you favor or oppose such laws?" The non-Southern middle-class whites again indicate a commendable level of liberal virtue, 88 percent favoring such laws. Once again, despite the fervid assertions, the equivalent blue-collar group also shows that same high level of virtuous sentiment, in this case the figure being 89 percent.

What about housing? This is an area in which, once again, there is fierce anti-black and necessarily anti-equalitarian sentiment present; or at least so it is said. In 1963, NORC asked the following question: "If a Negro with the same income and education as you moved into your block, would it make any difference to you?" The percentages of blue-collar and white-collar respondents saying "no difference" were 72 and 71 respectively. Once again, the image of the liberals as a beleaguered minority is not supported; and, once again, the assumptions that liberal virtue resides in the middle class and that intolerance is disproportionately found in the working class are not supported.

It might be, to repeat the previously mentioned objection, that the finding is "pre-backlash." But when the same question was asked in April 1968, the result did not indicate a "backlash" or "reaction" at all; it showed rather an increase in tolerant sentiment in both groups, the respective figures then being 83 and 88 percent.

One might haggle over the wording of the question and object that the "same income and education" phrase might obscure the "real" distribution of opinion. A question asked by the University of Michigan Survey Research Center in its 1964 election study does not contain that kind of clause; it asks: "Which of these statements would you agree with? White people have a right to keep Negroes out of their neighborhoods if they want to. Or, Negroes have a right to live wherever they can afford to, just like white people." The percentages favoring open housing were 72 among the blue-collar workers and 80 in the white-collar ranks. The same question, when asked four years later during the 1968 election campaign, found 84 percent of the manuals and 84 percent of the nonmanuals favoring the open-housing option. There was, it will be noted, no reaction in the course of the intervening four years, with the long-term trend of recent years toward ever higher levels of tolerance continuing unabated.

When asked about school integration a similar result appeared. The 1963 NORC question read as follows: "Do you think white students and Negro students should go to the same schools, or to separate schools?" Of non-Southern manual workers 79 percent and of the nonmanuals 81 percent said they should go to the same schools. The same question was asked in April 1968, the percentages being 80 and

89 for manuals and nonmanuals respectively. Again, the evidence provides no indication of a reaction.*

Not all the evidence is as positive as these results. A 1968 statement read: "White people have a right to keep Negroes out of their neighborhoods if they want to, and Negroes should respect that right." In this case somewhat lower percentages disagreed, that is, took the tolerant position, the figures being 45 and 63 percent for manuals and nonmanuals respectively. This result comes from the same study that asked about the Negro with the same education and income moving in. The discrepancy between the two results may mean that some whites, particularly those in the manual ranks, subscribe to an equality position and to a "neighborhood autonomy" position at the same time. Even in this case, were the nervous liberal once again to feel beleagured, it should be noted that there are still some 45 percent of the blue-collar workers who are with him on this matter. There is no warrant for seeing the wall of opposition suggested by Walinsky's remark.

When questions were asked about closer contacts, the amount of approval fell off sharply from the high levels indicated in the questions about job equality, housing, and equal schooling. Asked about objections to one's teen-age child dating a black boy or girl, the percentages with "no objections" fell to 6 and 13.

To summarize the evidence briefly: among non-Southern whites there is immense support for equality with respect to jobs, housing, and educational opportunities. In both these areas, contrary to widespread alarm, there is very little difference between manuals and nonmanuals in their stated positions. When it is a question of closer contacts, much less equalitarian sentiment is indicated, and in these cases there are some larger differences between manuals and non-manuals.

The responses among Southern whites are quite different, as may well be expected. The overall levels of tolerance are considerably lower, and there are also rather consistent and fair-sized differences between

---

* People who find such responses difficult to believe, perhaps because they are some-how attached to the idea that manual workers must be a repository of bias, will some-times ask the question: How do you know that they are *really* expressing their genuine feelings when they respond in the polls? Aren't they perhaps giving what they think are the proper or expected answers, while in their actual conduct they go by different, less attractive values? There is of course no way of discounting this possibility entirely — with regard to blue-collar workers who are polled, or with regard to *anyone else*. But my own assumption would be that such a response bias is more likely to occur among middle-class respondents, who are much more involved with current views preaching or assuming tolerance, than among blue-collar workers, whose milieu might be more amenable to a frank expression of intolerant attitudes.

manuals and nonmanuals. It is in the South that one finds a relatively intolerant working class. The respective percentages approving of a Negro moving into their neighborhood were 55 and 63. The percentages favoring integrated schools were 35 and 64. But, even in the South, there are some striking exceptions. Taking the April 1968 question on equal job opportunities, the percentages of manuals and nonmanuals taking the tolerant position were 79 and 77.

The focus on the "competition for jobs" appears, therefore, to be misleading. This study indicates that four-fifths of the Southern white workers hold an equalitarian position on that question. A majority of the white workers also take an equalitarian position on the housing question. The situation is less favorable with respect to school integration, but even here one-third of the white workers take the tolerant position.

These attitudes also vary considerably within the South, the lowest tolerance appearing in the Goldwater or Wallace states and the highest in the border states. Even these attitudes are not constant, for in recent years they have shown the same tolerant trend found elsewhere in the nation. The percentages favoring integrated schools in 1963, for example (as compared with the 1968 figures cited in the previous paragraph), were only 21 and 49.

If one did not make the regional separation but simply presented the overall figures for manuals and nonmanuals in the entire nation, the result would obscure the fact that the class differences do *not* appear in the non-Southern states. The conventional presentation, in other words, lends credence to the notion of working-class intolerance by averaging diverse regional patterns.

Against this survey evidence, to be sure, one has the evidence of the elections, both the 1964 and the 1968 presidential elections having involved attempts to stimulate a backlash. Such evidence, involving as it does a kind of behavior (as opposed to the mere expression of opinions to pollsters), is of a much "harder"ʾ character. And, as is well known, in both elections the white working class is supposed to have indicated its preference for those proffering backlash appeals. Theodore White, for example, tells us that the "disturbance of spirit" felt by white workingmen in 1964 was "absorbed in the Goldwater vote."

Once again we may ask, is that true? The University of Michigan's Survey Research Center's 1964 election study shows only 20 percent of the non-Southern white workers supporting Goldwater in that election, a level of Republican sentiment well *below* normal levels. Rather than absorbing the "disturbed spirits," the Goldwater candidacy repelled hundreds of thousands of them. Among relatively low-income middle-class groups, approximately a third favored Goldwater. Among the high-income middle-class group, which for short we may call the upper-middle class, approximately half favored his candidacy. In the case of the upper-middle-class white Protestants, the level of Goldwater support ran to 70 percent. And it would be a mistake to write these voters off as untutored *arrivistes,* since 22 percent of that group had at least some college education and another 42 percent had finished college or gone on for a higher degree.

Speaking of that other remarkable event of the 1964 campaign, the appearance of George Wallace on the national scene, Theodore White observes:

> ... Wallace astounded political observers not so much by the percentage of votes he could draw for simple bigotry ... as by the groups from whom he drew his votes. For he demonstrated pragmatically and for the first time the fear that white working-class Americans have of Negroes. In Wisconsin he scored heavily in the predominantly Italian, Polish and Serb working-class neighborhoods of Milwaukee's south side. . . .

That is all true enough, Wallace did score heavily to take approximately one-third of the votes there. The only point omitted in White's account is that Wallace drew almost twice as high a percentage in the elegant north-side suburbs. Outside of the ghetto, his vote in that primary was *lowest* in white working-class neighborhoods. In general, the richer the suburb the higher the Wallace percentage. In Dane County, which contains the state capital, the most elegant suburb, Maple Bluff, also had the more elegant level of Wallace support. It seems likely that much of this Wallace vote came from those out to punish the Democratic "favorite son," a governor who had brought in a sales tax. Such misrepresentation of the sources of Wallace's 1964 strength is quite widespread. The political sociologist Seymour Martin Lipset, for example, writing in *Encounter* later that year, claimed that Wallace "received his highest vote in the predominantly Catholic working-class areas of Milwaukee. . . ." One fact that has been completely overlooked amidst the talk of a *growing* reaction is that Wallace's vote in the South Side of Milwaukee was considerably lower both in percentage and in absolute numbers in the 1968 presidential election than in the 1964 presidential primary.

All this, however, is mere play as against the most telling demonstration of the "working-class racism" thesis: the vote for Wallace in the 1968 election. Again, taking the words of the eminent commentator Theodore White, we learn that

> No less than 4.1 million [of Wallace's 9.9 million votes]
> came from the Northern and Western states; and these were, over-
> whelmingly, white workingman votes. . . . Despite all the influences
> of the media, all the pressure of their labor leaders, all the blunders
> and incompetence of the Wallace campaign, they had voted racist.

Again, is it true? Did *they* vote racist?

According to most political surveyors, the best available studies of the American electorate are those undertaken by the Survey Research Center of the University of Michigan. Taking their study of the 1968 election and examining the non-Southern white respondents and their political preferences, one finds that Theodore White's claim is not supported. Of the non-Southern blue-collar workers, 9 percent voted for Wallace as against 8 percent of the equivalent white-collar workers. The manual–non-manual difference in Wallace support is a matter of *one* percentage point.

In assessing this "difference" it is worth remembering that as a result of migration the non-Southern manual ranks contain a somewhat larger percentage of white ex-Southerners than do the non-manuals. And one should also bear in mind that the non-Southern middle-class ranks gain a special edge in "liberalism" as a result of the disproportionate number of Jews present there. Without these two special contributions, it seems likely that even this one-percent difference would disappear.

In the South, by comparison, the traditional hypothesis is supported. A sizable minority of the white workers, some 39 percent, favored Wallace, as did approximately one-third of the lower-income middle class. Only one-eighth of the Southern white upper middle class favored Wallace, most of them preferring Nixon.

A discussion of the 1968 election by Seymour Martin Lipset and Earl Raab, based on Gallup data, shows results that are very similar to those of the Survey Research Center study. Here the difference between the manual and nonmanual vote for Wallace was a matter of four percentage points within the non-South populations. In the South the difference was again considerably greater. These authors also added the percentage of those who "considered Wallace" in the course of the campaign and, looking at the "Total Wallace Sympathizers," came up with a larger difference, one of twelve percentage points. Whether "considering Wallace" derived from *sympathy* for him or from the absence of a more attractive alternative is not indicated in Lipset's presentation. The frustration of the voters in that election is indicated by one poll result which showed that 43 percent of the electorate were not satisfied with any of the three candidates who had presented themselves. In any event, a majority of the manual workers who "considered" Wallace eventually rejected him so as to yield the 4 percent difference.

There is a striking congruence between these voting results and the attitudinal evidence discussed above. Outside the South, there were no class differences on those issues which were presumably of key concern, manuals and nonmanuals alike showing very high tolerant–equalitarian percentages. The voting evidence shows much the same pattern, a very limited attraction to the Wallace appeals and essentially the same level of such interest indicated by both groups. The Wallace appeal, incidentally, was exactly the same in both the lower-middle and upper-middle-class segments.

One might add further details to this picture of the Southern Wallace vote. It was a vote centered in smaller communities and middle-sized cities. In those locations he took approximately two-fifths of the total as against less than one-fifth in the larger cities. Intolerance in the responses to the attitude questions is also concentrated in the same communities. Why do the smaller Southern communities have the outlook they do? It might be owing to the influence of fundamentalist Protestant sects preaching the inferiority of the sons of Ham. It might be owing to competition for jobs, although rural blacks are in general located in different areas from the majority of rural and small-town whites, the former being found disproportionately in low-land plantation areas and the latter in the uplands and hill country.

Another question deserving some attention is stimulated by this discrepancy between the evidence presented here and the productions of liberal intellectuals. One might sum it up with a modification of a current slogan: they are "telling it like it isn't." How come?

There are a number of reasons. Most of the Gallup presentations during the 1968 presidential campaign made no separation by region, thereby averaging in two divergent patterns. The Southern pattern would come through in the nationwide figure and suggest general, across-the-board confirmation for the "working-class authoritarianism" thesis.

Another tendency involves the magnification of small percentage differences. The Gallup results throughout the campaign showed the manual workers to be only a few percentage points ahead of the nonmanual categories in their level of Wallace support. The relationships indicated in the monthly polls were somewhat erratic, and in some cases the manual percentage even fell below that of some of the nonmanual groups. Despite this, the formulations tended to be categorical; it was the "racist workers" and the virtuous (or "moderate") middle class. Where some conception of *relative* magnitudes was indicated the tendency still was to magnify the differences—as, for example, in Theodore White's use of the adjective "overwhelming."

Some data presentations make use of attitude scales. In such cases a range of questions would be used, some having high, some middling, and some low tolerance response levels. They would then be combined so that the result would, typically, be single-scale scores rather than a number of percentages for each of the separate questions. This allows some methodological gains and a considerable degree of economy in the presentation of findings. In the case of the NORC studies reported here, it would mean combining the questions on jobs, housing, and schooling (which showed either small or no class differences) with the questions on more intimate contacts (which did show such differences). The overall result, mixing as it does two diverse orientations, would hide the lack of difference in those areas of greatest public concern. In this case the conventional wisdom would gain some support even if there were a separate presentation by region.

Some presentations have shown tolerance and intolerance by educational level (presumably a surrogate for or close equivalent to occupation). These presentations characteristically show a very strong relationship and one is invited to translate the result back to the "obvious" implications for the poorly educated and the well-educated occupational groups. But education is a poor surrogate for occupation, for the simple reason that education is very strongly related to age. And what is showing up in this education-tolerance relationship seems to be that older people are less tolerant than younger people. Put somewhat differently, this means that older, small-town, or rural (and poorly educated) Southern women are less tolerant than young, urban, non-Southern (and college-educated) men. Put still another way, this means that there are a lot of other factors operating besides education to yield those handsome distributions.

The evidence presented here is not entirely new. Similar results have appeared from time to time, but because they do not support dominant preconceptions, they have generally been ignored. Some ten years ago Charles Herbert Stember reviewed a large number of national studies in his book *Education and Attitude Change* (published by the Institute of Human Relations Press, New York, 1961). He found that many of the conventional judgments were unfounded or at least not as clearly and unambiguously supported as some have thought. His summary conclusion reads: "Socioeconomic status has no uniform effect of its own on attitudes toward the rights of Negroes." Regrettably, his work has not gained the attention it deserves, and one result is that the conventional wisdom persists. One study that presented evidence challenging the conventional wisdom was treated as follows by two sociologists: "There is just too much independent evidence that prejudice toward Negroes is inversely associated with current occupational status for us to contemplate seriously the possibility that the zero order associations revealed by this data are substantively correct." The "independent evidence" they then cite consists of three community studies and one very erratic sample of veterans. All of those studies, incidentally, involve very small percentage differences.

Intellectuals of a literary persuasion are compulsively hostile to systematic data presentations, preferring instead their own "free" and uninhibited associations stimulated by the *New York Times* accounts of the day's events. A few thousand construction workers, following a scenario very similar to that of the motion picture *Z,* attack peace demonstrators on Wall Street, and for these intellectuals those few thousand become the "typical" blue-collar workers. The available evidence does not support that interpretation. Yet demonstrations against open-housing marchers (once again in the notorious South Side of Milwaukee) are presented as further proof of the sentiments of the entire population in that area. Lost from view was a small survey of the area's population, which indicated that 70 percent of it favored open housing.

It is correct that most incidents of black-white conflict occur in white working-class neighborhoods on the edge of the ghettos. But then, one might ask, where else could they occur? In order to have conflict one must have contact. For there to be conflict between upper-middle-class whites and blacks, one or the other of them would have to go on a long march or take a long bus ride. Where that has happened—as, for example, when open-housing marchers went to two upper-middle-class suburbs in Milwaukee—the receptions were similar to the marches to the South Side working-class areas. The location of the conflict, in most cases, is determined by urban social geography. It is a serious question, however, as to whether the actions of small minorities of counterdemonstrators (many of whom are not from the immediate area) speak for or express the feelings of the majority of white workers. The evidence reviewed here would indicate that they do not.

The point, in short, is that literary-political intellectuals read their special preconceptions into the day's news. In this respect they exhibit all the perceptual biases and distortions that have been so amply documented in experiments in social psychology. A review of "the nation's malaise" by any of these writers will dwell on an assortment of awesome backlash campaigns. Such an account would have mayors Stenvig of Minneapolis and Yorty of Los Angeles figuring very prominently. When one asks, however, about Mayor Peter Flaherty of Pittsburgh and Mayor Sam Massell of Atlanta—both of whom beat back the established powers in their respective cities, fighting all the standard weapons in the backlash arsenal—the characteristic response is, who are they? In such a case, the literary intellectual has either submerged the evidence or, worse, failed even to see it. In the antiseptic language of the social sciences, this would be called "selective perception."

If one compulsively rejects systematic evidence and has a trained, aesthetic disgust when faced with "data," with numbers, percentages, or correlation coefficients, then clearly that kind of contact with reality is never going to affect one's understanding. In great measure, the understanding that then comes to dominate has roughly the same basis as that of neighborhood or backyard gossip. Interpretations are passed around within a narrow circle of acquaintances. Those people within that circle support and mutually reinforce each other so that in time their special understandings appear to be indisputable.

Such selective perception and continuous misreading of the evidence gives rise to the alarm felt by liberal policy-makers and, in turn, provides the basis for "go slow" policies and "benign neglect." The evidence reviewed here indicates that the policy-maker genuinely concerned with equality and human decency has considerably more support for his initiative than he ever dreamed.

The evidence reviewed here covers events through November 1968. One of the difficulties of survey research is that the day after one can always say, "That was yesterday." In some ways "backlash" is an indestructible hypothesis. Throughout the 1964 election campaign commentators of all varieties were predicting it, regardless of the evidence of the pollsters, and only when the result was in did they, for a moment at least, desist. There was a period of quiescence and then again, slowly, the hypothesis reappeared in all its glory for its George Wallace flowering. Once again, the result did not match the grim prognostications of the professional alarmists and, in the face of some more positive results in the 1969 elections, the concern again faded. But then, prior to the 1970 congressional elections, there it was again. It was difficult to add up the results of that year's elections as evidence of the efficacy of hard-line, backlash campaigns, and so the sounds of alarm again faded away.

There is little point in making a priori stipulations as to what the evidence on that "day after" will or will not hold. It is always possible that the long-term trend toward greater tolerance might be, or might already, since 1968, have been reversed. It is also possible that in some localities there could be tensions that would reverse the national trend. But the evidence above suggests the need for some restraint before jumping to a conclusion based on impressions or on a few spectacular or dramatic events. The mistaken conclusion can, in some circumstances, give rise to the very eventuality one would ardently wish to avoid.

Bibliographical Note

This article is based on Chapter 11 of my forthcoming book *Class and Political Orientations in the United States.* For additional evidence, see Herbert Hyman and Paul Sheatsley, "Attitudes Toward Desegregation," *Scientific American,* July 1964, pp. 16–23; see also, Mildred A. Schwartz, *Trends in White Attitudes Toward Negroes* (Chicago: National Opinion Research Center, *Report No. 119, 1967*); and my chapter, "Black Demands, White Reactions and Liberal Alarms," in *Restraining Myths and Liberating Realities* (forthcoming).

On the misrepresentation of the Wallace phenomenon in Wisconsin in 1964, see Michael Rogin, "Wallace and the Middle Class: The White Backlash in Wisconsin," *Public Opinion Quarterly,* Spring 1966, pp. 98–108. The scenario of the Wall Street construction-worker events is covered by Fred Cook in "Hard Hats: The Rampaging Patriots," *Nation,* June 15, 1970, pp. 712–719. The persistent dovishness of blue-collar workers in anti-war referenda is shown by Harlan Hahn in "Correlates of Public Sentiments about War: Local Referenda on the Vietnam Issue," *American Political Science Review,* December 1970, pp. 1186–1188, and in his "Dove Sentiments Among Blue-Collar Workers," *Dissent,* May-June 1970.

Women Who Work in Factories
Judith Buber Agassi

The current feminist literature largely ignores women who work in factories and their special problems. Is this justifiable? Is industry truly a declining sector in the economy, employing an ever-decreasing percentage of the labor force while the service sector keeps expanding? Women in the academy and the mass media have been organizing to demand their rights; so have some welfare mothers, domestic workers, and white-collar workers. Have the voices of the blue-collar women not been heard because their numbers are declining to a point where improving their conditions is not worth the effort?

Statistics show no such decline. The proportion in the United States of women among industrial workers — as well as the proportion of women industrial workers among all working women — has remained stable. This is borne out by the latest figures available from the U.S. Department of Labor, covering the years 1967, 1968, and 1969. In those three years the numbers of blue-collar women were 4.597 million, 4.9 million, and 4.974 million. The proportion of women among all employees in industry was 27 percent, which seems constant for these years (I cannot check the data with absolute accuracy). The percentages of blue-collar women among all working women was 16.7

JUDITH BUBER AGASSI, an Israeli, teaches political science at Haifa University and is a research staff member of the Center for International Studies at the Massachusetts Institute of Technology. She is at work on a comparative study of blue-collar women.

percent, 17.3 percent, and 17.1 percent. Looking at the 1960s as a whole, the proportion of women among operatives and in industrial crafts, though constant among employed women, has slightly declined in the total population. Of much more significance, however, is the continued concentration of blue-collar women in the lower skills and the backward branches of industry.

It is said that the storm of automation is already reducing the number of male industrial workers and soon will affect women, too. Such forecasts may sound reasonable and simple, but the realities are complex and varied. The influence of women workers on the development of industry undoubtedly is limited. But if this influence were channeled through large-scale union and political organizations, more effective action could be planned.

It is a serious mistake to think that a number of industrial working women may lose their jobs without affecting the general position of women in the labor market. Janice Neipert Hedges of the Bureau of Labor Statistics pointed, in June 1970, to the oversaturation in such typical women's professions as nursing, teaching, and social work—at a time when the proportion of women, and especially of married women, in the labor force is on the constant increase. She warned that if women will not branch out into the main growth occupaions, the competition will become cutthroat, especially between young and older women entering or re-entering the labor market. Clearly the job situation of all working women will be adversely affected by a serious shrinkage in *any* part of the still limited women's labor market.

Do Women Have a Future in Industry?

To answer this question, let us first discuss whether industry has a future as an employer. In the popular literature there lingers the nightmare utopia of the 1950s: the workerless factory. But our recent experience has proved that this is merely a remote possibility—with the one exception of power stations, where we now find a minuscule labor force. True, much semiskilled machine-tending and many old industrial skills are becoming superfluous with the advance of automation. In such sectors of industry where continuous flow processes have been automated, there have been spectacular reductions of manpower. But in other sectors, reductions have not been drastic. In most industries, automation is far from complete and will remain partial for the foreseeable future. Besides, all automated production processes need programming, and constant maintenance and supervision. The more varied the product, the more human work is required.

Supply, warehousing, the shipping of materials and parts and finished products, as well as related accounting—all these require extensive manpower even under the most streamlined conditions.

What is more, the very process of automation has created many new jobs that require new skills. And as automation reduces costs and makes feasible the mass production of a whole range of new products, new industries spring up. Although these automated manufacturing industries will continue to employ human labor, women are in danger of losing their workplace because they only possess inferior skills and are concentrated in industry's most backward sections.

The old industrial craft skills that survive automation include those of industrial electricians, carpenters, pipefitters, machinists, tool- and die-makers, and draftsmen—and, as we know, women's share in these old skills is minimal. But now to the new skills that are developing in the automobile, aircraft, office machines, household appliances, air conditioning, radio and television, and computer industries. These new skills are used both in industry and in retail—in installation and maintenance, i.e., in the services. Until recently, few women workers were trained in these new craft skills. In the technical occupations on the borderline between blue and white collar—such as electrical, electronic, and chemical technicians—women, too, have only made limited entry and work mainly in the lower ranks. All this demonstrates that women workers in industry are concentrated in semiskilled and low-skill jobs—using hand tools, some electrically powered and some not. Some women operate simple, manual, old-fashioned machinery, the sewing machine or its analogue, or feed and tend isolated semiautomated machines, such as the buttonhole or soldering machines. And women do the assembling, checking, pressing, folding, packing, stacking, and stamping of products.

In theory, then, automation or increased mechanization will abolish the great majority of industrial jobs now held by women. What may follow?

Certain technologically backward industries, which employ large numbers of low-paid and low-skilled workers, may simply disappear from the U.S. economy or from whole areas of the country, priced out by rival industries employing cheaper and more stable labor. This has recently happened in the shoe industry, largely undercut and priced out by competitors from Italy and Spain, and also in the New England textile industry, which moved South during the '30s and is now endangered, together with the clothing and plastics industries, by competition from the Far East. The same is happening in food industries that did not modernize.

Protectionism may, in all these cases, draw out the process

of mechanization. Yet, since about half of the industrial women workers in the U.S. are concentrated in clothing, food, and textiles, nearly half of the women's jobs are in jeopardy—which means well over two million. If we add other backward industries with great numbers of women workers—such as footwear, plastics, toys, costume jewelry, and notions—we can add almost another half-million. The displacement of women workers from all these industries would be a disaster for all working women in the economy.

But the end of these industries and jobs is not inevitable. Although all their production processes pose special problems, they can largely be overcome. Through the resolute introduction of high mechanization or automation, productivity in these industries could be raised to such levels where they could compete with low-wage countries while paying acceptable United States wages. There are already blueprints for prototypes of such fully or semiautomated machinery for these branches, and some of the new machinery is in production, though not in the United States.

The obstacles to modernization are many: the financial weakness of small businesses; the load of old buildings and old machinery; the traditionalism and lack of boldness of management; and, also, government protection. But the women workers themselves provide the most serious obstacle: as long as women are willing to fill these demanding, high-speed, mind-dulling, and nerve-racking dead-end jobs for wages lower than those of most male workers, management will not invest in modernization.

In the lowest-paying industries, the supply of native women workers has nearly dried up, and the remaining native labor force consists largely of middle-aged and older women. New employees are drawn from a few remaining immigrant communities. In the greater Boston area, these women workers used to be French-Canadians. Now they are Portuguese immigrant women who usually arrive with limited schooling (Portugal has only four years of compulsory education), know little English, have a mother or mother-in-law to look after their babies, are used to low pay, and urgently need ready cash. Most of them find jobs in the needle trades. Yet the girls of the next generation, born in the United States, won't do this kind of work. And so this labor supply is scarce and will become scarcer. Now is the time to demand changes in these industries—before unplanned modernization will result in unemployment for large numbers of women workers, exacerbating the disadvantageous position of all women workers, in or out of industry.

But will not modernization reduce and thoroughly change jobs, and remaining jobs be declared men's work? Will not women be pushed out of their old strongholds in one way or another?

Such displacement of women could be blocked by an agreement between employer and union guaranteeing the jobs of those now employed. (There are major precedents of unions protecting male workers whose jobs have been threatened.) The resulting, inevitable reduction could be achieved gradually, through normal turnover. To be sure, if these industries were to expand rapidly through modernization, there would be no need for reducing the labor force. But whatever happens after modernization, women should push for the training of women workers in preparation for new, upgraded jobs. This strategy has just been adopted by the German textile workers' union, whose membership is largely female.

So much for the future possibilities in the backward, traditional women's industries producing food and clothing. Let us now turn to the future of a second concentration of women workers, employed in the electrical and electronic industries. Here basic production is technologically ultramodern; yet in the production departments one rarely finds a woman. The women still work in assembly, adjustment, drilling, spot-welding, soldering, threading, lettering, calibrating, checking and rechecking of tiny components—at jobs where the technology is backward or spotty, at jobs still performed by hand-and-eye coordination.

A parallel situation holds in the ultramodern chemical industries, especially in pharmaceuticals. In such jobs as the filling of containers, packing, stamping, and labeling, modern technology stops, and women go on performing their old jobs. Professor Günther Friedrichs, a European expert, reports that there are solutions to nearly all the problems of automatic assembly in packing, whatever the size of components or containers; but these solutions are not applied because it is cheaper to employ women.

Assembly methods in the prosperous and until recently rapidly expanding electronics industries resemble those in backward industries—modernization is undercut by cheap labor, and most women are in the two lowest wage grades. Yet pay in electronics is relatively high, and women still are considerably better paid here than, say, in the needle trades.

Some of the electronics firms recruit only high school graduates; some have abolished the piecework method, which remains pervasive in the traditional women's industries. While most women workers in electronics still do routine and repetitive work and have little chance for advancement, the loss of their jobs—if they were to be displaced by greater automation—would of course be a heavy blow. In

the recent recession, considerable numbers of part-time women workers in electronics, especially those on mothers' shifts, have already
lost their jobs.

The only way out of the present decline in the number of employed women workers—whether caused by recession or competition
of cheaper Asian labor—seems to be a campaign for the resolute upgrading of the technology, demanding guarantees that women employees will be trained for the new, upgraded job. Many women have
developed considerable yet unused mechanical skills and knowledge,
and management would profit were it to consult them on ways to overcome weaknesses in existing semiautomatic production processes.
The upgrading of production processes *and* jobs might soften the blow
of an otherwise disastrous cut in the female work force.

But to achieve equality for women in industry, an all-out onslaught is
needed on the so-called man's jobs—this is the only way to improve
the general skill level of women. How can it be done?

At least as important as the women workers' demand for training, wherever automation is in the offing, is their need for resolute
entry into industrial craft skills requiring training and still wholly
staffed by men. I have in mind such skills as those of electricians,
draftsmen, and machinists, all the new photographic skills used in
printing, and, also, various precision jobs. As we have learned from
the Bureau of Labor Statistics, the greatest increase in industrial employment is expected among the new craft skills needed for the checking, maintenance, installation, and repair of new machinery—from
aircraft and automobile to dishwasher and percolator. These jobs are
somewhere between industry proper and services. Some of these
craftsmen now work in industry, some are employed by industry but
outside it, others by independent service firms, and some operate as
independents. The most important barrier keeping women out of such
occupations has been their inability to procure training—especially
in older crafts; they are excluded by the men who control the training—sometimes employers, sometimes unions. Training for the
newer crafts is increasingly provided by vocational schools, community colleges, and the armed forces, especially the Air Force.

Here, as we know, a major obstacle has been the sex-typing
that both girls and their parents have accepted as a matter of course.
But this seems to be changing. Now that the Air Force, for example,
has started training women in the new aviation skills, there may be a
turning point and precedent for a new tradition—training women on
an equal basis with men in industrial crafts. Recent data on women
enrolled in vocational schools for training in various crafts related to

appliances are also encouraging, though still too low to change the imbalance. There has to be a far greater number of technically skilled women before a campaign for equality of opportunity in skilled and supervisory industrial jobs can succeed. As long as there is only an insignificant number of skilled women in a given occupation, it is hard to convince men that women are in earnest about equality.

Can Equality Ever Be Achieved?

The question of equality pertains both to what kind of equality we wish to achieve, and in what respect men and women are potentially equal. Concerning industry, the second question can be rephrased: Are women, potentially, as technically proficient as men? A recent psycho-technical survey of U.S. school children shows that girls' all-round technical ability, on the average, equals that of boys. Obviously, for adults this is not true—presumably because of lack of training and opportunity for women, not to mention the strong psychological factor which causes many women to suppress technological ability because it is considered unfeminine.

The question of equality, therefore, is rooted not in techno-logical ability but in women workers' special needs as mothers. In the work life in industry, as in the work life in other branches of the economy, the norms were created by men. These norms demanded a continuous work life, the eight-hour day plus overtime and shift work, interrupted only by weekends, holidays, annual vacations, and brief sick leaves. When women entered industry, they were expected to satisfy these norms; they still are. Any deviation, by men or women, is considered a weakness that will result in certain penalties. Since working mothers can hardly fully conform to these norms and since by now many women workers are mothers, employers (who usually are males) still regard female labor with strong reservations; and women, even known campaigners for women's rights, accept these norms and find themselves in a weak position.

These rigid and accepted norms are outmoded and bad, almost as much for men as for women. Yet employers and unions make rules and regulations favoring immobility and uninterrupted work life, which are detrimental both to the individual and the economy. The introduction of study sabbaticals, for example, and exchange programs obviously is beneficial; they have trickled down to the lower levels of management, but hardly at all to workers. The recent introduction of the ten-hour day, four-day week is creating an entirely new pattern, where men's lives are divided into nearly two halves, one in industry and one with the family. This, then, is the right time to examine the possibility of adapting the norms of work life to needs of working mothers, so that they can advance in their work life without being forced to neglect their children or suffer from constant strain.

My major point here is that changing the norms of work life for working mothers may benefit them and our whole society. As things stand, working mothers seldom conform completely to the norms: they have to leave work in emergencies, and/or work part-time, and/or interrupt their work life for some years. For all this they are penalized. They receive lower pay; for example, the hourly pay for a six-hour day is significantly lower than that for an eight-hour day. They lose seniority through interruptions or never acquire it when working part-time. They lose pension rights and security at every inter-ruption, or never acquire them at part-time work; in many firms even steady six-hour-a-day mother-shift workers have no job security. And, of course, women in general are frequently excluded from either train-ing or promotion out of fear, or on the excuse that they may quit.

If the part-time work most common among and satisfying to working mothers were to become normal, women would be much hap-pier in their work life, and in a better position to catch up in techno-logical skills.

These suggestions are not mere dreams—they have partly been achieved in Western Europe. In all of Western Europe paid ma-ternity leave has acknowledged the fact that working women bear children. In the United States this is still in the stage of a government "recommendation." In some countries, much more far-reaching ac-commodations are on the way. German unions, for instance, now demand an eighteen-month optional, unpaid maternity leave with full protection of seniority and pension rights, as well as leave in case of sick children. In Sweden a more radical solution has been adopted: working women have the right, during their careers, to work up to fifteen years part-time, without loss of rights for training, promotion, etc. In Sweden this provision has caused deep changes in attitudes, leading to the highest labor participation of women and their highest pay ratio in the West.*

Absence of adaptive legislation is matched by an absence of community services, such as a full range of day-care centers, nursery

---

* It is true that traditional protective legislation for women, such as laws against assign-ing women to lift heavy weights or against exposing them to moral danger by employ-ment after midnight, are now the subject of considerable debate by women trade union-ists, some of whom argue for the abolition of such protective laws. Undoubtedly, both here and in Europe, many of these laws are used to stave off equality, and to justify the exclusion of women from better jobs.

schools, kindergarten classes, school lunches, early afternoon supervision for school children, and community summer camps. Only in the
last two years or so has anything been done regarding day care, and
this mainly in metropolitan centers; much of it is still too expensive
for the average working mother. Throughout most of suburban and
small-town America, nursery school, and sometimes even kindergarten, is still provided only privately, at a high price and for short
hours. Most grade schools do not provide school lunches, and afternoon supervision is a rarity. That so many mothers work, nonetheless, is a sign of their ingenuity, but also a cause of unnecessary and
harmful stress.

If all these ideas were successfully implemented, more mothers
would work in industry; more would work full-time and would have
longer work lives; and more jobs would be created in the child-care
field. The chief beneficial effect on the economy in general would be
a more rational distribution of the burden of social services and social
security in a society with a rapidly growing retired population. Also,
of course, as more women develop a meaningful life outside the home,
they will be enabled to overcome passivity and limitations. Once
women workers are recognized as both workers and women, not only
will their chances to work increase, but also their chances for more
challenging jobs, which will be a positive compensation for domestic
chores.

Why should the United States, the most technologically advanced industrial nation, be so backward in both legislation and services for working mothers? Only a few years ago it was a widespread
view that the American abhorrence of ideology has prevented the
development of the strong feminist ideology that is essential for a
strong feminist movement. Recent experience, however, makes it
superfluous to debate this point: there is plenty of ideology around
today, feminist and otherwise, but unfortunately few social scientists
have thought out the problems and possible solutions regarding women
in industry. Most of the literature concerning women's rights centers
around the professions. Today's feminist movement is decidedly
upper middle class in orientation, with the typical slumming tendencies
of middle-class radicals who, except for their own kind, notice hardly
anyone but welfare mothers.

The reason for the conspicuous backwardness of the U.S. in
legislation and services for the working mother lies in the historically
weak position of women in the union movement and in industry. This
goes back as far as the nineteenth century. While all over Western
Europe it was taken for granted that working-class wives would go
to work in the factory, in the United States up to the '30s married

women, even in the working class, were expected to stay home. The exceptions were the most newly arrived and needy immigrants, and Southern blacks.

While in Western Europe it was the norm for workers' daughters to enter industry upon leaving school at the age of fourteen, in the U.S. free public education kept many workers' and farmers' daughters in school up to the age of sixteen or even eighteen, thus also qualifying them for clerical jobs. Besides, the United States was the first country to provide a great number of clerical jobs for women, and many young working-class girls chose office instead of blue-collar jobs. And so even the positive aspects of American society have contributed to the present backward position of women in industry. These positive aspects include prolonged public education, relative prosperity that has enabled most working-class wives to stay home – and the relative flexibility of the American class structure which permitted the daughters of workers to enter middle-class jobs.

The American people need to be awakened to the problems of working-class women, and then much can be done to make their lives easier through the development of services and legislation comparable to the best in Western Europe.

Black Workers and the Unions
Ray Marshall

A major cause of conflict between white union members and black workers has been union control of jobs. Historically, labor unions have mainly been controlled by whites, with a few exceptions such as the Brotherhood of Sleeping Car Porters (BSCP) and some black locals in the Carpenters, Longshoremen, Bricklayers, Cement Masons, Laborers, and Musicians. In the South most of the strongest local unions—those in printing, railroad, and construction crafts—were controlled by whites, even though blacks have had some locals of craftsmen in the travel trades, laborers, and longshoremen. Historically, these white-dominated unions have been used to ration scarce job opportunities to particular groups of white workers, and the black unions were successful where there were already large numbers of black workers before the unions came on the scene.

From the inception of the AFL in 1886, Samuel Gompers and its other leaders were committed to organizing without regard to race or religion. Ideologically, Gompers never abandoned his opposition to excluding Negroes from AFL unions, but during the 1890s he apparently surrendered to the reality of racial discrimination. While em-

RAY MARSHALL is chairman of the Department of Economics and director of the Center for the Study of Human Resources at the University of Texas, Austin. He has written extensively on labor economics and minority problems, including Human Resources and Labor Markets, *co-authored with Sar Levitan and Garth Magnum.*

249

phasizing that it was good unionism to organize regardless of race, creed, or color, he finally decided that it was better to organize blacks and whites into segregated locals than not to organize at all.

In view of widespread union discrimination, it was perhaps natural for such Negro leaders as Booker T. Washington to ally themselves with powerful employers who were willing to cooperate with them to obtain a steady supply of cheap, nonunion labor. Since both Abraham Lincoln and many of these employers, especially in the North, were Republicans, it was equally natural for black leaders to be Republicans, creating another source of conflict with the predominantly Democratic unions. Washington and other Negro leaders were convinced that the profit motive and economic productivity would overcome racism and gain respect for Negroes. In his famous Atlanta Exposition address in 1895, Washington advised Negroes to shun politics and acquire the necessary skills to meet the competition of white workers.

The extent to which Negroes were used as strikebreakers probably has been exaggerated, but blacks did play an important role before the 1930s in meat packing, steel, coal and ore mining, automobiles, and railroads as strikebreakers. And while white workers also were extensively used to break strikes in these industries, Negroes, seeming far more conspicuous, were far more resented. By World War I Negro-AFL relations were, to say the least, strained.

The transformation of the Negro population from rural Southern to urban Northern is one of the most significant developments in American history. In contrast to only 12 percent in 1910 and 26 percent in 1930, by 1970 over half of all American Negroes lived outside the states that had made up the Confederacy, and more than 90 percent of employed Negroes worked outside agriculture.

This urbanization increased the Negroes' political power, especially in the North where they had the right to vote and could maneuver within the two-party system. In turn, this growth of black political power created leverage with which black leaders could accelerate racial changes in the South that, in the long run, might be even more important than those in the North. The urban environment, North and South, raised the Negro's aspirations and caused him to demand equal education, civil rights, and job opportunities.

After 1935 the CIO challenged AFL affiliates, causing them to relax some of their racial restrictions. In order to appeal to the large numbers of Negroes in the mass production industries, the CIO adopted an equalitarian policy at the outset. John L. Lewis's United Mine Workers had long had a favorable reputation among Negroes because of its steadfast refusal to sanction discrimination. Unlike

AFL craft unions, the CIO's unions had no control over employment and therefore had to organize black employees if they wanted to succeed in collective bargaining. Because it had broader social objectives and less economic power than the AFL, the CIO also needed Negro support for its legislative programs.

The CIO's efforts to gain support among Negroes included financial contributions to such organizations as the NAACP and Negro churches and newspapers; the adoption of equalitarian racial policies; and the service of its leaders in such organizations as the NAACP and the National Urban League. While the NAACP and the Urban League remained skeptical of the AFL even during the 1930s, their leaders urged Negroes to join the CIO. This position, however, did not go unopposed within the black community; anti-union sentiments were deeply embedded among the black bourgeoisie. Yet a cooperative relationship between the CIO and the Negro community soon proved mutually beneficial.

All this is not meant to imply that CIO units automatically followed equalitarian policies while all AFL locals discriminated against and were shunned by Negroes. At the time of their merger in 1956, the AFL probably had at least as many black members as the CIO. Moreover, some CIO locals barred Negroes from membership, and others permitted segregated locals. But the most serious problem for Negroes in the CIO was that of segregated seniority lines which restricted Negroes to menial and disagreeable jobs. These seniority arrangements were not caused entirely by unions, of course, but collective bargaining formalized such arrangements, and white CIO members vigorously resisted their elimination.

When the AFL and CIO merged, race relations in America were in considerable ferment, caused largely by the results of the black migration out of the rural South. In some ways, the Negro's position was worse in the North. Although Negroes had inferior status in the South, they were able to develop institutions—schools, churches, professional and fraternal organizations, and unions—which they controlled within the limits imposed by institutionalized segregation. The Southern Negro community also produced its own civil rights organizations and business and professional leaders, and while in general Negroes were relegated to inferior occupational positions, they had some good jobs at least within the Negro community.

In the North, on the other hand, Negroes controlled very few institutions; even civil rights organizations were more under the control of white liberals than was the case in the South. In the South, the targets for civil rights groups were fairly open and easily understood, whereas in the North, institutionalized racism was more subtle and more difficult to combat. Moreover, the pervasive influence of the ghetto had a debilitating effect on blacks, unmatched by the simpler problems of the rural South.

The AFL-CIO merger coincided with ideological attacks on unions from several quarters. Nor did these attacks come entirely from labor's traditional enemies on the Right. They came also from liberal and left intellectuals. Some of these had backed unions during the 1930s but became disenchanted because of what they saw as the labor movement's willingness to accept the "Establishment." Some left-wing critics considered discrimination to be closely related to the labor movement's other defects. Since, according to this view, the labor movement openly supports the capitalist system, it also helps sustain the racism that is part of that system.

The Negro's sense of frustration and powerlessness in the ghetto produced a resurgence of black nationalist feeling, especially among Negro males suffering from unemployment, underemployment, and unjust welfare systems. It is therefore not surprising that many young Negro males resorted to militancy and revolutionary rhetoric in order to protest their conditions and assert their manhood.

Relations between unions and blacks were also strained by differences over the enforcement of civil rights measures. Although unions had played a vital role in the passage of civil rights legislation, they had been critical of some of the ways this legislation was implemented. The concept of "affirmative action" to be undertaken by government contractors was a particularly important source of conflict. The rationale behind this concept was a conviction held by government officials and some black leaders that the mere elimination of overt discrimination would lead to relatively limited advances by Negroes. Contractors were therefore required to take "affirmative action" to ensure that Negroes were recruited for jobs or upgraded into positions from which they had previously been excluded.

Conflict over this concept resulted in part from its lack of operational precision: no one could say exactly how many Negroes should be hired or admitted to unions. To cope with this problem, those entrusted with enforcing equal-opportunity provisions of government contracts often implied that employers and unions were expected to meet racial quotas. This, in turn, caused many unions and white workers to conclude that the federal government was determined to give Negroes preferential treatment over whites.

One of the most important controversies over preferential treatment in the building trades came in the summer of 1969, when the Department of Labor issued a plan for government contractors in the

Philadelphia construction industry requiring builders to "set specific goals of minority manpower utilization." Although the Department of Labor declared that these specific goals were "not intended and shall not be used to discriminate against any qualified applicant or employee," the Philadelphia Plan was widely criticized by contractors and unions as requiring quotas and preferential treatment. Union leaders argued that the Philadelphia Plan would not guarantee jobs for blacks in the construction industry because it would be possible for contractors merely to meet their requirements by moving black workers from nonfederal to federal projects. In the construction industry it is much more important to be attached to the labor market than to a specific job. Following this principle, unions, contractors, and civil rights organizations in Chicago and other cities developed the so-called "hometown" plans, based on outreach and voluntary-negotiation concepts. For its part, the Labor Department did not object to such plans and, indeed, seemed to have a preference for them; but it was convinced that such pressure as that imposed by the Philadelphia Plan was necessary in order to get unions and contractors to adopt so-called voluntary plans. At this writing, neither the Philadelphia Plan nor the hometown plans have been greatly successful. The lessons learned to date, however, make it clear that the outreach concept—whereby special organizations recruit, tutor, and place minorities into jobs or training positions—has been the single most successful way of getting blacks into construction jobs.

At the beginning of the 1970s, many white trade unionists were hostile to racial quota or "goal" systems and other such programs. They were also very much concerned about neighborhood integration, especially in the North. What is not clear is the extent to which these attitudes were racially inspired or were a reflection of economic forces. For example, many white workers have considerable investments in their homes and feel that neighborhood integration would cause a deterioration in real estate values. Neighborhoods in transition also seem to be characterized by high rates of crime, inflicted to some degree on the families of white workers, although blacks themselves clearly bear the heaviest burden. It is therefore too simple to brand the white worker a racist because he is concerned about adequate protection or the value of his house.

How important is race in the constellation of factors that produce dissatisfaction in white manual workers in general and union members in particular? Although some observers claim to see evidence of "backlash" in white worker attitudes, the opinion polls give mixed results. For example, union members on the whole were slightly more favorably inclined than others toward passage of the Civil Rights Act of 1964, as indicated by the Gallup Poll of December 31, 1963, which asked, "Would you like to see Congress pass the Civil Rights Act (1964)?"

	Percent in Nonunionists (3,214)	Percent in Union Members (575)
Yes	59.4	63.8
No	32.4	27.5
Not sure	8.2	8.8

However, a later poll taken by Louis Harris (April 15, 1968) found that union and nonunion workers responded as follows to the question, "Have Negroes tried to move too fast?"

	Percent in Total	Percent in Union Members	Percent in AFL-CIO	Percent in Teamsters
Too Fast	61	69	63	66
Too Slow	9	6	6	4
About Right	20	18	24	11
Not sure	10	6	6	19

These figures suggest that many union members who favored the Civil Rights Act of 1964 also thought that Negroes had tried to "move too fast," although this too is far from conclusive because the responses are not controlled for other factors (income, education, region, etc.) which might have influenced attitudes on the speed of racial progress.

Community race sentiments, as reflected in legislation, influence the attitudes of white union members toward race relations within unions. One of the main influences of law is to fix moral authority for various practices. Even when it contains inadequate enforcement powers, civil rights legislation is important because it establishes a positive influence for racial equality. Although law does not automatically change conduct, it undoubtedly causes a shift toward the sentiments expressed by the legislation.

The positive role of law will be undermined if it is incompatible with underlying political reality or fundamental concepts of justice. For example, while most white workers are apparently convinced that people should not be economically disadvantaged solely because of race, they clearly disagree with Negroes over the extent to which racial discrimination is responsible for the black workers' economic disadvantages. Blacks are likely to give heavy weight to discrimination, while whites assign more weight to "qualification." To some extent this is a problem of semantics. When white workers use the term "racism" or "discrimination," they are likely to mean specific overt acts. For blacks, racism often means institutionalized behavior patterns that make it difficult for blacks to upgrade themselves. The tendency to blame white racism for the Negroes' plight has therefore generated hostility among whites who might concede that blacks face institutionalized segregation but who nevertheless do not consider themselves personally responsible. Indeed, it probably requires a high level of abstract sophistication to feel a personal sense of guilt for racial discrimination. Workers are more likely to be concerned with concrete circumstances than with abstractions.

Because of attachments to their neighborhoods and their unions, some ethnic groups have demonstrated what seems an inconsistent pattern of strong pro-Negro attitudes on the job and in the union and strong anti-Negro attitudes in neighborhoods. This occurs because different sets of forces determine behavior in each circumstance. Good trade unionism requires equality of all workers on the job, while a strong neighborhood attachment can mean trying to keep outsiders with a different culture from encroaching on community institutions and undermining property values.

White unionists can naturally be expected to resist measures that threaten their job security. Negroes are therefore likely to make their greatest progress during periods of tight labor markets. This is not to argue that a tight labor market would be a sufficient cause for black economic progress. Much depends on whether people are able to take advantage of job opportunities as they become available. Tight labor markets operate much faster to change the demand conditions than to generate supplies of labor in order to meet the demand. Therefore, unless training enables blacks to meet job qualifications, a tight labor market will not necessarily help unemployed black workers.

Tensions among blacks, intellectuals, and white workers are infused with considerable class prejudice in that the conflict over job equality is partly a conflict over job status. The white workers likely to show the greatest resistance to blacks on the job are those who feel their work should have higher status than generally accorded by public opinion. This is one reason for the resistance to blacks by craft unions in the building, printing, and railroad crafts.

But the implications of this problem are not limited to the class or status feelings of white manual workers. To some extent, intellectual and middle-class whites are likely to exhibit stronger biases against white workers than they do toward blacks, from whom they are largely insulated. Intellectuals are inclined to romanticize blacks, much as they romanticized workers at an earlier time. Academic

whites often see no inconsistency in demanding four-year requirements for B.A. degrees, while condemning electricians for requiring
four years, mostly spent at work, for apprenticeships. Middle-class
critics are convinced that it does not take four years to become an
electrician, although few of them know much about the jobs they are
criticizing. They know only that manual jobs have lower status than
professional occupations and therefore should require little formal
preparation.

By now there is a long history of black workers organizing themselves
to promote their interests within the labor movement. Some of these
organizations have been made up of local craftsmen in a particular
industry – such as construction, the railroads, and longshoring – where
white-controlled unions would not accept black workers on equal
terms. Local black construction workers' organizations currently
exist in a number of major cities.

   The most viable black labor organizations have been those
working within the labor movement, such as the Brotherhood of
Sleeping Car Porters, formed originally by A. Philip Randolph and a
group of Socialists in 1925. Not only have Randolph and the BSCP
worked within the union movement to advance the interests of black
workers, but they exercised an influence far out of proportion to their
numbers. Randolph has been instrumental in establishing a variety
of black labor organizations formed for such diverse purposes as saving the jobs of railroad workers threatened by discriminating unions,
promoting black civil rights interests, and leading the March on Washington movement which forced Franklin D. Roosevelt to create the
first Fair Employment Practices Committee.

   When the AFL-CIO merger was being discussed in the mid-
1950s, black trade unionists held a number of meetings in major cities
to exert influence on the civil rights policies of the new organization.
There was some apprehension among Negroes in the CIO that the
new federation would be dominated by white AFL leaders. Ironically,
however, no black leader in the CIO could match A. Philip Randolph's
stature in the Negro community, even though his union was affiliated
with the AFL. The difference, of course, was Randolph's record in
fighting for Negro rights and the fact that his organization was made up
almost exclusively of blacks, making it possible for him simultaneously
to promote Negro and trade-union objectives without alienating his
constituency.

   The merger was accompanied by increasing tensions between
blacks and the labor movement, not because of a deterioration of the

position of black trade unionists (the AFL-CIO's civil rights position was much stronger than that of the CIO had been, and two Negroes were elected to the AFL-CIO Executive Council), but because the black community grew more and more impatient with discrimination. Black union leaders were reminded by the Negro press that the AFL-CIO admitted unions whose constitutions restricted membership to whites. AFL-CIO affiliates in the skilled trades barred Negroes from membership by informal means or permitted blacks to be organized into segregated locals. Black leaders were not much impressed with the argument that many Negro workers preferred segregation, since corruption and communism would not have been permitted just because local members preferred it. And many blacks, in this last decade of militant assertiveness, were convinced that union leaders were not doing all they could to eradicate racism within their organizations.

As a consequence, black trade unionists have organized themselves within unions in order to get blacks elected to union positions, to overcome discrimination, and to promote Negro and union objectives. One such local organization was the Trade Union Leadership Council (TULC), organized in Detroit in 1957 and strongly influenced by black leaders within the United Auto Workers. The latter were concerned about what they considered the decline of black union influence in the UAW after Walter Reuther consolidated his leadership. The TULC therefore sought to strengthen the influence of black trade unionists, to increase union support for civil rights objectives, and to promote union causes in the black community.

At the national level, A. Philip Randolph and other black trade unionists organized the Negro-American Labor Council (NALC) in 1960 to pursue objectives similar to those of the TULC. The NALC grew out of the discussions of black trade unionists at the 1958 and 1959 NAACP conventions and was strengthened by a well-publicized debate between A. Philip Randolph and George Meany at the 1959 AFL-CIO Convention. The underlying issue was the priority to be given civil rights and trade-union objectives, but the formal issue was the admission of the International Longshoremen's Association (ILA) to the AFL-CIO in spite of ILA's record of segregation. Randolph demanded that the AFL-CIO take action against unions that permitted segregated locals. Meany defended the admission of the ILA and the "right" of blacks to maintain their own unions.

A number of developments caused relations between many black trade unionists and the AFL-CIO to improve markedly during the early 1960s. A high point came when Martin Luther King, Jr., said at the 1961 AFL-CIO Convention:

Negroes are almost entirely a working people. There are pitifully few Negro millionaires and few employers. Our needs are identical with labor's needs – decent wages, fair working conditions, livable housing, old age security, health and welfare measures, conditions in which families can grow, have education for their children and respect in the community. . . .

The two most dynamic and cohesive liberal forces in the country are the labor movement and the Negro freedom movement.

During the 1960s, radical blacks attacked black leaders who were attempting to work within the labor movement. Militant white racists were, at the same time, attempting to counteract labor's support of Negro organizations and programs. Neither of these movements gained more than local support, though the black separatists were able to form a few dual unions in isolated places, and some trade unionists were drawn to George Wallace during the 1968 election.

Black and white trade unionists now are brought closer together by the rapid growth of black political power in the South, which has resulted from voter registration drives and the Voting Rights Act of 1965. Indeed, the election of blacks to political office on a scale unprecedented since Reconstruction and the growing political power of blacks have had a perceptible impact on Southern politicians. Black and white trade unionists therefore consider union-black-liberal coalitions to have increasing promise in the South, as the Republican party gains power and splits the white vote along economic lines.

A. Philip Randolph, Bayard Rustin, and Norman Hill formed a new movement in 1964 to organize black trade unionists in the A. Philip Randolph Institute. Its philosophy is that Negroes need the help of large sectors of the white community, especially of the unions, in order to bring about the kinds of institutional reforms that will make a difference in the lives of most blacks. These leaders reject black separatism as unworkable.

The Institute has organized fifty local Randolph Clubs in thirty states and is in the process of strengthening these affiliates and of organizing new ones, especially in the South. The black trade unionists' successes in the South undoubtedly are largely the result of growing black political strength in that region and of the fact that Southern black unionists operate in political climates where liberal forces have been weak and unstructured, thereby giving greater influence to any well-organized group.

The success of the Randolph Institute's program will depend in part on its ability to organize black trade unionists into a political force with sufficient power to produce tangible changes in the lives of black people. There is no denying the political potential of the black trade unionist, especially in the South. There are probably between 2.5 and 2.75 million black union members in the United States, about half of whom are concentrated in the South. Blacks hold elected positions at almost every level in these unions and often exercise considerable influence in internal affairs, even if rarely in proportion to the black union membership. Black trade unionists have been particularly influential in internal union affairs in such places as New Orleans, Memphis, and Miami, where there are local Randolph Clubs.

The Randolph Institute program also will depend on the black trade unionists' ability to gain support within the black community. On race questions the black community is united, but when it comes to economics, splits are likely to develop. Although it is difficult to generalize, black union leaders rarely seem to have high status in the black community. The leaders of black opinion have been primarily preachers, professionals, and sometimes businessmen catering to the black community. There is no way of knowing its current intensity, but the black middle class, historically, has had strong anti-union sentiments. Anti-unionism has been encouraged by the black press, which tends for the most part to be economically conservative and nonunion. Black professionals also are prepared by their own experiences to exaggerate racism in the labor movement. With few exceptions, such as A. Philip Randolph, the black press rarely gives much attention to black trade-union leaders. Indeed, even such otherwise excellent sources as *The American Negro Reference Book*, edited by John P. Davis, have almost no reference to black trade unionists or the role of unions and collective bargaining in advancing Negro interests.

Despite this neglect, black unionists are in an excellent position to provide economic and political leadership. For one thing, few other leaders of any other American institution, including universities and churches, have experienced as close a relationship with whites as have black unionists. Their experiences certainly have been more useful in this regard than those of black professionals or businessmen who apparently are at least as biased against manual workers as most middle-class whites. I say "apparently" because the role of black trade unionists in the black community is a matter that needs much greater exploration than it has received.

There is much evidence of a sense of frustration among white workers, but we do not know the extent to which this mood is produced by racial factors and the extent to which it has other causes. Nor do we know the extent to which the mood of union members differs from that of white nonunion workers.

Nevertheless, I am persuaded that a number of conclusions

would survive careful documentation. The first is that there is likely to be very little resistance by whites to further advances by blacks on the job. The extent of this resistance will be determined by whether programs developed to equalize job opportunities for blacks recognize the fears and interests of whites. This is particularly likely to be true where demands are made for quotas or preferential treatment— especially if these cause Negroes with less than minimal qualifications to be hired ahead of qualified whites in order to compensate for past discrimination. Regardless of short-run consequences, this kind of "preferential treatment" will in the long run perpetuate inequality.

This, however, is not an argument against special programs making it possible for blacks to meet the same entry-level qualifications and performance standards required of all workers. Such special programs can do a great deal to overcome the effects of institutionalized discrimination.

Public officials and other opinion molders can moderate conflict between black and white workers by recognizing a number of realities. The first of these is that hostile racism, whether black or white, must consistently be challenged. The second is that programs must be built which pay careful attention to the legitimate interests of the various groups while counteracting demands that are racially motivated. Third, many of the frustrations of various racial and ethnic groups are based on fear, others on myth. Perhaps the myths can be overcome by presenting factual evidence. But whether this is possible or not, efforts should be made to avoid appealing to the racist attitudes of blacks or whites. It is extremely shortsighted, in my opinion, for higher-income groups to think they can solve the nation's domestic problems by playing off one group of workers against another. It is equally important for unions to build programs that prevent employers' playing off black and white workers against each other.

I am persuaded that it was entirely correct to give priority to black employment problems, because this was and is our most disadvantaged group. But public programs for the disadvantaged erred in not considering the legitimate concerns of white workers.

The program advocated by the Randolph Institute seems to me to be soundly conceived, even though it is far from certain that it will succeed. There is little doubt that the social and economic problems confronting manual workers in general, and poor workers in particular, will require concerted national programs. And these programs are not likely to be adopted without racial unity among all workers. White workers cannot build lasting economic security at the expense of black workers, and lasting economic security for blacks cannot be built at the expense of white workers. The transition to political action will require black and white leaders who are able to move from protest to programs.

Finally, it seems fairly certain that black political power will increase, even though blacks rarely will be effective in separatist movements. It will, however, be extremely difficult to translate the Randolph Institute's philosophy into an effective national program that would make possible an effective coalition. Getting blacks registered is not the same as getting them to vote or electing candidates who will fight for programs to really improve the workers' lot. Moreover, getting blacks organized into unions is not the same as negotiating good contracts. All this remains to be done.

Last Chance for Desegregation
Richard J. Margolis

Will Black and White Workers Live Together?

> *As soon as it is admitted that the whites and the emancipated blacks are placed upon the same territory in the situation of two foreign communities, it will readily be understood that there are but two chances for the future: the Negroes and the whites must either wholly part or wholly mingle.*
>
> — Alexis de Tocqueville

Early last June a rumor spread through Rosedale, Queens — a blue-collar community of Irish, Jews, and Italians — that a black man had bought a two-family house there and planned to move in with his white wife, his black brother and sister-in-law, and ten black children. The neighbors' reaction was conventional. With picks and axes they rampaged through the house, shattering windows, ripping out fixtures, flooding the basement, and scrawling graffiti on the walls: "We hate niggers. . . . Stamp out niggers." Others stood outside and cheered. No one called the police. (The rumor proved unfounded. Actually, the house had been bought by two Chinese brothers, one of whom was married to a white woman. *They* never moved in.)

On the same day, by coincidence, President Nixon issued a major policy statement on housing and race. He began with the usual pieties, deploring racial discrimination and extolling justice; but then he proceeded to take a hard line against what he called "forced integration," by which he meant federally supported efforts to move black families out of urban tenements and into decent suburban dwellings. "We will not seek to impose economic integration on existing local jurisdictions," the President reassured white suburbanites. He thus

RICHARD J. MARGOLIS writes on social issues for magazines, foundations, and government. His book of poems for young people, Looking for a Place, *is recently published.*

262

threatened to snuff out the few embers of integration that his Secretary of Housing and Urban Development, George W. Romney, had bravely been fanning. Romney's constant plea to suburban officials had been to loosen local zoning restrictions and accept their "fair share" of subsidized low- and moderate-income housing. Now the President was saying they need not listen.

The two "statements" made that day last June—one by the man in the White House, the other by a mob in Queens—would seem to reflect America's continuing commitment to some form of apartheid, no matter what the social cost. Indeed, much of the segregation we now endure is a product of these two forces—upper-middle-class manipulation of our land and our laws for political and financial profit, and ad hoc blue-collar violence.

Through the years blue-collar families have gained nothing from this casual alliance, other than the consolation, perhaps, of social superiority over blacks. (Even that dubious advantage is disappearing.) In fact, white working-class families have nearly always suffered from the segregating system. Their panicky reaction to black move-ins both lowers their property values and, as a rule, forces them to flee to newer, more expensive neighborhoods.

The depth of white panic should not be underestimated (although that is precisely what some leaders of the latest "white ethnic" renaissance—of which more later—seem to be doing). To many white people segregation has the force of natural law. A few years ago in Skokie, Illinois, about eighty-five white residents met to protest the presence of the town's first black family. Until 1949, when the U.S. Supreme Court struck down restrictive covenants, Skokie had been almost exclusively a WASP suburb. But in the '50s thousands of Chicago's Catholic and Jewish families, most of them only a few years and dollars removed from their blue-collar origins, had moved in. Now they were frightened. "I moved out here so my kids could have grass and trees and sunshine," a young father shouted. "And now look what's happening!" He was clearly under the impression that blacks blotted out the sun.

People who suffer from such primal fears are likely to make the rest of us suffer, too. Their terror seeps into the body politic, with the result that our leaders fail to pursue those policies which might deliver us from apartheid. Nevertheless, the two segregating impulses mentioned above—blue-collar panic and white-collar profiteering— appear to be weakening; or, to put it more precisely, a new set of circumstances may be rendering segregation less interesting to the establishment and integration less odious to the public. It is already too late for Americans to slip through the horns of Tocqueville's un-compromising dilemma. Ultimately, it seems to me, we are more likely to "wholly mingle" than to "wholly part."

The new set of circumstances can be quickly summarized. First, the laws of the land now explicitly forbid racial discrimination in housing. The force of these laws (and several Supreme Court decisions) does not ensure desegregation, but for the first time in history it offers fair-housing supporters a legal base from which to operate. Second, the establishment — especially the federal establishment — now tends to favor a certain amount of ghetto dispersion; the new attitude reflects a complete reversal of traditional federal thinking. And third, the current housing shortage, which for blue-collar workers will get worse before it gets better, makes possible a grudging but useful coalition between white ethnics and blacks, both of whom seek better housing.

These factors do not guarantee desegregation of our cities and towns; but they do offer reasonable grounds for hope and action.

There has always been a kind of Gresham's Law at work in the civil rights movement, in which the obvious issues have tended to drive out the more complicated ones. Liberals spent decades, for example, trying to abolish lynching and the poll tax, before making any serious effort to attack segregation per se. As late as 1962, President Kennedy was capable, without irony, of telling a delegation of black leaders that he saw no need for new civil rights legislation.

Then, for a variety of reasons, the logjam began to break up; and now we appear to be heading, with many painful detours, toward at least partial desegregation of our schools. Neither Mr. Nixon nor Mr. Wallace has been able to alter that drift of affairs. When the citizens of Mobile decided to heed federal busing guidelines rather than the rantings of their governor, something fundamental, perhaps revolutionary, had occurred. Similarly, when school systems throughout the North started to desegregate — not because segregation was wrong but because it was illegal — we were getting very close to the heart of the matter.

All this activity is prologue to the main event: the breaking up of our black ghettos and the concomitant integration of our white suburbs. That fight, as we shall see, has yet to be waged. It remains one of the toughest challenges in the '70s.

There was a time, not very long ago, when desegregation of our neighborhoods was viewed as a relatively simple matter by most of its supporters. It seemed then to depend upon a "change of heart" among white residents, a sudden seizure of conscience that would magically open the ghetto gates. Accordingly, fair-housing enthusiasts preached tolerance to real estate brokers and signed petitions pledging to welcome black neighbors, provided those black neighbors had a suitable income. All this was naive but understandable. Over the years a substantial segment of the white population has, in fact, undergone just such a change of heart. National polls invariably indicate that at least half the white population "would not object" if a black family moved next door. But the ghetto gates have remained closed.

It soon became clear that many whites were capable of deploring neighborhood segregation without necessarily abolishing it. At this point the emphasis switched from conscience to legislation, and during the '50s many states and cities passed laws banning discrimination in various types of housing. Today twenty-six states and more than two hundred cities have such laws on their books. Still, the ghetto gates have remained closed.

During the '60s anti-segregationists pinned most of their hopes on federal reforms, beginning with President Kennedy's 1962 Executive Order which barred discrimination in new housing that was federally financed or insured. Then, in 1968, both Congress and the Supreme Court struck blows at segregation which many observers at the time considered decisive. The Congress passed a fair-housing law that banned discrimination in virtually all of the nation's 65 million housing units; the law applied not only to landlords and sellers but also to banks, insurance companies, and real estate brokers.

Almost simultaneously the Supreme Court affirmed the old Civil Rights Act passed in 1866, which forbids racial discrimination in the sale or rental of all housing and land. "When racial discrimination herds men into ghettos and makes their ability to buy property turn on the color of their skin," said the justices, "then it . . . is a relic of slavery. . . ."

Even then the ghetto gates did not open. Why not? The reason most frequently advanced, both by the New Left and the old Right, is that blacks no longer wish to integrate white neighborhoods (if, indeed, they ever did). There is some truth in this. In a study on *Protest and Prejudice,* Gary T. Marx notes that less than a third of the urban blacks he interviewed preferred to live in racially mixed neighborhoods, and only 4 percent would choose neighborhoods that were "mostly white." Yet most blacks seem to recognize the theoretical truth that the road to better housing usually leads to neighborhoods beyond the ghetto. A 1969 *Fortune* survey, for instance, indicates that 93 percent of the nation's blacks favor desegregation in housing.

A far more likely reason for the failure of legal reforms to produce fair housing is white ambivalence. A nation that wants it both ways—to mingle and to part—has a tendency to make laws it will not enforce and promises it will not keep. In general, and despite new pride and militancy among blacks, *the main barrier to neighborhood desegregation remains white intransigence, not black clannishness.* In any case, the new laws are on the books and the new promises are on our conscience. We can cash them in whenever we're ready.

I concede, on the face of it, that we do not appear to be ready. All the indices of recent years suggest that whites and blacks are more rigidly and irreversibly estranged from one another today than ever before. Thanks to sociologist Karl E. Taeuber we have a rough statistical index of our madness. Taeuber used 1960 census figures to analyze the degree of racial segregation in 207 cities, placing them on a scale from zero (no segregation) to 100 (absolute segregation). The *least* segregated city, San Jose, California, had an index rating of 60.4. Half the cities had segregation ratings above 87, and one-quarter exceeded 91. Only eight cities were rated below 70.

The migrations of the sixties have brought us still closer to total apartheid. Today only 7 percent of our suburban population is black, while more than half of all American blacks live in central cities. At least four cities already have black majorities. If the trend continues for another decade, the 1980 census will list more than fifty cities with black majorities.

It is all too easy to interpret these events fatalistically, that is, as the inevitable product of powerful and impersonal forces that sweep all before them. After all, the two great migrations — that of blacks from rural South to urban North, and that of whites from cities to suburbs — have been going on for generations. Back in 1890, Jacob Riis noted that "New York has been receiving the overflow of colored population from Southern cities. In the last decade this migration has grown to such proportions that it is estimated that our Blacks have quite doubled in number since the Tenth Census." During the same period Alexander T. Stewart, a New York department-store magnate, conceived the idea for a planned residential development in Garden City, Long Island, and thus inaugurated what might be called the Age of the Suburbs.

Most authorities, of course, attribute these twin migrations to industrialization, that is, to the new farm machinery that drove people off the land, and to the automobile that allowed others to move out to the suburbs. These are undeniable facts, yet they do not take into account the vital role racism played in the process. Not only did racism impel millions of black people northward, it also drove millions of white people outward to places like Garden City. It would have been more logical, after all, for blacks to have moved to suburbia, where land was cheaper and where the environment more closely resembled that of their rural origins. But it was not logic that moved populations. Riis cites the maxim of New York City's landlords: "Once a colored house, always a colored house" — a sure sign of creeping segregation.

It was clear from the start that "drawing the color line" was good business. By creating artificial housing shortages for black families, landlords were able to charge outrageous prices for shoddy housing. This cruel game is still being played. A post-riot study of Watts, for example, revealed that greater congestion had led to higher rents — this despite more than 100,000 housing vacancies in greater Los Angeles. Similarly, in Chicago almost half the black families earning $7,000 or more live in substandard dwellings; for white families with comparable incomes the figure is 6 percent.

Nor can anyone doubt that the white stampede to suburbia has filled the pockets of many businessmen — land speculators, realtors, bankers, home builders, and road builders, to name a few. In fact, one could make a fairly strong case for neighborhood segregation as a pillar of the American economy. Few suburban land developers would disagree with Mr. Dooley's dictum: "Life'd not be worth livin' if we didn't keep our inimies."

It is far from accidental that for generations real estate firms and lending institutions viewed racial segregation as axiomatic. "A Realtor should never be instrumental in introducing into a neighborhood . . . members of any race or nationality . . . whose presence will clearly be detrimental to property values in the neighborhood." This was the official opinion of the National Association of Real Estate Boards as late as 1957.

The point to remember here is that segregation did not simply "happen"; it was assiduously planned, promoted, and pampered by those who had most to gain from it. Eventually, it came to be taken for granted, a fixed shadow on our social landscape. City planners with Ph.D.'s drew their blueprints for future communities in black and white; school systems quietly shifted their boundaries to arrange for what they would later call de facto segregation; and, most significant of all, the federal government allied itself with the forces of segregation.

From the moment the government entered the housing business, back in the early '30s, it also entered the segregation business. In 1938 the official Federal Housing Administration (FHA) *Underwriting Manual* cautioned home buyers: "If a neighborhood is to retain stability, it is necessary that properties shall continue to be occupied by the same social and racial group." (*"Once a colored house, always a colored house."*) The manual recommended use of restrictive covenants to keep out "inharmonious racial groups," and even provided a model restrictive covenant for readers too innocent to write their own.

In another manual, not revised until 1949, FHA urged its mortgage valuators to consider whether "effective restrictive covenants against the entire tract are recorded, since these provide the surest protection against undesirable encroachment. . . ." It warned valuators to beware of "adverse influences," such as "infiltration of business and industrial uses, lower-class occupancy and inharmonious racial groups."

Other federal agencies were behaving no better. The Home Owners Loan Corporation, for example, which was organized in 1933 to buy up and refinance delinquent mortgages, sold houses *only* to members of the dominant race in a given neighborhood. And the public housing agency early established a policy of "racial equity"—a polite way of saying separate but equal housing—which to this day is honored by a majority of local housing authorities.

The government did its work well. It fixed segregationist patterns in thousands of new suburbs, where 80 percent of all new housing is now being built. Since World War II the FHA and the Veterans' Administration together have financed more than $130 billion in new housing. Less than 2 percent of it has been available to nonwhite families, and much of that on a strictly segregated basis. "It is one thing," notes Gunnar Myrdal in the *American Dilemma,* "when private tenants, property owners and financial institutions maintain and extend the patterns of racial segregation in housing. It is quite another when a Federal agency chooses to side with the segregationists."

There remains both within the federal government and the housing industry a considerable amount of segregationist sentiment. As recently as last summer, for example, an investigation by the U.S. Commission on Civil Rights revealed that federally subsidized houses—especially those subsidized by the Section 235 mortgage-assistance program—were being sold along the same old segregated lines: inner-city houses to blacks and suburban houses to whites.

But segregation has become less fashionable within the Establishment, with the result that the private prejudices of government and industry leaders are less frequently translated into public policy. Indeed, public policy seems now to be moving, albeit unenthusiastically, toward desegregation.

In *Politics of Federal Housing,* Harold Wolman cites results of interviews he conducted with sixty-seven members of "the decision-making elite" in formulation of housing policy. These included HUD officials, White House officials, congressmen, state and municipal government leaders, home builders, bankers, labor leaders, and a few civil rights representatives. Wolman asked them, among other things, whether they thought public policy should be directed more toward: (a) improving housing conditions within the ghetto; (b) dispersing the ghetto; or (c) both in about equal proportions. Only eight of the sixty-seven favored dispersing the ghetto, while nineteen favored improving it. But thirty-one wanted "both in about equal proportions." (The remainder either voiced a different opinion or no opinion.)

Furthermore, twenty-three of the "influentials" thought more federal control was needed in forming low-income housing policies, thus appearing to embrace President Nixon's nemesis—"forced integration." (Twenty-eight of the respondents favored more local control.) In general, one can conclude from Wolman's data that the people who make housing policy nowadays, while not exactly the avant garde of integration, are considerably more sympathetic to notions of desegregation than were their predecessors. It was the policy-makers of the '30s and '40s who laid the ghetto's cornerstone; and it is that cornerstone at which some of their successors are now beginning to chip away.

The public, meanwhile, may also be adjusting gradually to a desegregated future, but the transformation is no more inevitable than was segregation fifty years ago. It will have to be planned and even popularized. In particular, desegregationists will have to find an accommodation with blue-collar families, who offer us the paradox of simultaneously being the most obdurate of segregationists and the most promising candidates for integration. Historically, the Northern white blue-collar worker has been among the first to insist on his racial prerogatives. Frederick Douglass found this out when as an escaped slave in 1838 he secured a job on a shipbuilder's wharf in New Bedford, Massachusetts, the heart of abolitionist country. On his first day at work, "I was told that every white man would leave the ship in her unfinished condition if I struck a blow at my trade upon her." Douglass, a skilled calker and copperer, had to settle for common, unskilled labor at half the pay.

In those days integrated employment seemed a more serious threat to whites in the North than did integrated housing. But after Emancipation, as blacks began coming North in greater numbers, the residential neighborhood became a symbol of white supremacy. It was meanly defended. In the years immediately after World War I, for example, dozens of blacks were killed for venturing across the community color line, and scores more were beaten and sent packing.

"Where will these people live?" asked Clarence Darrow of a Detroit jury in 1925. Darrow was defending Dr. Ossian Sweet, a black physician accused of committing murder while protecting his house against a white mob. (The neighborhood Sweet had moved into was a bastion of first-generation white ethnocentricity.) "The colored people must live somewhere," Darrow continued. "Somewhere they must live. Are you going to kill them? Are you going to say they can work but cannot get a place to sleep? . . . Oh, gentlemen, what is the use! You know it is wrong. Everyone of you knows it is wrong."

In 1951, to cite a later instance, Harvey E. Clark, Jr., a black war veteran, tried to move his family into a $60 apartment in Cicero, Illinois. A mob, aided by local police, started fires in the building and forced Clark to flee at gunpoint. "Get out of Cicero," the police chief told him, "and don't come back to town or you'll get a bullet through you." A year later an investigating grand jury—with "a passion for irrelevancy," as the late Charles Abrams observed—indicted an NAACP attorney defending Clark as well as the owner of the apartment house, her lawyer and her rental agent, charging them all with conspiracy to injure property by causing "depreciation in the market selling price." (The indictments were later dropped.)

But surely the reader is familiar with this melancholy history. I have dredged up a bit of it here not to indict the past but to clarify the present. For it is clear that the Rosedale incident is but the latest footnote to a very old story.

It is well to state this plainly, because white ethnics nowadays are getting more than their fair share of sentimental whitewash. When the television comedy *All in the Family,* about a "lovable bigot" who doesn't want any "coons" living next door to him, attracts 100 million weekly viewers and wins an Emmy, the cause of desegregation has not been served.

Similarly, when the sociologist Andrew M. Greeley, in *Why Can't They Be Like Us?* absolves white ethnics from violent tendencies, one wonders at his grasp of history. "White ethnics are afraid of violence," Greeley assures us. "There was much of it in their past, both in this country and in Europe. . . . They now have much more to lose than they did in the past. The threat of violence implies that their efforts may have been in vain, and that their hard-won gains are in jeopardy." It is true, of course, that most white ethnics, like everyone else, are nonviolent in most contexts; but not always in the context of race relations, and hardly ever in the context of neighborhood segregation. When protesting blacks prepared to march through Cicero for the announced purpose of desegregating that town, the white residents were hardly "afraid of violence." The protesters deemed themselves lucky to finish their trial march alive.

Everything Greeley says about white ethnics could be said, *mutatis mutandi,* about blacks. There was much violence "in their own past." Their gains were "hard-won" and are "in jeopardy." Yet when Greeley discusses the blacks, he chooses to see them through the eyes of his white ethnics: "I must still insist that violence in American cities is real. Many streets are unsafe, most parks are unsafe . . .; quiet residential neighborhoods are open to easy attack, and the threat of violent eruption hangs over the city each summer. . . ." As if the streets in Rosedale are any safer for blacks than the streets in Harlem for whites!

What this amounts to, it seems to me, is old wine in new bottles; but now it is sanctified by the mass media as "lovable" and advertised by academics and others as harmless, or even healthy. The rhetoric of this new movement often has a familiar aura. Speaking at one of several recent conferences devoted to white ethnics, a Baltimore lady named Barbara Mikulski declared: "The ethnic American is sick of being stereotyped as a racist and dullard by phony white liberals, pseudo black militants and patronizing bureaucrats. . . . He himself is the victim of class prejudice." To be sure, the white ethnic *is* frequently a victim of class prejudice. But such belligerent apologias, replete with *their* stereotypes, are not reassuring. They could as easily have been spoken by a Rosedale rioter as by a Baltimore orator.

Some civil rights spokesmen who should know better have adopted a similar propaganda line. The Urban League, for instance, has published results of a national survey claiming to prove that "white 'native' Americans are more likely than Polish, Irish, or Italians to have anti-black attitudes." But the Urban League does not say what proportion of those anti-black native Americans live in the South, where most whites are WASPS.

One need not look far to see what the Urban League is driving at. It is the old dream of a blue-collar coalition between blacks and whites. "Close to half . . . of all households of Irish, Polish, or Italian origin are in manual occupations, or in so-called blue-collar work," notes the League. "They therefore may identify with many of the problems of lower-income minority members. Many of the white ethnics, in fact, work as peers with blacks, Puerto Ricans and Mexican-Americans. . . ."

The fallacy in all this is not that such a coalition is impossible — it *is* possible, provided we do not confuse white ethnics with white knights; the fallacy lies in the assumption that a coalition can be easily achieved, that white ethnics are psychologically "ripe" for it. The current vogue of glossing over historic conflicts between blue-collar blacks and blue-collar whites may undermine our last chance to form an effective coalition based on realities rather than myths.

For desegregationists the key reality today is a cruel housing shortage that for decades has plagued blacks and white blue-collar families as well. The situation is roughly as follows: In 1968 the Congress committed the nation—in principle at least—to the "construction or rehabilitation of 26 million housing units" during the next ten years. The figure reflected official estimates of what America would require if every family were to be decently housed. (According to the 1970 census, 4.3 million of our dwelling units are "substandard.")

These goals, in the opinion of many observers (including Mr. Romney), have been grossly understated. Yet even they are not being met. Tight money and inflated building and land costs are the reasons. The average new house today costs about 30 percent more than it cost in 1967, and payments have shot up 56 percent in that period.

The result is that many low- and moderate-income families are compelled to live in crowded, substandard housing. And the present "housing boom," which will probably produce more than two million new units, has done little to relieve the pinch. Mainly, this boom is for the affluent. The mobile home industry is breaking all sales records because mobile homes are the only dwellings most blue-collar families can afford to buy. But mobile homes are far from satisfactory: they provide less space for the money and tend to depreciate at a faster rate than does conventional housing. The mobile-home boom is a function not of public preference but of public desperation.

So far the Nixon administration has done little to redress the housing inequity. In fact, in 1971 the President released $2 billion in previously impounded "Special Assistance" money to keep the lid on the mortgage market for nonsubsidized, high-priced housing. Originally, Congress had intended this money to aid low- and moderate-income housing.

It seems likely, then, that the pressure for low-cost housing will continue to increase, and that this pressure will be generated at least as much by white ethnics as by blacks. If the two can work together, they will hasten the day when the Congress must act; and when that happens, the federal government will go into the housing business on a scale unprecedented, not only in central cities but in the suburbs as well.

Yet everything in our history suggests that a large portion of white America will try to secure better housing without paying the price of desegregation. If we allow this to occur, then in a relatively short time the nation will proceed to subsidize total apartheid through the construction of some thirty million housing units, about half again the number of units now extant. On the other hand, if whites and blacks, liberals and trade unionists, make desegregation a non-negotiable item, there may still be time to undo the work of the past hundred years—that is, to get ourselves together. In any event, America will soon learn whether the two races are fated to wholly mingle or wholly part.

Bibliographical Note

The best historical survey of segregated housing in the U.S. can be found in Charles Abrams, *Forbidden Neighbors* (New York, 1955); for more recent history, see James L. Hecht, *Because It Is Right* (Boston, 1970). The federal government's role in segregation is documented by Gunnar Myrdal, Richard Sterner, and Arnold Rose, in *American Dilemma* (New York, 1944), and more recently by Richard and Diane Margolis in a pamphlet, "How the Federal Government Builds Ghettos" (New York: National Committee Against Discrimination in Housing, 1967).

Current attitudes toward segregation among the federal "elite" have been studied by Harold Wolman in *The Politics of Federal Housing* (New York, 1971). See also *A Report to the President: AFSC Experience and Recommendations re: Executive Order 11063 on Equal Opportunity in Housing* (Philadelphia: American Friends Service Committee, 1967).

For a look at blue-collar fears pertaining to interracial housing, see *Forbidden Neighbors,* as well as Kenneth G. Weinberg, *A Man's Home, a Man's Castle* (New York, 1971). See also portions of Mike Royko's *Boss* (New York, 1971), particularly chap. 2.

Current blue-collar or "white ethnic" attitudes toward race are subject to debate. For one point of view see Andrew M. Greeley, *Why Can't They Be Like Us?* (New York, 1971); see also Stephen Clapp and Geno Baroni, "I'm a Pig, Too," in the *Washingtonian,* July 1970. For another viewpoint, see Timothy Lee's article, "Rosedale: Might Makes Right," in the *New York Post,* June 30, 1971.

The best continuing source of information on the national housing shortage and federal nonsolutions is *The Low-Income Housing Bulletin,* a monthly published by the Rural Housing Alliance, Washington, D.C.; see especially the issues of December 1970 and September 1971.

Sweet and Sour Notes
Irving Howe

On Workers and Intellectuals

The working class is a social presence; the proletariat, a historical potential. No one can question the place of the workers in the industrialized countries: their politics, their role in the work process, their ways of life. They exist, they constitute a distinctive class, they are a force. But the proletariat as agent of revolution—this remains a problem, an enigma, perhaps a delusion. For some it is still an indestructible hope; for others a burned-out disappointment.

The working class is a reality, the proletariat an idea. The reality occupies physical and social space, the idea survives in the minds of intellectuals. Surviving in the minds of intellectuals can sometimes endow that idea with great power and thereby transform it into a new social reality. Yet this seems least likely in the advanced capitalist countries, the portion of the world Marxism declared to be center-stage for the proletarian drama. Perhaps, then, there is something wrong with the idea.

Where the working class has refused to accept the historical role of recreating itself as a revolutionary proletariat, a phalanx of disabled theoreticians, intellectuals, and functionaries searches desperately for a connection, some way of linking their idea with the reality. Perhaps, they speculate, all that is needed is patience; per-

IRVING HOWE is editor of Dissent *and the author of, among other books,* Decline of the New, Steady Work, *and* A World More Attractive, *and co-author, with B. J. Widick, of* The UAW and Walter Reuther.

haps a new strategic policy; perhaps a shock administered to the sullen flesh of the working class. But the reality proves intractable, the connection is not found, and some, in the sardonic words of Brecht, begin to wonder whether it might not be better to create a "new" proletariat.

The social class or group that remains most attached to the idea or potential of the proletariat, to the hope that it will yet appear in heroic and transfiguring guise, is . . . not the working class itself, indeed, almost anyone but the working class. Sons of millionaires, Hegel-stricken professors, street desperadoes, Latin guerrillas — none of whom have the slightest connection with the working class as it exists — *they* are caught up with the idea of the proletariat.

Not, to be sure, because they have much interest in or sympathy with the actual experience of the discrete human beings who compose the working class. No; they are social engineers, candidates for tomorrow's politburo, in search of a revolutionary motor by which to start up the quest for power. What obsesses them is, above all else, the image of revolution, revolution as act and will, revolution apart from, perhaps against, the laws of history or the inertia of the masses. The future society interests them less than do visions of power, and visions of power less than does the brilliant apocalypse of revolution. Bastard descendents of Sorel, they live by visions of final conflagration.

Marxism declared that history, having presumably been subjugated once and for all to scientific law, has assigned to the working class the task of creating itself as a proletariat and thereby liberating all of humanity. It was a vision of great power: the "chosen" class. But suppose the working class refused the honor? Or proved incapable of fulfilling the assignment?

Confronting this possibility, Trotsky said that in such an event it would be necessary for socialists to remain partisans of the enslaved, even if the latter could never throw off their enslavement. Morally admirable, his answer is politically unsatisfying because it depends on a refusal to consider any middle term between absolute revolution and unending oppression.

This refusal is perpetuated, though seldom with Trotsky's grandeur or purity, by those neo-Marxists who have recently discovered Lukacs and Marcuse. They, too, enjoy the positing of inflexible alternatives: either the working class performs the tasks assigned to it by history (that notorious scold) or it shows itself to be a historical nullity, a class doomed never to fulfill its potentiality through a conquest of power.

Lukacs seems to believe the assignment will yet be completed, Marcuse that the date for completion has long since past. Yet they are not as far apart as might seem. Marcuse has given up on the

working class—it has disappointed him—and he scoffs at it as "integrated," "one-dimensional," and worse. Lukacs remains, apparently,
an orthodox Marxist. But his famous "voluntarism," in *History and
Class Consciousness,* is not merely a persuasive rebuke to the passivity of the old-line European Social Democrats who acquiesce in
the status quo by ceding socialism to the automatic laws of history;
it is also a counsel of desperation, and sometimes a signal for desperadoes, since it rests on a tacit recognition that the working class has
indeed failed to elevate itself to a proletariat, or at least shows little
aptitude for doing so by itself. Consequently, Lukacs places an enormous stress on the "voluntarism" of the revolutionary vanguard, that
is, the self-appointed intellectual elite of the Communist parties. By
no very subtle methods, this elite takes over or "replaces" both the
working class as it is and the proletariat as it should be but is not. Why
this notion should appeal to deracinated intellectuals who propose to
substitute guerrilla terrorism for the self-activity of the masses needs
no elaboration. A reviewer of Lukacs's book makes the point neatly:

> Certainly when Lukacs effects his divorce between an abstract prole-
> tarian class-consciousness, whose concrete embodiment is the
> authority of the Communist Party, and the empirically observed
> thoughts and feelings of proletarians submitted to that authority,
> he opens the door wide for a return to a regime of "reified" laws and
> institutions, in the form of the party and its discipline, imposing a
> false consciousness or ideology on the mass of workers.—*Times
> Literary Supplement* (London), June 6, 1971

Must we accept the categorical either/or? Suppose that the
Leninist option is false and that we need not choose between the working class as proletarian savior and the working class as supine victim.
Suppose it persists in finding its own ends and its own way, neither
the precise ends of Marx nor the fixed way of Lenin. Suppose it
chooses to be neither the agent of world transformation nor the
eternally crushed victim of exploitation. To all the neo-Marxists, with
or without Hegelian trim, this is the one possibility that seems most
irritating. It disturbs their sense of symmetry.

Or suppose, again, that the working class in the advanced
countries chooses the path the neo-Marxists call "embourgeoisement,"
a phrase that has never been known to frighten a single worker in the
entire world. For what the use of this phrase "embourgeoisement"
really signifies is a contempt for the daily experience and aspirations
of the workers. In social reality, the process that provokes this term
of excoriation is the gradual strengthening of the independent institutions of the working class within the welfare state, a society retaining

essential elements of capitalism yet steadily modifying them. The working class becomes more firmly established within the society, gaining greater control over the terms and conditions of its life than it has ever had in the past — certainly, greater control than any working class enjoys in a Communist country.

The workers choose their own path. Marxists had always said, "The liberation of the working class is the task of the workers alone." It now seems, however, that many of these Marxists intended a secret codicil: "Yes, but only if that liberation occurs within the delimited avenues to which we, mentors of the working class and creators of the proletariat, have assigned it."

Nowhere, neither West nor East, has the liberation of the working class yet occurred in the sense that Marxists envisaged. Perhaps what they envisaged must now be seen as a historical limit to be approached, rather than a fixed goal to be achieved. In any case, it is useful to ask: Where, to use a Marxist category, do the workers come closer to constituting "a class for itself" — where do they have more independence, assertiveness, dignity, and a greater sense of their potential: in England, not yet visited by the revolution, or, Russia, fifty years after it has occurred? In Sweden, where not a large enough portion of the means of production has been nationalized, or in China, where too large a portion has been nationalized?

History refuses to perform by blueprint. The working class in the West is neither promethean nor servile. With time there remains the possibility that, envisaging new goals and finding new allies, it will move beyond the incremental politics to which it is committed in the welfare state and toward its own version of socialism. If so, it will have no need for commissars who would discipline it or *enragés* who would terrorize it.

The working class may yet find its own images of potentiality, surely less dramatic than those assigned to it by Marxist intellectuals, but also, one may suppose, less bloody, less apocalyptic, less sacrificial.

I turn to a narrower theme, but no less abrasive: the relations between intellectuals and unionists.

Most intellectuals and most unionists neither know nor care much about the other. Across chasms, people do not quarrel. Only when they are, or once were, close to each other do they grow heated in debate. The disputes occur between the small number of intellectuals still attached to the idea of unionism and the small number of unionists still concerned with what intellectuals say.

Let's rehearse the case against the radical intellectuals as an intelligent unionist can make it, a case often valid and sometimes devastating.

Intellectuals have always nourished abstract ideas and sentiments about the people who lead or belong to unions: they have never been willing to see unions as they actually are. A few decades ago, those ideas and sentiments were enthusiastic, out of sympathy for the dramatic struggles of the unions, and sometimes misguided, out of a wish to gratify socialist expectations. Only seldom have intellectuals bothered to look closely at the lives of workers or the workings of unions; only seldom have they understood what is distinctive about the role of unions in American society. If they had, they could not seriously have supposed that unions in the United States can be expected to behave according to models drawn from the European experience.

Looking for a proletariat where none is to be found, the radical intellectuals suffer disillusionment. From disillusionment they turn savagely against the workers, condemning them for a failure to be what they, the workers, never dreamed of becoming. If not dismissed *en masse* as "one-dimensional" (a complaint from which you and I do not, of course, suffer), the workers are sneered at as overfed slobs named Joe and Archie.

This is the stereotype, even caricature, favored among many leftist intellectuals during recent years, and it surely is enough to sour even the most imaginative unionists against intellectuals as a group.

If unionists had listened to the Stalinist intellectuals, they would have committed suicide, first through "dual unionism" and the theory of "social fascism," and then in another dozen ways. If they had listened to the left-socialist intellectuals, they would have been persuaded that the Wagner Act was a step toward "fascism," thereby refraining from the organization of the millions of workers that in fact occurred during the 1930s. If they had listened to the Trotskyist intellectuals, they would have remained indifferent to the outcome of World War II on the ground that it was "imperialist" on both sides.

Not a pretty list—though one that could easily be extended. The advice of the radical intellectuals to unions has often been disastrous, quite as their tone has been arrogant. I draw a one-sided picture, deliberately, to stress why the suspicion with which even sophisticated unionists look upon left-wing intellectuals is not without some basis in reality.

Let's turn now to the case that the intellectuals could make against the unionists, often valid and sometimes devastating.

The run-of-the-mill union leadership has usually been trapped in a crude pragmatism, according to which it confined itself to the rituals of collective bargaining, and has failed to see that external social events might undermine or undo even the best of contracts and that there were many critical problems affecting workers that no contract could even begin to cope with.

In its own way, the union leadership has been as ideological as any of the radical intellectuals—only theirs has been an unacknowledged and inadequate ideology. The most bitter experiences have been required to teach the unions that they had to confront the larger social issues; that they needed intellectual help and guidance on a range of problems from trends in employment to foreign policy; that pure-and-simple unionism is as obsolete as laissez-faire in economy. The unions, to be sure, have become major agencies for social reform within the welfare state, but by now the limitations of that policy, essential though it remains, are becoming evident. All officials and office holders, including those in unions, yearn for stasis; reality is so cruel as to deny it.

Valuable as the unions' achievements have been in regard to domestic legislation, they have sadly failed to cope with the kinds of problems that arise *after* the welfare state is instituted. On a whole range of social (as distinct from economic) issues, the unions are tongue-tied or retrograde. With respect to major new constituencies—the young, the academics, the "new class" of technicians, the middle-class reformers—the unions often take a hardbitten attitude, as if intent on driving off potential allies. On questions of foreign policy, many unions remain locked in a Cold War rigidity, victims of Lovestoneism.

And then there's the record, spotty in general and disgraceful in some particulars, of the unions regarding internal democracy. Little wonder that idealistic youth, only a few decades ago so warmly inclined toward unions, now feels a mere indifference toward them. A process of petrifaction has set in, and while the unions continue to do well in their own province, they cannot be hailed as they were only a few decades ago.

Again, a one-sided picture, drawn deliberately, to stress why the suspicion that even sympathetic intellectuals have toward official union policies is not without some basis in reality.

These two outlines of caricature—unionists toward intellectuals, intellectuals toward unionists—have the value of rendering sharply feelings that are sometimes suppressed for reasons of tact. Yet, once stated, of what use are they? Surely, not for purposes of mutual dissociation. Socialists, no matter how critical of unions, want to remain their partisans. Perhaps one value in bringing these feelings out into the open is to clear the air a little, and thereby begin the slow work of reknitting cordial relations.

Beyond that, it might be useful to recognize that—apart from the rightness or wrongness of the points made by either side—some of the conflicts between intellectuals and unionists are not only unavoidable but even fruitful. Often, the two deal with problems different in character and scope, so that the strengths of one may well be the weaknesses of the other. It is the job of intellectuals to speculate, generalize, try to see problems from some imagined moment in the future. It is the job of unionists to grapple with urgencies, gain rapid tangible advantages for their constituents, hold firmly to the obligations of the present. Only rarely do intellectuals make good union leaders, or union leaders good intellectuals.

The point should not be overstressed, if only because it might make things too easy for both sides. For if each performs distinctive functions which the other cannot, they also overlap in their interests and work. As our society grows more complex and intractable, unionists discover that they have to double as intellectuals and intellectuals that they have to involve themselves in immediate problems.

Some intellectuals have wanted, during the last two or three decades, to participate directly in the life of the unions, mostly as technicians and staff men who put special skills at the service of the leadership. By now there is hardly a union leadership that doesn't recognize the need for economists, writers, time-study experts, and the like.

Though not myself directly involved, I have been able to watch the experience of such intellectuals for some years now, and so far as I can see, it has by no means been without strain and disappointment. The problem is this: very few union leaderships are prepared to recognize that the intellectuals whom they employ must be allowed—at least if they are to remain intellectuals (and if not, what use can they be even as technicians?)—the kind of independence of thought and statement that the academy allows professors. Even to make such a comparison would strike many union leaders as absurd.

They feel, whether or not they say, that if those economists, writers, and other experts work "for us," then they had better toe the line in public. Mostly, it's a gut feeling owing partly to the proprietary sense that union leaders develop toward their organizations, but also to the rough-and-tumble tradition, not exactly conducive to intellectual nuance, that has dominated many unions. By and large, both because of tight employment conditions and the submissive idealism of some labor intellectuals, the leadership has had its way. In some unions, with heavy hand; in others, more delicately. For the labor intellectuals themselves, the problem has always been difficult: they usually lacked any "mass base" in a local or other segment of the union for which they worked, so that they were totally dependent on the goodwill of the leadership; they were not, as a rule, much good at intra-union politics, so that they could seldom maneuver between one group of leaders and another: and sometimes they were themselves half-persuaded of the rationales that were improvised for depriving them of public independence.

Because of the difficulties in which they found themselves, a good many labor intellectuals — I'd guess, the more gifted ones — have gradually and quietly drifted away from their union posts and moved into the academy. One understands their motives: they are genuinely attached to the idea of unionism and have worked hard in its behalf, yet they wish to enjoy the autonomy that intellectuals attached to universities command.

Among more sophisticated unionists — those who don't just content themselves with telling you who's boss — there is often heard the argument which asserts that unions are combat organizations requiring a degree of discipline that precludes complete freedom of public speech for any of their officers or employees. This argument has a certain plausibility, but the more you think about it, the more inclined you are to consider it specious. If, let us say, a trade union is engaged in a bitter strike, it surely has a right to expect that its economist will not at that moment issue a public statement denouncing the strike strategy or the bargaining demands. There, indeed, some collective discipline seems appropriate. But if an intellectual employed by a union writes in his own name to express views on economic policy, political candidacies, and the Vietnam War that are at variance with those of his union's leaders, he should be able to do so in complete freedom and without jeopardizing his job. He should feel as free as a professor; but in truth, he seldom does.

These days young people, whatever their other merits or demerits, tend to cherish the right of independence and to be very skeptical about claims for organizational discipline. On the whole, that's fine. If, however, the unions continue to display their traditional attitudes toward intellectuals, they simply are not going to attract the brighter and more gifted young people, the kind they urgently need in a variety of posts. What they will attract will be time-servers and yes-men, of whom there is already no shortage in the ranks.

Finally, it is a matter of principle — the point Herman Benson brilliantly argues in his article — that if unions are to be persuasive in their claims to constitute a major defense of democracy, they must show themselves to be democratic within their own life. They are being asked to respond to a social and moral pressure that—fitfully, erratically, but significantly—extends throughout our society; and it is good that they should be asked.

IV. Class and Ethnicity

New Ethnicity and Blue Collars
Andrew M. Greeley

Cultural Pluralism in the Working Class

It is a truism among liberal academics that we have a lot to learn from the blacks, a truism I fully concede. Yet, does any liberal academic believe in his heart that we have much to learn from the Poles or the Italians?

I have asked this question in order to suggest that racism in the United States is but a manifestation of a much wider bigotry. And I would submit that this larger bigotry can be found precisely among those so ready to confess their guilt over racism and to insist that the rest of us confess, too. Bigotry against those who are "different" may well be less intense in the United States than in any other large nation, but it's still here, and while blacks suffer the most, they are by no means the only ones. Robert Coles has documented in his *Middle Americans* the strange, complex mixture of bigotry and enlightenment in middle America. It would be interesting if some similarly sensitive author documented the bigotry in intellectual America. We have permitted ourselves to be deceived by the research showing

ANDREW M. GREELEY is director of the Center for the Study of American Pluralism at the National Opinion Research Center, and a lecturer in sociology at the University of Chicago. Among his books are Why Can't They Be Like Us? *and* The Denominational Society. *This essay is from his new book,* That Most Distressful Nation: The Taming of the American Irish, *copyright © 1972 by Andrew M. Greeley, and printed here by permission of the publisher, Quadrangle Books.*

that prejudice scores go down as education goes up. We have rarely if ever asked whether the better educated get higher scores simply because they are likely to know in advance the "right" answers.

The fundamental assumption behind distrust of diversity is that it ought to go away unless it is the diversity based on social class — and that *this* diversity only is "rational." American theory endorses cultural pluralism, but our behavior insists on as much assimilation as possible, as quickly as possible. Many liberals were properly horrified in the era of Senator Joseph McCarthy when, as Pat Moynihan put it, Fordham men were investigating Harvard men. The Irish Catholics and their Italian successors had become "superpatriots." Only rarely did anyone bother to ask whether there were fierce pressures at work demanding that they become superpatriots, if only to establish that they were Americans just like everyone else.

Underlying the assumption that all diversity except that of social class ought to go away is a basic model, which either in pop or sophisticated versions permeates much of social science. It is an evolutionary model that sees the human race moving from *Gemeinschaft* to *Gesellschaft* — from community to association — from the sacred to the profane, from the particularistic to the universalistic. The great men of proto-sociology — Tönnies, Tröltsch, Weber, Durkheim — all chronicled the end of a peasant, feudal era and the beginning of a modern, urban era. *Gemeinschaft* was dying, they thought, and the rationalized, bureaucratized city was replacing the tribal, ascriptive society of the peasant commune. Ties of blood, faith, land were becoming less important. What counted was one's place in the technostructure. It was important what one did, not who one was. The bureaucrat must treat all men evenhandedly because in the world of rationalized bureaucracy all men were interchangeable. Ties of common faith, common ancestry, common race could be expected quickly to vanish.

For Max Weber the disappearance of *Gemeinschaft* was not something to be especially happy about. He, Tönnies, and others felt a distinct nostalgia for the world that was disappearing and grave unease about the new one emerging, but many of their successors have taken the evolutionary model not merely as description but as norm. The irrational — that is, the sacred, ascriptive, particularistic — was not only going away, it *ought* to be going away. Men not only were organizing themselves around the dimension of social class, but this was the way they *ought* to organize themselves. Communities based on common kinship or faith or historic experiences were "irrational" and hence immoral. They belonged to a past the evolutionary process was inevitably leaving behind.

One can leave to such existential philosophers as Gabriel Marcel and political critics as John Schaar the question of whether the bureaucratic model is adequate for human life. One can also assume that most sociologists are now sophisticated enough to realize that *Gemeinschaft* has survived and is doing nicely. Yet the pop version of the *Gemeinschaft-Gesellschaft* model has become an accepted part of conventional wisdom. If men would stop defining themselves as Irish or Italians or Catholics or Missouri Synod Lutherans, they would be better human beings, and our society also would be better.*

A number of damaging results flow from the conviction that these irrational diversities ought to go away.

(1) The demand for cultural pluralism is confused with a demand for separation and, since separation is bad, so is cultural pluralism. Very recently, an exception has been made for blacks; now it is more or less conceded among American elites that separatism —for blacks—is good. These elites don't seem to understand that American blacks are not asking for separation from the rest of society but for the right to develop their own culture within the society. Research done at the University of Michigan shows that large majorities of blacks are in favor of black studies while only tiny minorities are seeking a black nation. The research demonstrates that what we are dealing with in the black-pride phenomenon, even among the young, is not a desire to isolate oneself from the rest of American society but the right to have one's own particular heritage and culture respected as part of the society.

The blacks and the Spanish-speaking Americans may force on mainstream America that cultural pluralism which we have honored in theory and rarely accepted in practice, and eventually they may persuade mainstream America that cultural pluralism is not separatism. For the Germans and the Irish, it's too late. Their ethnic heritage has been strangled, but black and Spanish-speaking Americans may make it possible for Italian and Polish Americans to keep alive in the larger American context something of the past from which they came.

---

* Professor William Simon has gone so far as to suggest that my insistence on the importance of primordial ties reflects the official position of the Catholic Church. Apparently he doesn't realize that the Catholic Church is quite incapable of having official positions anymore, and that it is terribly uneasy about the rediscovery of ethnicity. American Catholicism has done all it could to promote the elimination of ethnic differences—in its own efforts to prove that it is as American as anyone else, if not more so—and now suddenly discovers the process may have been a mistake and needs to be reversed. With one or two exceptions, such as Michael Novak, American Catholic intellectuals have shown little taste for the revival of interest in ethnicity. Of course, it's hard for them because their ethnic past has only recently been forgotten.

The sociologist Paul Metzger has argued persuasively the case for cultural pluralism. He notes that

> Sociologists, by and large, have accepted the image of Horatio Alger in the Melting Pot as the ideal definition of American society. Although they have repeatedly documented the discrepancy between social reality and cultural myth in America, they have also taken the view that the incorporation of America's ethnic and racial groups into the mainstream culture is virtually inevitable.... Successful assimilation, moreover, has been viewed as synonymous with equality of opportunity and upward mobility ... assimilation is viewed as the embodiment of the democratic ethos.

Metzger offers three conclusions:

> (a) The belief that racial assimilation constitutes the only democratic solution to the race problem in the United States should be relinquished by sociologists.... The assimilationist strategy overlooks the functions which ethnic pluralism may perform in a democratic society....
> (b) To abandon the idea that ethnicity is a dysfunctional survival from a prior stage of social development will make it possible for sociologists to reaffirm that minority-majority relations are in fact group relations, and not merely relations between prejudiced and victimized individuals. As such, they are implicated in the struggle for power and privilege in the society....
> (c) To abandon the notion that assimilation is a self-completing process will make it possible to study the forces ... which facilitate or hinder assimilation or ... which generate the sense of ethnic and racial identity ... It is certainly within the province of sociological analyses to point to the possibilities of conscious intervention in the social process (by either the majority or the minority group) to achieve given ends.*

Metzger's conclusions seem eminently sane. For American society is a complex society in which the idea of assimilation and homogenization is an absurd one.

(2) A second result of adherence to the assimilationist model is that we misunderstand the American political structure. Elite groups assume that "issue politics" are the issues of social class; for, after all, social class is the only "rational" difference in the society. If we are to have a rational politics, we must have a politics of social class

---

* L. Paul Metzger, "American Sociology and Black Assimilation: Conflicting Perspectives," *American Journal of Sociology,* January 1971, pp. 628–629, 643–644.

in which men are divided into liberal and conservative, depending on whether they take the position of the rich or the poor. The black phenomenon can be fit into this image of politics by assuming that all blacks are poor—or identify with the black poor—and, hence, belong on the "liberal" side. It's a little more difficult to figure out why most Jews are liberal because social-class position should put a considerable number of them on the side of the conservatives.

The conviction that social-class politics are the only kind of rational politics shows the grip Marxism of a sort has on the minds of most American intellectuals. But from the very beginning, American politics were denominational and regional. The framers of the Constitution were already operating within the framework of a cultural consensus that saw the need to recognize that regional and religious diversity necessitated toleration for pluralism.

The political structure of the early years of the Republic reinforced that consensus. However much the ideal of assimilation might be urged, it was nevertheless essential to recognize that in addition to social class issues, there were also issues of race, religion, and nationality. Our elites rail against these issues as ethnic politics, without realizing that ethnic politics is part of the very fabric of American life. The attempt to impose the European Left-Right continuum simply does not correspond to the nature of American politics. Worse, it fails to recognize one of the most important accomplishments of American life. We have learned not only to harmonize social class diversity within some kind of civil and political unity—however tenuous at times—but also to harmonize, more or less, regional, religious, ethnic, and racial diversity.*

An emphasis on the politics of "rational issues," that is, issues of social class, ignores the richness and success of the American political enterprise. Conflict between capital and labor is, somehow, rational and legitimate. Conflict between black and Pole or, in New York, between black and Jew, over access to the land of the city, is irrational and illegitimate. It is all right for society to develop mechanisms to deal with the former conflict in the political order, but it is immoral for society to develop mechanisms for trying to deal with the latter problem—or, if mechanisms are to be developed, they must be based on the assumption that one side is moral and the other not.

(3) Since it is assumed that most ethnic groups ought to vanish

---

* I do not hesitate to say "racial diversity," because the overwhelming evidence of survey data is that blacks still accept the American political structure and, indeed, are optimistic about their future gains within that structure.

(except for Jews, blacks, Spanish-speaking Americans, and American Indians), and since it is also assumed that most ethnic groups have no contribution to make, it is scarcely worth learning anything about them. Italians provide pizza, Poles provide Polish jokes, and the Irish provide corrupt politicians. The Greeks, the Latvians, the Slovaks, the Slovenes, the Luxembourgers, the Armenians? Well, they're all going to go away, too. The blunt truth is that many members of those elite groups who read the *New York Times* and the *Washington Post,* and also *Commentary* and the *New York Review of Books,* know more about Nigeria than about the Northwest Side of Chicago, and have a much better understanding of the issues facing Britain in its entry into the Common Market than of the issues facing American Poles and Italians. The myths that the hard hat supports the war and the white ethnics are racist are myths that persist in the face of overwhelming statistical evidence to the contrary, in part because the opinion-making intellectual and political elite really don't think it worth the effort to learn anything about the alleged hard hats and racists.

Such ignorance can be useful. In a city like Newark, the decision to base promotion in the school system on racial factors rather than test scores is a decision that benefits the blacks to the disadvantage of the Italians. There is no getting around it: as long as the decision is limited to the school system and to the city of Newark, anything done to help the blacks will hurt the Italians. The latter group may argue that nobody sought balance for them thirty or forty years ago. They wonder why, just as they have begun to make it on their own, they are to be punished for a social injustice with the creation of which they had little or nothing to do. If one knows something about Italian Americans, one might even think this would be a gross injustice and that if anybody is to be selected by society to pay the price, it certainly ought not to be the Italians. But this would make things much too complicated. Far better to mark the Italians down as victims and proceed with one's plans. How to justify such a strategy? It's easy. Italians, after all, are white ethnic racists who refuse to confess their guilt.

(4) Ethnicity is immoral—when it isn't a white ethnic racist cop-out. There are two versions of the charge of immorality; one from militant blacks and their white supporters, and the other from the mainstream white liberals. Wherever the subject of ethnicity is discussed, there is always a black person present who shakes his head and says he wonders why this interest in ethnicity seems to have come precisely at the time when American blacks are finally beginning to get some tiny fragments of justice. It looks to him, he observes, as though the concern for ethnicity is simply one more form of white

racism. Such an observation, while perhaps understandable, is socially and politically obtuse. *The new consciousness of ethnicity is in part based on the fact that the blacks have legitimated cultural pluralism as it has perhaps never been legitimated before.* Other Americans, observing that now it is all right to be proud of being black, wonder, quite reasonably, why it is not all right to be proud of being Italian or Polish. Perhaps more important, without some kind of fundamental consensus from, if not the active cooperation of, white ethnic Americans, the reasonable goals of American blacks will not be achieved.

If positive cooperation is not possible, it still is true that in most large American cities, black goals are not going to be achieved without at least passive consent of substantial numbers of white ethnics. The response is that the white ethnics are so racist, even passive consent cannot be expected. Research shows that the ethnics are no more racist than anyone else, and that the Irish are second only to Jews in their score on pro-integration scales; but such evidence is systematically ignored by those convinced it can't possibly be true.

The other objections to the concern for ethnicity come from those mainstream American liberals who are still dogmatically convinced that ethnic diversity is a "bad thing." Professor William Simon, for example, sees life as so narrow, dull, provincial, and frustrating in white ethnic communities that the best thing we could do is help their few sensitive young people to break out.

In both cases, the conclusion from the implicit model is the same. Diversity is bad. The inevitable corollary of such a conclusion is that those who are different from us should change because, obviously, we can't be expected to change.

So powerful is the model that says social-class differences are good and/or rational, and that ethnic, racial, and religious differences (with exemptions for blacks and Jews) are bad and/or irrational that many of the agencies becoming involved with research on ethnic groups justify it by saying that what they are in fact interested in is "blue-collar" workers. It is very difficult to persuade elite Americans that there are many blue-collar workers in the cities who are not "ethnic" (read Italian or Polish), and that there are many ethnics who are not blue-collar workers. The notion that there are upper-middle-class Polish and Italian suburban professionals runs so contrary to the social geography of many of the liberal elite that they seem quite incapable of believing that such people exist. I certainly do not want to suggest that the present plight of the blue-collar worker is not worth considering, but I must insist that the blue-collar worker is one thing and the ethnic is something different, and while there is a partial overlap, it is not complete.

Obviously, I have a model of my own, and its broad outlines, I suppose, are implicit in my railing against the official one. What has happened with the urbanization and industrialization of society is not the replacement of *Gemeinschaft* by *Gesellschaft,* but rather a tremendous expansion of human relationships, and most of the new relationships — with the bus driver, the traffic policeman, the department-store clerk, the government bureaucrat, the personnel officer at the factory — are in fact *Gesellschaft* relationships. But because whole new areas of relationships have been created, it does not follow that the old forms of human relationships have been eliminated. It merely means that they no longer exhaust the totality of life.

We now must turn to a question that is both central and difficult. What is the relationship between ethnicity and social class? Are blue-collar ethnics influenced more by their blue-collar status or by their ethnicities? The question is fairly simple to phrase, but there is no simple answer.

There are three different perspectives from which ethnic groups are viewed by contemporary American sociologists. The first is taken explicitly by Herbert Gans in his brilliant book *The Urban Villagers.* Gans sees the behavior of the Italians in a community threatened by urban renewal in Boston as essentially working-class behavior and not as behavior uniquely Italian.

The second perspective is employed by Daniel Patrick Moynihan and Nathan Glazer in *Beyond the Melting Pot.* Glazer and Moynihan see the ethnic groups of New York City as essentially interest groups. There is no longer a substantial cultural component attached to membership in an ethnic community, but the communities will persist in any case because, through the course of history, they have become super-interest groups whose numbers perceive political and economic advantage in sustaining cooperation with each other.

The third perspective is advanced by Peter Rossi (mostly in personal conversations) and suggests that, in addition to a social-class component and an interest-group component, ethnic communities are still the bearers of cultural traditions. Passed on in the early socialization experience, these traditions take the form of subtle differences in what people expect from those with whom they have close relationships.

In the present state of research, it is impossible to say what blend of the three perspectives is most useful for understanding ethnic diversity in American society. But on the basis of research in progress at the National Opinion Research Center, the following assertions can tentatively be made:

¶ Considerable ethnic diversities persist even when social class is held constant. The work being done by Norman Nie and Barbara Currie confirms my own earlier research showing that political and social attitudes differ significantly among various ethnic groups even when social class is held constant. Work I am doing with William McCready indicates that even when social class is held constant there are very considerable differences among ethnic groups in personality orientations, occupational values, expectation toward spouse and children, and quantity and quality of intimacy in family relationships.

¶ Some ethnic groups have become indistinguishable in their social-class distribution from the rest of American society. The Irish, the Scandinavians, and the Germans, in particular, are no more likely to be "blue-collar" or "working-class" than any other Americans from similar regions in the country.

¶ While it is hard for some observers to give up the notion that most, or all, white ethnics are blue-collar workers, the notion is inaccurate. Even the recent immigrant groups from Eastern and Southern Europe have substantial middle- and upper-middle-class components. Not all blue-collar workers, even in Northern cities, are ethnics, and not all ethnics are blue-collar workers.

¶ Some ethnic groups have managed to maintain a very high level of internal cohesion, despite the fact that most of their members have entered the middle and upper middle class. Rural communities of Germans and even Luxembourgers in the Midwest have become quite prosperous without ceasing to be ethnic, while even in large cities the Greeks have managed to maintain strong internal bonds, though they are spatially diffused and quite successful economically.

¶ Some blue-collar ethnics are more "liberal" on both matters of race and peace than their nonethnic blue-collar counterparts. The Italians and the Irish, in particular, are more "liberal" than typical Americans, even when social class and region are held constant. Similarly, all the Catholic ethnic groups are more likely to be Democrats even when social class is held constant.

¶ While the Poles are no more liberal on matters of race and war than their white Anglo-Saxon counterparts, neither are they any less so.

¶ The work of Nie and Currie, recently confirmed by work done in Boston by Wilson and Banfield, shows that the ethnic groups are not any more "private" or "particularistic" than other Americans and, if anything, are less so. The work of Nie and Currie also indicates that those ethnics who have some kind of formal affiliation with an ethnic organization or engage in some kinds of explicitly ethnic behavior are likely to be the most liberal on matters of race and peace.

With the previous assertions in mind, we can now address ourselves once again to the question: Is social-class loyalty or ethnic loyalty more important to the blue-collar ethnic? The answer seems to me that this is not a very good question. I suspect that most blue-collar ethnics do not think in terms of "loyalty" to either social class or ethnic group. The amount of explicit identification with either or both probably varies from time to time and situation to situation. The two pertinent questions ought rather to be:

(a) What kind of behavior is predicted by social class and what kind by ethnicity—quite apart from any explicit or conscious loyalty to either social class or ethnic group?

(b) Under what sets of circumstances does conscious identification with either social class or ethnic group or both become pertinent and important?

It must be confessed that at present we know very little about the answers to these critical questions. What we do know, however, enables us to say that to see the world of the ethnic in terms of *either* social class *or* ethnic groups is far too simpleminded. One might also hazard the suggestion that the evidence reported above about the greater "liberalism" of ethnics, particularly those with some kind of conscious ethnic identification, would indicate that the survival of ethnic groups may turn out to be a very good thing for improving the quality of American life.

In what Peter Rossi calls the "public sphere," the rational principles of the technostructure prevail. In the private sphere, men still are inclined to choose to be with "their own kind of people." There is, of course, considerable overlap. Real estate, construction contracting, law, medicine, the church, and politics are part of the public sphere, but are still organized in many cities around ethnic, religious, and racial diversity. When it comes to choosing relationships where either intimacy or trust is involved, there is still a strong tendency to choose people of whom we can say in effect, if not in fact, "Your mother knew my mother."

The ethnic groups did not come into being in the Old World; they are American creations. In the Old Country the immigrants were citizens of towns, not of nations. They *became* ethnics in the United States, partly because the larger society has defined them as ethnics, but partly also because it was in their own interest to become ethnics. Political power could result from ethnic cohesiveness, and the ethnic collectivity could provide social support for its members. It was useful to be able to say to the personnel manager at the factory, "My mother knows your mother." He would be less cold to you, and you might be more likely to get the job.

In my model, then, ethnicity is one form of *Gemeinschaft* that has survived in a rationalized, bureaucratized society, and one of the criteria we have for finding role opposites with whom we are able to relax as a prelude to intimacy. I am not suggesting that a sense of presumed common origin (Max Weber's definition of ethnicity) is the only criterion around which an intimate relationship can be established; I am suggesting merely that ethnic collectivity is one of the sources available for finding self-definition and social location.

Men will necessarily differentiate themselves. What is important is whether these differentiations can become socially constructive. Lévi-Strauss has pointed out that in primitive tribes the totemic clans are always made up of animals of the same class of beings. Thus, one can have a tribe in which there is a bear totem and a lion totem and a tiger totem, and another tribe that will have an eagle totem and a falcon totem; but one will never have in the same tribe (unless it be the National Football League) eagles, lions, falcons, and bears. The reason for this, Lévi-Strauss says, is that the purpose of the totemic clans is to differentiate the tribe as a prelude to its reintegration. The tribe achieves structural integrity not by homogenization but by diversification. It may very well be that both because they provide self-definition and also substructure within the larger society, ethnic groups are a strong, positive social asset.

Data available to us at the National Opinion Research Center show that the more involved a person is in his own ethnic heritage, the less likely he is to display signs of racism and bigotry. Many of our colleagues react to this finding with complete disbelief, for if it is true, the official model is no longer acceptable, and my alternative model becomes plausible. If so, we may have to let Poles continue to be Poles, and may even require of the Irish that some of them learn what it means to be Irish again.

The self-hatred of many American intellectuals is so great that they seem quite incapable of even considering the possibility that something good has happened in the United States. In fact, we Americans have learned how to integrate, more or less well, more or less justly, in a rather brief period of time, a fantastic variety of racial, ethnic, and religious groups. We have been helped by our economic wealth and we have not made a perfect job of it by any means; but, given the size and heterogeneity of American society and the fact that it was put together quickly, the amazing thing is that it works at all. Yet for some bizarre reason, we would like to be persuaded that our success has come not from learning how to deal with diversity, but rather from having eliminated diversity.

As a result, when we discover that some groups are considerably less satisfied with their share in society than others, we are quite incapable of applying the wisdom of our own experiences to these newly discovered problems. We are a nation that has discovered once again, perhaps definitively, the fact of human diversity. And now we act as though we had discovered this fact for the first time, and had absolutely nothing in our past experience that would help us understand how one copes with it.

I have chosen to write what may seem an abrasive article, if only because previous efforts to break through the conventional wisdom have been so completely unsuccessful. Sometimes I think that Mr. Pope is right, that if we were not all born little Tories and little Whigs, then we were born either little assimilationists or little pluralists. Yet we need not be what we were born. Like most good Irish Americans, I was firmly persuaded for many years that all Catholic ethnics had to become good Americans, which of course meant good Irish Catholics. I was persuaded by the official version of American Catholic history (so far as there is any) in which the bishops who struggled against the German and Polish claims for "separatism" were the heroes and the bishops who pushed "separatist" positions were the villains. I now understand that the Irish hierarchy at the turn of the century (with one or two exceptions) was no more tolerant of diversity within the Church than the WASP political leadership was tolerant of diversity within the country. Great injustice was done to Polish and Italian Catholicism by Irish leadership, and I suspect it is still being done.

The temptation to see pluralism ending with one's own group is apparently a universal temptation. One hears that blacks and Puerto Ricans, too, say of each other, "Why can't they be like us?" But if the temptation is universal, in the present state of American society it is a temptation to which we should not succumb. Diversity is not going to be eliminated; we must improve our abilities to live with it.

We may even begin to enjoy it. The time may come when the most desirable neighborhoods in the large cities are those with people of widely different ethnic, racial, and religious backgrounds. Only the very rich may be able to live in diversified neighborhoods. Who knows, perhaps the time will even come when American fathers and mothers will worry and sweat and slave so that they can make enough money to move into a neighborhood where their children can have the advantage of being reared in an atmosphere of diversity. It may even be seen as an advantage so important that, compared with it, a college education will pale into insignificance.

How Important Is Social Class?
Dennis H. Wrong

The Debate Among American Sociologists

The old question of why there has been no socialism in the United States has often been answered by referring to the racial, ethnic, and religious divisions within the ranks of labor — which are the result of successive waves of overseas immigration and the partial incorporation into the labor force of the rural blacks. Accordingly, the American Left has been impatient with the ethnic loyalties and animosities of American workers, seeing them as fossilized survivals that retard the growth of class-consciousness. Radicals have charged the ruling classes with deliberately fomenting racial and religious prejudice as part of a divide-and-rule strategy. Yet liberal pluralists have argued that multiple loyalties to class and interest organizations, nationality groups, and churches have enabled the United States to maintain a stable yet flexible social order, and to avoid those bitter conflicts in which class, ethnic, and religious divisions are superimposed upon one another. Both radicals and liberals have joined in deploring the race-consciousness of American workers, who have so often excluded Negroes, Orientals, and Mexican Americans from their organizations, thus subjecting these groups to relatively unrestrained exploitation.

DENNIS H. WRONG is Professor of Sociology at New York University and editor of Contemporary Sociology. *He is the author of* Population and Society *and* Power.

These attitudes now have been modified by what Andrew Greeley has called "the legitimation of ethnic self-consciousness." New Left radicals and those liberals influenced by them have supported the growing ethnic solidarity of blacks, Chicanos, and American Indians. But they have looked with disfavor upon the revival of ethnic sentiments among whites — seeing them, not inaccurately, as a response to the new black militancy. Having written off the working class and its unions as a force for major change, the New Left is prone to dismiss the stirrings of ethnic awareness among blue-collar workers as no more than tokens of the incurable racism of the American society. Older socialists, though they have abandoned the millennial expectations of classical Marxism, have retained their attachment to the proletariat, accepting it as it is, "warts and all," as a force for peaceful democratic change. And many of them have, as a result, adopted a newly sympathetic attitude toward the American workers' ethnicities. Both ideological orientations — the emphasis of the New Left on racial pride and Third World nationalism, and older leftists' acceptance of the American working class in its full concreteness — have aroused new interest in the tangled web of class and ethnic identifications in American society.

Less politically committed social analysts also have tended to minimize the role of ethnic groups in American society, seeing them as destined to disappear within a few generations. In the 1950s, religious identifications were thought to be acquiring new significance in an emerging "mass society" in which even objective class inequalities were supposed to be diminishing. A religious revival was widely proclaimed, and some survey researchers claimed that "religious affiliation" was becoming the crucial "variable," supplanting class, ethnicity, and rural-urban residence in accounting for surviving differences in behavior within an increasingly homogenized society. Religious organizations were seen as replacing the old ethnic associations founded by immigrants in providing individuals with secure group membership and social and emotional support as a protection against the impersonality of the larger society. Will Herberg's *Protestant-Catholic-Jew* and Gerhard Lenski's *The Religious Factor* were the two most impressive books representing these tendencies. Lenski, however, has recently conceded that "... *The Religious Factor* is, at best, a picture of an era that has ended." *

Sociologists and a host of popular social critics who exaggerated and

---

* Gerhard Lenski, "The Religious Factor in Detroit: Revisited," *American Sociological Review,* February 1971, p. 50.

oversimplified their conclusions called attention in the 1950s to new forms of community life in the expanding suburbs. Although it was recognized that economic and ethnic segregation was maintained and even increased in the suburbs, suburbia was seen primarily as a new and relatively classless way of life, supplanting the old ethnic urban neighborhoods. It was thought to represent the future to which surviving working-class, lower-class, and ethnic subcultures would eventually succumb under the impact of continuing prosperity. Most of the commentary on suburbia was derisive in tone, and by the early '60s many sociologists were refuting negative stereotypes that had often originated in popularizations of earlier studies by their colleagues. *

Some stressed the persistence of class differences, even in suburbia itself, as against the view of a standardized suburban lifestyle embracing almost everyone. A smaller number argued that ethnic differences had far from disappeared. But even Nathan Glazer, who had insisted for years on the neglected and often subterranean influence of ethnic ties in American life, recently conceded in his introduction to a new edition of *Beyond the Melting Pot* that he and Daniel Patrick Moynihan had underestimated the durability of ethnicity in 1963, when they had concluded the first edition with the sentence "religion and race define the next stage in the evolution of the American peoples." †

In the early '60s, attention shifted from religion and suburbia back to the inner city and, to a lesser extent, to the rural and small-town South and the border-state region. The reason, of course, was the black revolution and the rediscovery of poverty. Racial discrimination and economic deprivation, victimizing a sizable minority of the population, seemed more significant than the largely symbolic religious and intra-middle-class differences stressed in the previous decade. The gradualist view of poverty as confined to "pockets," destined to be wiped out in the course of continued economic growth, no longer seemed plausible. Nor did the comfortable liberal notion that the elimination of racial discrimination was the "unfinished business of American democracy," bound to be achieved painlessly within a few decades. By the end of the '60s, the student and youth revolts and the emergence of a new feminist movement had added age, generation,

---

* For a summary of this debate, see Dennis H. Wrong, "Suburbs and Myths of Suburbia," in Wrong and Harry L. Gracey, eds., *Readings in Introductory Sociology* (New York, 1967), pp. 358–364.
† Nathan Glazer and Daniel Patrick Moynihan, "Introduction to the Second Edition: New York City in 1970," *Beyond the Melting Pot* (Cambridge, Mass., 1970), pp. vii–viii.

and sex to the list of major group identifications seen as shaping values in America.

Clearly, the shifts in the attention of social analysts from class to religious and residential, race, sex, and generational divisions reflect real discontinuities in the recent development of American society. But the mass media, with their voracious appetite for novelty, pick up and publicize each new group that comes into focus, enhancing the impression of discontinuity and casting into outer darkness the "*Other Americans*" or "forgotten men" or "silent majorities," who then have to be "rediscovered" when the currently fashionable group has been overexposed.

Yet even the most scrupulous, perceptive sociological studies of different segments of American society give rise to disagreements as to exactly *which* group memberships or cultural identities account for the attitudes and life-styles that even their critics concede they accurately describe. I shall give several illustrations of such controversies that arise out of the interpretation of the findings of some of the more influential recent sociological studies, stressing those bearing on class and ethnicity. Sociological research, to be sure, reveals the multiple affiliations and identities of its subjects; but sociologists, sometimes out of a polemical desire to refute prevailing scholarly or popular stereotypes, often stress the primacy of one set of social or cultural determinants over others. Even when this is avoided, the precise way in which age, generation, class, religion, ethnicity, race, and residence interact to produce a subcultural profile poses a difficult problem of analysis.

The sociologist Herbert Gans has insisted on the primacy of class, viewed as the resultant of income and educational and occupational opportunities, in shaping group values and behavior. Gans's first book was *The Urban Villagers,** a study of an Italian community in the West End of Boston, which was influential in mobilizing liberal intellectuals against urban renewal projects that destroyed cohesive neighborhoods. Gans insisted that his subjects' way of life reflected a generic working-class rather than a specifically Italian American subculture, pointing to patterns of family structure, sex role and courtship practices, and other values that West Enders shared with a wide variety of ethnically different working-class communities, including the culturally homogeneous British working class. In a review of the book Peter Rossi, one of the few leading American sociologists of Italian American origin, demurred. He invoked "memories of my childhood

---

* New York, 1962.

and adolescence in New York City during the twenties and thirties" to argue that "there is much more characteristically Italian (or perhaps more generally Latin) in the social organization of the West End than Gans would have the reader believe." *

In a later study of a planned suburban community in the Philadelphia area, *The Levittowners,*† Gans attacked the "myth of suburbia," arguing that the move to the suburbs had not fundamentally changed class-determined life-styles and that the major conflicts in the multi-class community he studied arose out of clashes between upper-middle-class, on the one hand, and lower-middle and working-class values and interests, on the other. Gans has also been a major critic of the notion that there is an at least semiautonomous "culture of poverty," insisting that the behavior of the poor is essentially a response to economic deprivation and lack of opportunity.

Bennett Berger's *Working-Class Suburb* was an earlier study attacking the suburban myth. It described, unlike *The Levittowners,* a purely working-class planned development in San Jose, California. Like Gans in *The Urban Villagers,* Berger argued that his subjects embodied an "incipient native white working-class culture" destined to replace older ethnic cultures, although in contrast to Gans the main thrust of his argument was directed against the claims of suburban residence rather than of ethnicity as a shaper of life-styles. "We have no clear images of *American* 'working-class style,' " Berger wrote,

> precisely because the lowest positions on our socioeconomic ladder were traditionally occupied by the most recent groups of European immigrants, each of which, as they arrived, pushed earlier groups of immigrants up. Our images of working-class life, consequently, are dominated by ethnic motifs. But the end of mass immigration from Europe may promote the development of an indigenous white working-class culture in the United States in the near future.... The blue-collar work force is likely to remain at between 20 and 25 million for some time to come, and it is extremely doubtful that Mexicans, Puerto Ricans, and Negroes will constitute the major part of this industrial labor force. Moreover, the facts of color, marginal occupations (largely not unionized), and ghetto residence are likely to sustain the ethnicity of these groups for the foreseeable future and isolate them from the native, white working-class culture apparently incipient in the San Jose suburb.‡

---

* From Peter Rossi's review of *The Urban Villagers,* in the *American Journal of Sociology,* November 1964, pp. 381–382.
† New York, 1967.
‡ Bennett Berger, *Working-Class Suburb* (Berkeley, 1960), p. 95.

Berger's interpretation of his own evidence did not pass un-
challenged. In a review, Harold Wilensky argued that since Berger's
community was only two years old at the time of the study, he had not
given its residents sufficient time to develop such suburban middle-
class patterns as the *Kaffee Klatsch* among wives, joining voluntary
associations, becoming active in the church and PTA, reading con-
sumer-oriented magazines, and raising their aspirations for their
children.* Wilensky also claimed that Berger's own evidence suggested
that some of these patterns were beginning to appear, although they
had not been present in the grimy industrial slum Berger's respondents
had inhabited before moving to the suburb. Wilensky concluded of
Berger's community that "it looks like a suburban variant of lower-
middle-class culture."

In a later publication, Wilensky forcefully generalized his
viewpoint, maintaining that

> ... in the United States and in other rich countries, class conscious-
> ness among manual workers is a transitional phenomenon charac-
> terizing workers not yet accustomed to the modern metropolis and
> the modern work place; that a clearly defined working class no longer
> exists, if it ever did; that much behavior and many attitudes said to
> be rooted in class are instead a matter of race, religion, ethnic origin,
> education, age, and stage in the family life cycle.
>
> Insofar as class categories remain at all useful, the line
> that divides stably employed, well-educated, well-paid workers from
> the lower class is becoming more important than the split between
> upper working class and lower middle class.†

The Gans-Rossi difference was over the relative importance
of class as against ethnicity, but Berger and Wilensky disagreed over
whether there are distinct lower-middle and working-class subcultures,
although Wilensky was evidently inclined to attach more importance
than either Gans or Berger to suburban residence as producing at
least a "variant" of lower-middle-class culture. Wilensky's later
statement, however, downgrades the significance of class as such. But
he fails to distinguish between politically militant class-consciousness
in the Marxist sense and the more common emphasis in American
sociology on class as the shaper of life-styles and the source of a diffuse "consciousness of kind" that is hardly the same thing as Marxist
class-consciousness.

---

* From Harold Wilensky's review of *Working-class Suburb,* in the *American Socio-
logical Review,* April 1961, pp. 310–312.
† Harold Wilensky, "Class, Class Consciousness and American Workers," in William
Haber, ed., *Labor in a Changing America* (New York, 1966), pp. 12–28.

The concept of class has been used with reference to American life in three distinct ways. First, there is the Marxist model of classes as rival groups organized and mobilized for conflict arising out of clashing economic interests. Wilensky correctly questions the importance of this kind of "class-consciousness" in the United States today and even in the past. Except perhaps for a few brief moments in the 1930s and in particular regions or industries, the American working class has not conformed to the Marxist model. There has never developed here a network of working-class interest associations and trade-union or party-created institutions sufficiently far-flung and powerful to constitute a distinctive subculture resembling the "nation within a nation" formed around the SPD in Imperial Germany.* The distinctive working-class way of life and "we-them" consciousness described by such English writers as Richard Hoggart, Raymond Williams, and E. P. Thompson has scarcely even been present in America.

Most American sociologists have favored a noneconomic conception of "social class," defining classes as aggregates of persons or families differing in values and behavior and forming a rank order of status levels. Most research on class in American communities has employed, at least implicitly, this view of classes as ranked subcultures. The studies of W. L. Warner and his associates in the 1930s and 1940s were pioneering examples. The much-criticized idea of a "culture of poverty" doubtless initially caught on so quickly because it was consistent with this approach.

However, when such sociologists as Herbert Gans and Bennett Berger insist on the importance of class in American life, they suggest a third conception. Essentially, they stress the role of economic inequalities in shaping people's aspirations and outlooks. Classes in this view are neither solidary groups mobilized for social conflict nor more diffuse groups sharing a common life-style and status pride. Rather, classes are groups whose members' aspirations and opportunities, beliefs, and life-styles—far from reflecting a coherent self-sustaining culture or subculture—are basically shaped by their market position in the national economy, and, to use a formulation of Max Weber's, by their differential "life-chances" in the commodity, credit, and labor markets.

Neither the alternative subcultural nor the unequal life-chance views conceive of classes as sharply defined groups inspiring intense loyalties and becoming the focus of self-consciously affirmed identities. True, such analysts as Veblen, the Lynds, Mills, and, more recently,

---

* Guenther Roth, *The Social Democrats in Imperial Germany* (Totowa, N.J., 1963).

G. William Domhoff have imputed at least a modified form of Marxist class-consciousness to American upper or "ruling" classes.* And some versions of the subcultural model have pictured classes as membership groups creating strong identifications, at least at the local community level. But these partial exceptions either exclude the vast majority of Americans or confine, in Stanislaw Ossowski's phrase, "class structure in the social consciousness" to the local community.†

This is significant because it means that class fails to lend itself to the interpretation most favored by American sociologists to account for both changing and constant group loyalties and the process of identity formation in America: what might be called the "protection-against-anomie" theory. Sociologists have contended that strong social bonds and identities based on religion, ethnicity, locality, and occupation have persisted or developed in America because they provide emotional security and a sense of community in the face of the impersonality and rapid social change of the larger society. The fierce peer-group loyalties—often affirmed as "generational" solidarity— of the young, the appeal of communes, and the new popularity of encounter and sensitivity-training groups, all are recent phenomena readily explained in these terms. The "quest for community" as a reaction to the forces promoting anomie—whether these forces are primarily identified with capitalist market relations, industrialization, urbanization, bureaucratization, or all of these together—has long been a major theme of sociological thought going back to nineteenth-century thinkers, in particular to Durkheim and Tönnies.

But the influence of class on conduct in America cannot be understood in terms of this theory, for neither classes nor associations based explicitly on class bonds and interests have been recognized objects of loyalty or membership groups with which people could proudly identify. Frank Tannenbaum's *A Philosophy of Labor* ‡ is one of the very few efforts by an American to present trade unions as *Gemeinschaften,* protecting their members against the impersonal forces of industrial society rather than as limited economic-interest organizations. But even Tannenbaum was suggesting a potential role rather than describing an actual one. Milton Gordon in his *Assimilation in American Life* § argues that the combination of ethnic origin and class position has produced a group or collectivity he calls an "eth-

---

* However hardheaded corporate elites may have been in protecting and advancing their own interests, even in the 1930s the claim by upper-class conservatives that FDR was "a traitor to his class" had a forced, anachronistic ring.

† Stanislaw Ossowski, *Class Structure in the Social Consciousness* (New York, 1963).

‡ New York, 1951.

§ New York, 1964.

class," and that this is the largest "reference group" with which Americans feel a positive sense of identification. People define themselves, Gordon maintains, primarily as upper-middle-class Jews, working-class Poles, or lower-class blacks rather than by class or ethnic origin alone.

De Tocqueville was the first to suggest that the leveling of class distinctions in the United States created the risk of an atomized, anonymous society, threatened by the "tyranny of the majority," and he saw the American predilection for forming voluntary associations as a response to this situation. Nearly a century later, such European theorists of "mass society" as Emil Lederer and Hannah Arendt held that the decline and breakup of social classes under the impact of war, inflation, and depression had produced a spiritual homelessness conducive to the rise of totalitarian movements that adopted slogans promising the restoration of brotherhood and community. But in America, groups other than classes have played an intermediate role between the family and the total society, protecting the individual from anomie.

Sociologists have used the protection-against-anomie theory to account for everything from rises in the birth rate to the appeal of fanatical ideological movements; so it hardly suffices to explain why particular groups become major carriers of identity. "Why," Andrew Greeley asks,

> was not social class the membership around which American city dwellers could rally, as it was in England? Why have the trade unions rarely, if ever, played quite the fraternal role in American society that they have in many continental societies? Granted that urban man needed something to provide him with some sort of identification between his family and the impersonal metropolis, why did he stick with the ethnic group when there were other groupings to which he could make a strong emotional commitment? *

Why, moreover, do different groups — churches, suburban communities, ethnic groups — appear to succeed one another as centers of "belongingness"? To a degree this is, as I have already noted, a matter of appearance encouraged by fashions in sociological theorizing and the nervous faddishness of the media. As Greeley observes:

> The relevant issue for social research is not whether one [means of self-definition] replaces the other or even whether these factors are

---

* Andrew M. Greeley, *Why Can't They Be Like Us?* (New York, 1971), p. 40.

being replaced by yet another means of self-definition. The important question is, rather, under what sets of circumstances, which kinds of people find what sources of self-definition pertinent. When, for example, do I choose, explicitly or implicitly, to define myself as Irish, when as Catholic, when as Irish Catholic, when as an academic, when a Chicagoan, when as an American? *

But what, then, of the current "resurgence of ethnicity" noted by such sociologists as Greeley himself, Glazer and Moynihan, and increasingly publicized by the media? Obviously, the new assertiveness of blacks and the adoption of separatist slogans by some black militants have provided the occasion for a newly self-conscious and unapologetic ethnicity among whites. Yet this cannot be dismissed, as it so often is, as a mere cover for racism. Glazer and Moynihan suggest that

> ethnic identities have taken over some of the task in self-definition and in definition by others that occupational identities, particularly working-class identities, have generally played. The status of the worker has been downgraded; as a result, apparently, the status of being an ethnic, a member of an ethnic group, has been upgraded. . . . Today, it may be better to be an Italian than a worker. Twenty years ago, it was the other way around.†

Such an emphasis on ethnicity rather than class or occupation reflects a general shift away from work identities and the workplace, which now has been noted in a variety of contexts for two decades. Even New Left radicals have argued that "the community" (the inner-city community, or ghetto) rather than the factory is now the major locus of social conflict. "Member of the community" and "community control" have acquired in much radical rhetoric the aura that once attached to "worker" and "workers' control." Christopher Lasch, a spokesman for this outlook, has advocated "building socialism" in the ghetto, although in his critique of black nationalism he asks, "Would self-determination for the ghetto threaten General Motors?" And he answers in the negative—which should be sufficient to dispose of "socialism in one community" as a primary objective in itself.‡

Recently, the assertion of a "generation gap," in which age and generation are regarded as crucial bases of identity and group allegiance, has been subjected to criticism that in many ways resembles

---

* *Ibid.,* p. 86.
† Glazer and Moynihan, *op. cit.,* pp. xxxiv–xxxv.
‡ Christopher Lasch, *The Agony of the American Left* (New York, 1969), p. 133.

the earlier debunking of the suburban myth.* Both critiques emphasized the persistence of class differences within, respectively, the younger generation and suburbia. College youth may have been attracted to the New Left and the counter-culture; but, it is pointed out, George Wallace also drew disproportionate support in 1968 from working-class and lower-middle-class youth. These polar outlooks attract, nevertheless, minorities: most young people continue to divide on political and social issues along the same economic and educational lines as their parents.

The restless hunger of many young people for new ideals and new forms of group life has obviously been influential out of proportion to the numbers involved. As if in response, the erosion of familiar moral landmarks has evoked self-conscious reaffirmations of traditional ethnic, religious, and territorial ties; this has, of course, happened often in the troubled course of modern history. Yet much as it has contributed to our understanding of the stresses of contemporary life, the emphasis of sociological perspective on anomie and "alienation," "the quest for community," "identity crisis," and "the need for participation" tends to lead to a relative neglect of the importance of the *economic*, of inequality in income and opportunity, as major determinants of the fate of individuals and groups. It has been the special merit of such sociologists as Herbert Gans and S. M. Miller to remind us of the continuing, pervasive influence of economic forces at the national level.

One may readily agree with Andrew Greeley that ethnic groups are not merely a cover for white racism, that they provide emotional support and prideful identities to their members, are a valuable source of diversity within American society, and that their legitimation need not result in the kind of divisiveness that prevents multi-ethnic coalitions in support of broad social goals. I also share Greeley's distaste for rootless "technological man" and for Warren Bennis's "temporary society," as well as for Robert Jay Lifton's "protean man"—and, more recently, for the ambivalent account by Greeley's fellow Irishman, William Irwin Thompson, of the "Los Angelization of America." †

It remains all too possible that the new positive valuation of ethnicity could become a matter of purely symbolic concessions, di-

---

* For a brief summary of the evidence, see Seymour Martin Lipset and Earl Raab, "The Non-Generation Gap," *Commentary,* August 1970, pp. 35–39.
† Greeley, *op. cit.,* pp. 98–99. Warren Bennis and Philip E. Slater, *The Temporary Society* (New York, 1968). Robert Jay Lifton, *History and Human Survival* (New York, 1970), chap. 15. William Irwin Thompson, *At the Edge of History* (New York, 1971), chap. 1.

verting attention away from the need for egalitarian economic reforms. This danger has often been pointed out in connection with black-studies programs, courses in Swahili, and plans to encourage "black capitalism" in the ghettos. Why should it be any less of a danger where the group pride of working-class "white ethnics" is involved? The likelihood of purely symbolic gains and "tokenism" seems somewhat greater than that white ethnic feelings will take an ugly racist turn and provide the basis for a fascist movement, although that possibility cannot be dismissed should American society face acute disaster.

One negative counterpart of close-knit group ties, and the support they provide for the individual, has been the stifling of impulses to freedom, self-determination, and striking out on new paths. If ethnic groups have often, as Greeley acknowledges, been a "mobility trap" for their members, may not heightened ethnic solidarity lead to an even greater sense of imprisonment for working-class boys and, especially, girls, who have become aware in recent years of new options in life-styles and career patterns and a more permissive hedonist ethos? The life-styles of ghetto blacks living on welfare in matrifocal families have often enough been held up by white liberals as models for emulation; and critics of the violence, family instability, lack of achievement orientation, and the many physical and mental pathologies prevalent in the black underclass have been accused of being "hung up on middle-class values." Such anthropological romanticism is unlikely to promote the kind of social change needed to eliminate ghettos, poverty, and racial discrimination. Are we to extend it to white ethnic groups, celebrate the cultural diversity of American society — and ignore its persisting economic injustices and the continuing arbitrary authority to which workers, both black and white, are subject on the job?

Despite the familiar claim that the ethnic diversity of the American labor force was a barrier to the birth of a powerful socialist movement, it is worth recalling that immigrant groups constituted the bulk of the membership of the newly created Communist party — or parties — after World War I.* Even 53 percent of the membership of the indigenous Socialist party was foreign-born by 1920.† The core of the New Deal coalition is usually described as consisting of labor and the urban minorities, though, to a considerable degree, these two groups contained the same people. If the Church of England, as the old saw has it, is the Tory party at prayer, it has been almost as true that

---

* Nathan Glazer, *The Social Basis of American Communism* (New York, 1961), chap. 2.
† James Weinstein, *The Decline of Socialism in America, 1912–1925* (New York, 1967), p. 328.

America's white ethnic groups have been the Democratic party and the union movement at home. Today "white ethnics" and "blue-collar workers" — when not the invidious "hard hats" — are terms often used interchangeably, each serving as a euphemism for the other in different contexts.

The revival of ethnic sentiments, therefore, need not be an obstacle to a coalition politics working through the Democratic party for reforms. One does not have to choose between extolling the new ethnicity, on the one hand, and ignoring or even deploring it, on the other. But recognition of the reality and the value of ethnic groups is no substitute for improving the school systems, reforming the tax structure, providing better housing, cleaning up the cities, and, in general, redistributing the good things of life in a way that will both increase the opportunities for individuals to escape from their ethnic communities, if they so wish, and improve the levels and quality of living in the ethnic communities themselves.

Index

310